On the Interpretation of Some Doubtful Words in the *Atharvaveda* and Other Essays

TARAPADA CHOWDHURY

MANOHAR
2023

First published 2020

Reprinted 2022, 2022, 2023

ISBN 978-93-88540-92-6

Published by
Ajay Kumar Jain *for*
Manohar Publishers & Distributors
4753/23 Ansari Road, Daryaganj,
New Delhi 110 002

Typeset by
Ravi Shanker
Delhi 110 095

Printed at
Replika Press Pvt. Ltd.

To the memory of my

Revered Gurus

Mahāmahopādhyāya Prof. Rāmāvatāra Śarmā

and

Dr. Kashi Prasad Jayaswal

Contents

Publisher's Preface

At the time of his untimely demise, around the middle of the twentieth century, Tarapada Chowdhury was rated among the foremost scholars of Vedic philosophy and philology in India, by scholars as diverse as R.R. Diwakar, Nalin Vilochan Sharma and Sarvapalli Radhakrishnan. Chowdhury in fact would contribute two chapters to S. Radhakrishnan's landmark *History of Philosophy: Eastern and Western* (2 vols.) brought out by George Allen and Unwin in 1952. One on 'The Vedas' and the other on 'Ramayana'. Both are represented in our volume. We start the volume with 'On the Interpretation of Some Doubtful Words in the Atharvaveda', Chowdhury's 1930 PhD thesis from University of London. A classic treatise, it is in Chowdhury's own words 'an attempt to find the value of a certain number of obscure words in the *Atharvaveda*. The suggested readings and meanings are by no means absolutely certain; they are to be taken for what they are worth. The main criteria (besides context) in determining them have been the following: (1) text criticism, (2) linguistics principles holding in the Indo-European or Indo-Aryan languages or in Sanskrit itself, (3) uses, remarks, or parallel passages in later literature and (4) facts otherwise known'. It is dedicated to Mahāmahopādhyāya Rāmāvtāra Śarmā, his guru at Patna University. In a singular recognition of its exellence, the thesis was published in full in *JBORS* in 1931.

Tarapada Chowdhury was also my grandfather. I never met him as he passed away 15 years before my birth. But stories of his polymath erudition and *panditai* were the staples of my childhood and growing up years in Patna, and I must admit I looked at them with the twin lenses of pride and scepticism. Not anymore. Now only the pride remains.

The volume also contains his short essay on 'Theism in Āyurveda', first published in *Kalyanakalpataru* in 1934. His long review article on 'The Uṇadisūtras' in its various recensions, looks at its importance as an authoritative guide to the position of the accent and the right sequence of sounds in a large number of nominal stems. Apart from being Head of Department, Sanskrit, Tarapada Chowdhury was also the first Head of Dept. Bengali at Patna University. His essay 'Some Phonetic Peculiarities of the Bengali Dialect of Manbhum' shows his lifelong love for the Bengali language, in particular the sweet yet robust variation spoken in his native Purulia, erstwhile Manbhum district of undivided Bihar.

The long essay, 'Linguistic Aberrations in Kālidāsa's Writings' brings the volume to a close and is a testament to his vast and eclectic scholarship. It is dedicated to his other great patron and mentor at Patna, Kashi Prasad Jayaswal. This volume brings together these classic essays (most of them out of print) on Vedic philosophy, linguistics and Indology for the first time under one cover. The essays have not been altered in any manner and have been reproduced in its original style when first published. We are grateful to the estate of Dr. Chowdhury for providing the essays and facilitating the curation of the volume.

I also wish to convey my profuse thanks to Dr. Michael Witzel, Wales Professor of Sanskrit at Harvard University, who read 'On the Interpretation' at short notice and pronounced it '. . . very good for its date, based on a thorough review of previous literature (including French and German), philology of the text and linguistic observations.' His validation firmed up my resolve to publish the volume under our own imprint. And in the end my heartfelt gratitude to Sri Ramesh Jain who agreed to bring out the volume in this, the golden jubliee year, of Manohar.

New Delhi
8 October 2019
(Vijay Dashami)

SIDDHARTH CHOWDHURY
Editor
Manohar

CHAPTER 1

On the Interpretation of Some Doubtful Words in the Atharvaveda

[The system of transliteration followed here differs from that adopted in the Journal in representing ऋ by r̥, ऌ by l̥, च by c, ड़ by ṛ, the Anunāsika[*] by ~, and in marking only the Udātta accent (′).]

Prefatory Note

This is an attempt to find the value of a certain number of obscure words found in the Atharvaveda. The suggested readings and meanings are by no means absolutely certain; they are to be taken for what they are worth. The main criteria (besides context) in determining them have been the following: (1) text-criticism, (2) linguistic principles holding in the Indo-European or Indo-Aryan languages or in Sanskrit itself, (3) uses, remarks, or parallel passages in later literature, and (4) facts otherwise known.

In suggesting an emendation of the text there is always a

Abbreviations

AB.=Aitareya Brāhmaṇa: Ait. Āraṇ.=Aitareya Āraṇyaka: Āp. Śr.=Āpastamba Śrautasūtra: ASS.=Ānandāśrama Sanskrit Series: AV.=Atharvaveda: Av.=Avestic: Baudh. Śr.=Baudhāyana Śrautasūtra: Beng.=Bengali: Bloomfield=M. Bloomfield, Hymns of the Atharvaveda, Sacred Books of the East, vol. 42: Boisacq=É. Boisacq, Dictionaire Étymologique de la Langue Grecque. BR.=Böhtlingk and Roth, Sanskrit Wörterbuch: Brugmann=K. Brugmann, Grundriss der vergleichenden Grammatik der indogermanischen Sprachen: Ch. 8=Chambers, No. 8, manuscript of the Atharvaveda: Dhanva. and Rāja.=Dhanvantari-and Rājanighaṇṭu: Dār.=Dārila, commentator of Kauśikasūtra: GBr.=Gopatha Brāhmaṇa: Geiger, Pali Gramm.=Pali Litteratur und Sprache by W. Geiger: GOS.=Gaekwad's Oriental Series: Grassmann=H. Grassmann, Wörterbuch zum Rigveda: Grill=J. Grill, Hundert Lieder des Atharva-veda: Guj.=Gujrati: H.=Hindi: Henry=V. Henry, French translation of books vii–xiii of the AV.: Ind. Stud.=Indische Studien: Kauś.=Kauśika Sūtra: Keś.=Keśava, commentator of Kauśikasūtra: KS.=Kāṭhaka-Saṁhitā: Ludwig=vol. iii of his Der Rigveda: Mān.

* First published in the *Journal of the Bihar and Orissa Research Society*, vol. XVII, 1930-1, pp. 25-100.

tacit assumption that (1) the mss. either originate from the same source or could possibly be compared with and corrected by each other, and that (2) the tradition has been for the most part a written one. The results speak for themselves: but the following facts may be considered. (1) Most of the mss. come from Gujarat (12 out of the 20 authorities of S. P. Pandit, who, at p. 16 of the introduction to his edition, admits giving mostly the Gujarat tradition); (2) S. P. Pandit, Atharvaveda, vol. III, pp. 216 and 315, remarks (on the basis of the traditional readings of certain words as compared with their developments in the later languages) that the tradition of this Veda is derived from mss. and is not strictly oral. As to the time when these graphic confusions [*viz.*, of *p* (प) and *y* (य), *kt* (क्त) and *tt* (त्त), etc.] may have occurred, Bühler's Palæographic Charts IV, col. XVI and VI, col. V show that about the sixth or seventh century A.C. the respective letters began to be sufficiently similar to be confused with each other.

ákṣu-

mṛtyór ā́ṣam ā́padyantā́ṁ kṣúdhaṁ sedíṁ vadháṁ bhayám: Índraś cā́'kṣujā́lā́bhyā́ṁ Śárvaḥ sénā́m amū́ṁ hatam. 8. 8. 18.

ákṣum opaśáṁ vítataṁ sahasrā́kṣáṁ viṣūváti: ávanaddham abhíhitaṁ bráhmaṇā ví cṛtā́masi. 9. 3. 8.

Śr.=Mānava Śrautaśūtra: Mār.=Mārāthi: MBh.=Mahābhārata: MS.=Maitrāyaṇī-Saṁhitā: Nigh.=Nighaṇṭu: Nir.=Nirukta: Nep.=Nepali: Oldenberg=Ṛgveda, Text critische und exegetische Noten. Pāṇ.=Pāṇini: Pet. Lex. or PW.=Sanskrit Wörterbuch by Böhtlingk and Roth: Pischel, Prak. Gramm.=Grammatik der Prakrit Sprachen by R. Pischel: Ppp.=Paippalāda rescension of the AV: PTS.=Pali Text Society: Punj.=Punjabi: RV.=Ṛgveda: Śāṅkh. Āraṇ.=Śāṅkhāyana Āraṇyaka: ŚB. or ŚBr.=Śatapatha Brāhmaṇa: SBE.=Sacred Books of the East: SPP.=Shankar Pandurang Pandit as editor of the Bombay edition of the AV.: TA.=Taittirīya Āraṇyaka: Tāṇd. Br.=Tāṇḍya Brāhmaṇa: TPr.=Taittirīya Prātiśākhya: TS.=Taittirīya Saṁhitā: Up.=Upaniṣad: v.=verse: Ved. Chrest.=Vedische Chrestomathie: Ved. Concord.=Vedic Concordance by M. Bloomfield: Ved. Myth.=Vedic Mythology: Ved. Stud.=Vedische Studien: Vj.=Vaijayantī of Yādavaprakāśa, edited by G. Oppert: VS.=Vājasaneyī-Saṁhitā: Wack.=J. Wackernagel, Altindische Grammatik: Walde=A. Walde, Indogermanisches Wörterbuch. Wh.=Whitney, Translation of the AV.

ā vāṁ dānāya vavṛtīya dasrā gór óhena Taugryó ná jívriḥ :
apáḥ kṣoṇí sacate māhinā vāṁ jūrṇó vām ákṣur áṁhaso yajatrā.
RV. 1. 180.5.

Previous Scholars: The commentary on both the AV. passages is wanting. Sāyana on the RV. passage takes *ákṣu-* as an adjective (=*vyāptaḥ*) qualifying *ṛṣi-* or *yajamāna-* understood; *apáḥ*, according to him, means either *antarikṣam* or *udakāni* ; *kṣoṇí* is either nom. du. (=*dyāvāpṛthivī*) or loc. sing. (=*bhūmyām*). 'Eine Art Netz', BR. 'Wagenachse', Nachträge to the shorter Pet. Lex. Geldner, Ved. Stud. 1,136f., equates *ákṣu-* with *jāladaṇḍá-* in AV. 8. 8. 5 and renders it with 'pole', which in RV. 1. 180. 5 is 'die Stange der Wagens=Deichsel'. He is not, however, sure of the epithet *sahasrākṣá-* in AV. 8. 8. 18. See also his notes, Trans. of RV. vol. I, pp. 233f. Henry (who renders with 'perche' in AV. 8. 8. 18) on AV. 9. 3. 8, Bloomfield, SBE 42, pp. 586 and 598, and Oldenberg, RV. 1. 180. 5, cannot accept Geldner's meaning because of the epithet *sahasrākṣá-*, which they understand to mean 'with thousand holes' (Bloomfield). Accordingly Bloomfield, *l.c.* p. 598, suggests that 'a covering of wickerwork' might be meant in AV. 9. 3. 8. This, of course, does not fit in with the other two occurrences of the word. Grill renders, 'Flechtennetz'.

It seems that *ákṣu-* is only a bye-form of *ákṣa-*, both originally meaning 'pole', but the latter eventually being restricted to the pole between the wheels of a chariot, namely, the axle. Such duplicate forms ending in *-a* and *-u* are not rare, cf. for instance: *kṛkavāka-* AV. 20. 136. 10: *kṛkavāku-* 'hen,' *krīḍá*-RV. 1. 37. 1, 5: *krīḍú-* 'playing' ib. 9. 20. 7, *tanyatā́*-f. RV. 1. 180. 12: *tanyatú-* 'thundering', *turváśa-* : *turvaśu-*, n. pr., *pā́da-* : *pādú*-RV. 10. 27. 24 'foot', *māyā́-* : *-māyú-* in *durmāyú-* RV. 3. 30. 15 'magic', *śayā́*-f. RV. 3. 55. 4: *śayu-* in *śayutrā́* ib. 1. 117. 12, 10. 40. 2 'couch', *śára-* : *śáru-* 'arrow', *harṣa-* : *harṣu* in *harṣu-mánt-* RV. 8. 16. 4 'joy', etc.

Prāk. *akkha-* has a meaning 'a measure of length, four cubits or twenty-four angulis',—Seth, Pāiyasaddamahaṇṇavo *s.v.*,—just the same idea as in the English measure of ength, 'pole'. Pāli *akkhavāṭa-* 'fencing round an arena for wrestling' probably contains *ákṣa-* in this sense. Beng. *ākh-* 'sugar cane', the *u* at the end of which is still perceptible in the pronunciation of Western Bengal, seems more likely to have come from *ákṣu-*, because of its resemblance to a bamboo pole, than from *ikṣu-*.[1] Beng. (Manbhum, dial.) has another word *ākhun* to denote a hooked bamboo pole, used for separating straw from corn.

It seems also probable that Gr. ἀξίνη 'axe, battle-axe'. Lat. *ascia* (<**acsia*, cf. *viscus* : ἰξός, *vespa*<* *vepsa*), Goth, *aqizi*, old H. Germ. *acchus*, Germ. *axt*, old Ice. *ex*, *ǫx*, Ang. S. *æx*,—Boisacq, Greek Dictionary, s.v. ἀξίνη— and Eng. **axe* are connected with *ákṣu*—*ákṣa-*, the meaning in these cases having conceivably been transferred from the 'handle of the axe' to the 'axe' itself.

We shall now see how this meaning suits the passages quoted above. In AV. 8.8.18 *ā́ṣa-* is an uncommon word, which Whitney, followed by Henry, emends to *óṣa-* and translates *mṛtyór ā́ṣam ā́padyantām* as 'let them go unto death's burning (?)'. He remarks, however, that only two of his MSS. read *óṣam*, all the rest *ā́ṣam*, 'which must accordingly be regarded as the traditional text, although unintelligible'. It is probably the same word as *āsá-* 'nearness' cerebralised by mistake, helped probably by the nearness of the preceding *r*.[2] *Mṛtyór ā́ṣam*, etc., can then be paralleled by 3. 11. 2**b**=RV. 10. 161. 2**b**, *yádi kṣitā́yur yádi vā páreto yádi mṛtyór antikáṁ nītá evá*. If this be acceptable, we may modify Whitney's translation thus: "Let them go unto the *nearness* of death, unto hunger, debility, the deadly weapon, fear; by *pole* and net, O Śarva, [do thou] and Indra slay yonder army". Poles of the net or the club are referred to as instruments of killing in the same hymn: v. 5, *antárikṣaṁ jā́lam āsīd jāladaṇḍā́ díśo mahī́ḥ : tenā 'bhidhā́ya dásyūnāṁ Śakráḥ sénām ápāvapat;* v. 11, *tṛṇéḍhv ènān matyàṁ Bhavásya;* and v. 12, *Sādhyā́ ékaṁ jāladaṇḍám udyátya yanty ójasā : Rudrā́ ékaṁ Vásava ékam Ādityaír éka údyataḥ*.

---

[1] *Vaṁśa-* is given as a synonym of *ikṣu-*, Dhanvantari- and Rāja-nighaṇṭu, ASS., p. 156. Hindi *ūkh* (besides *īkh*) is probably a case of assimilation, *ikṣuḥ*> *ikkhu*>* *ukkhu*> *ūkh*. Cf. Pr. *ucchu*=*ikṣu-*, Brugmann, Kurze verg. Gram. d. idg. Sprachen § 330.

[2] Such irregular cerebralisation is found elsewhere in the text. Cf., for instance, *ṛtúbhyaṣ ṭvā* 3. 10. 10, *sáṁ naṣ ṭébhiḥ* 2. 35. 2, *vi taṣṭhiré* 4. 6. 2, etc.

AV. 9. 3. enumerates the different things used in the construction of a *śālā*, a particular kind of thatched house still in common use in India. A description of a modern *śālā* with reference to the Atharvan hymn may be found helpful in properly understanding the hymn as a whole and the verse under discussion in particular. In the Mānbhūm district, before the walls are raised, a frame-work of the house is made by fixing posts (*upamít-*[1], v. 1) at short distances which are connected at the top by posts running all round (*parimít-*, v. 1). On these connecting poles rests one end of the slanting cross-poles (*saṁdaṁśá-*[2], v. 5), which, with their other ends, hold the dividing pole at the top (*páriṣvañjalya-*[3], v. 5, *viṣūvánt-*, v. 8).

These are laid over with sliced pieces of bamboo (prob. *paladá-*[4], v. 5 and 17) tied to the crosspoles by means of strings, made of a kind of grass, or bamboo-skins (v. 4). The top of this frame-work is then covered with straw, which is kept together by means of sliced bamboos spread upon it and tied to those below (v. 17). Walls are then raised, or, in some cases, the supporting posts are first connected by a net-work of rushes (v. 18), which is then plastered with earth. Sometimes the crosspoles of the thatch hang down a little beyond the walls and are then supported by a series of slanting poles, fixed against (*pratimít-*, v. 1) the outer sides of the supporting poles. Of furniture in such a house, two pieces are almost invariably

---

1 *Upamít-*, *parimít-*, and *pratīmít-* are all from the root *mi-* 'to build', 'to erect'. *Upamít-* is found also in RV. 1. 59. 1, 4. 5. 1, where a supporting pillar or post is intended, as well as *mít-*, ib. 10. 18. 12, with the same meaning.

2 *Saṁdaṁśá* usually means 'tongs'. These poles are so called, because each pair of them holds the ridge-pole as a pair of tongs. In Beng. they are called *kā̃ci* 'scissors', which gives the same idea.

3 *Páriṣvañjalya-* is probably a corruption for—*ṣvañjanya-*, 'that which is to be embraced (*viz.*, the ridge-pole, by the cross-poles on either side)'; cf. Ppp. reading, *pariṣvañcanadasya*. For interchange of *n* and *l*, cf. *kanyánā-* RV. 8. 35. 5 : *kanyálā-*AV. 'maiden', *péśanī-*f. : *peśala-* 'beautiful', *mulālí-*AV : *mṛṇālī-* 'lotus-stem', and Wack. 1. 175 (c). n.

4 *Paladá-* seems to be a Prakritism for *pra-rada-*, containing the root, *rad-* in the sense of 'scraping', 'slicing', 'splitting', cf. *tásara-* : *trasara-*, 'shuttle'.

to be found: the sling (*śikyá-*, v. 6), made of ropes, for hanging vessels on and the bamboo pole, sliced or intact, for hanging clothes on. The latter is hung down either from the crosspoles or from the ridge by means of cords tied to either end. When heavily laden, it would, of course, make a curve and thus resemble a head-band (*opaśá-*, for which see below). This must be intended by *ákṣu-* in the verse under discussion (*viz.*, 9. 3. 8); the epithet 'thousand-eyed (*sahasrākṣá-*)'—which, under any circumstances, would be an exaggeration—referring to its knotty joints. These, oval and slowly rising, resemble the eyeball to some extent, and for this reason they are often referred to as the 'eyes' of bamboo, cane, sugar cane, etc., in Bengali and other modern Indian languages.[1]

Accordingly, we may translate: "The out-stretched thousand-eyed pole, (like) a headband, hung down from (*ávanaddha-*) and tied on to (*abhíhita-*) the ridge, do we unfasten with our spell". The two epithets *ávanaddha-* and *abhíhita-* are significant as referring to the clothes-pole.

The RV. verse may be translated: "May I turn towards (*i.e.*, be inclined to give) a present for you, O wonderful ones, by the offering of a cow, like the aged son of Tugra (*viz.*, Bhujyu). Through your greatness, from water he goes to the earth; by you two (*vām*) his pole of distress is shattered, O adorable ones."

The pole here intended must be that, with slings at both ends, used for carrying loads (*vivadha-* or *vihaṅgikā-*, Hindi *bāhāṅg*), the idea being that he was thereby relieved of the load of distress that he had been carrying. I take here *apáḥ* as ablative singular of *áp-*, cf. Grassmann, s.v. *áp*, for use in singular; *kṣoṇí* as instrumental singular of *kṣoṇí-* 'earth', which is quite in consonance with the pada-pāṭha's considering it a *pragṛhya*, cf. Ved. Gr. § 72. 2 (c), and the pada-text of *āṣṭrí* AV. 6. 27. 3b, *mahí* 18. 1. 39b etc.; *māhinā*=*mahi*(*m*)*nā*, the first vowel lengthened for the sake of metre and then confused with *māhina-*, which accounts for the accent; cf. *páṭhiṣṭhām* AV.

[1] Nepali has *akhaṭo* for notches, which seems to be an extension of *akṣa-*.

14. 2. 6d (*patheṣṭhā́m*, RV. 10. 40. 13d), 'accented as if it were a superlative' (Wh.); and *vām* in **d** as instrumental dual, cf. RV. 1. 158. 3a, *yuktó ha yád vāṁ Taugryā́ya perúr ví mádhye árṇaso dhā́yi pajráḥ*, and ib. v. 4d, *mā́ mām édho dáśatayaś citó dhāk prá yád vāṁ baddhás tmáni khā́dati kṣā́m*. For the story of Bhujyu's deliverance from the waters onto the dry land, cf. RV. 1. 116. 3-5, 117. 14, etc.

ákṣya-

éhi jīváṁ trā́yamāṇaṁ párvatsyā́ 'syákṣyam : víśvebhir devaír dattáṁ paridhír jīvanā́ya kám. 4. 9. 1.

Previous Scholars : '*parvatasya trikakunnāmno gireḥ akṣam asi cakṣur bhavasi*'— Sāyaṇa. '. . . . bist eine Salbe vom Gebirge (?),'—Grill, who referring to 19. 45. 3 (*parvatīyam ā́ñjanam*), suggests an emendation to *ā́ñjana-*. Quoting Roth's opinion that *ákṣya-* may mean 'belonging to the eye, *i.e.*, an eye-ointment', he remarks that the characteristics of the remedy do not admit of such a limitation and that he can rather conceive of an epithet *akṣayya-* or *akṣ ara-*. "Come hither ! thou art the living, protecting eye-ointment of the mountain given by all the gods as a safeguard unto life."—Bloomfield, who remarks in the notes, "Aksham does not mean 'eye', akshyam is otherwise unquotable. Nevertheless we have translated akshyam, for the passage seems to be a tantalising reverberation of Śat. Br. III. 1. 3. 12 (viz., *yatra vā Indro Vṛtramahaṁs tasya yad akṣy āsīt taṁ giriṁ trai-kakudam akarot tad yad traikakudaṁ bhavati cakṣuṣy evai 'taç cakṣur dadhāti*). He refers also to MS. III. 6.3. and TS. VI. 1. 1. 5, each of which gives a version of the same story. "Come thou, rescuing the living one; of the mountain art thou for the eyes (?). . . ."— Whitney, who remarks, "The meter indicates that the true reading at the end of **b** is *ákṣyam*. . . .; but *ákṣya* is unknown elsewhere and its meaning in this connection is obscure."

The bad construction and obscurity of meaning which follow from the usual way of splitting **b** seems to suggest that we have to deal here with two words instead of three, viz., *párvatasya āsyákṣyam*, 'living in the mouth of the mountain'. This would be a fitting epithet for *ā́ñjana-*, one variety of the soft rock from which it is made being found in the cavities of some mountains, the other in the beds of certain rivers ; cf. v. 10, *yádi vā́'si traikakudáṁ yádi yāmunám ucyáse : ubhé te bhadré nā́mnī*. . . ., and *sauvīrāñjana-* and *sroto'ñjana-* in Vaidyaka, *e.g.*, Dhanva. and Rāja., p. 125, Bhāvaprakāśa, Śrīveṅkaṭeśvara Press ed., p. 43. *Āsyákṣya-* (to be read *āsiakṣia-*) contains the present stem of the root *kṣi-* 'to live' (cf. pres. *kṣiyanti*) followed by the suffix *-a*, formed like *cakram-āsajá-* RV. 5. 34. 6, *a-paśy-á-* ib. 1. 148. 5, *sadāpr̥ṇ-á-* ib. 5. 44. 12, etc., Ved Gr. § 115. 3a, which (denoting the agent) normally accent the suffix. The verse may thus be translated: "Come thou! rescuing the living one, who art a liver in the mouth of the mountain; given by all the gods, an enclosure, as it were, for life."

The confusion of the copyist of the pada-pāṭha is easily accounted for in the reminiscence of the story referred to above and in the fact that *ā́ñjana-* generally means an eye-ointment. I say, 'generally', because there are indications in the same hymn and elsewhere that it was applied to other parts of the body as well, being thus equivalent to an ordinary ointment or medicated oil. Cf. v. 4., *yásyā'ñjana prasárpasy áṅgam-aṅgam páruṣparuḥ : táto yákṣmaṁ ví bādhasa ugró madhyamaśír iva ;* v. 8, *tráyo dāsā́ ā́ñjanasya takmā́ balā́sa ā́d áhiḥ ;* and 19. 45. 5, *ā́kṣvaí 'kaṁ maṇím ekaṁ kr̥ṇuṣva snāhy ékenā́ pibaí 'kam eṣām : cáturvīraṁ nair̥tébhyaś catúrbhyo grā́hyā bandhébhyaḥ pári pātv asmā́n.*

In this connection may be considered *áhi-* in v. 8 quoted above. The present state of accent and the padapāṭha require us to take *ādahiḥ* as two words and the commentator accordingly explains *áhi-* as 'snake-poisoning.' But coming together with *takmán-* (fever) and *balā́sa-* (cold ?)[1] it would rather refer to some malady as Whitney also has suggested. No disease of the name, however, is known. I should think that it is one word, *ādáhi-* 'burning, *i.e.*, the sore caused by burning,' cf. *ājā́ni-* 'birth' RV. 3. 17. 3, *ābhogí-* 'enjoyment' ib. 1. 113. 5, *saṁtaní-* 'clashing noise', etc. As ointments, including medicated oils, are prescribed for fever, cold, and burnt-sores, in their various stages, this meaning would suit the context quite well.

ádrūkṣṇa-

yát te vā́saḥ paridhā́naṁ yā́ṁ nīvíṁ kr̥ṇuṣe tvám : śiváṁ te tanvè tát kr̥ṇmaḥ saṁsparśé 'drūkṣṇam astu te. 8. 2. 16.

---

[1] *Balā́sa-* is used frequently in the medical Śāstras as equivalent to *kapha-* or *śleṣman-* 'phlegm', 'expectoration.' Cf. Aṣṭāṅgahr̥daya, Sūtra. 23, 19; Uttara. 40, 31; and B.R., *s.v.*

Previous Scholars: '*tac ca vastraṁ saṁsparśe viṣaye adrūkṣṇam arūkṣam yathā mārdavam aśnute* (for *astu te*) *vyāpnoti gacchati tathā kṛṇmaḥ.*'—Sāyaṇa. '..nicht rauh sei's zur berürung dir'—Ludwig, p. 497. '..puisse ce contact t'être une caresse'—Henry. '..not rough to thy touch shall it be'—Bloomfield. '..be it not harsh to thy touch'—Whitney, noting that "SPP. reads 'with all his authorities' *ádrūkṣṇam* in **d**. Our mss. might doubtless all be understood in the same way, but some of them look more like *-ḍū-* or *-dū-*; *-rū-*, which our text unfortunately gives, is not found in any; neither *rūkṣṇa* nor *drūkṣṇa* appears to be met with elsewhere."

Ádrūkṣṇa- is undoubtedly the correct reading, which even the corrupt *'dukṣaṇam* of Ppp. points to. The word apparently contains the root *druh-* 'to harm', followed by the suffix *-sna*, Ved. Gr. § 118, and preceded by the negative particle. The absence of aspiration in *-dru-* points to the fact that *-kṣ-* in cases like this represents an earlier *-gẓh-*,[1] which has been lost in Sanskrit, Wack. I. § 209. a.

The lengthening of the root-vowel is similar to that found in *tīkṣṇá-* 'sharp': *tij-* 'to sharpen', *tigmá-*, TS. *hálīkṣṇa-*: VS. *halíkṣṇa-* 'a kind of animal', *śīkṣā-*: *śikṣā-* 'phonetics', which, according to Wack. I. § 39. n., have their *ī* from the desiderative, where *ī* is found several times before *-kṣ-*, partly in place of older *i*. To these may be added *níkṣaṇa-*: *nikṣ-* 'pierce,' and probably *dīkṣ-* 'to initiate a pupil': *diś-* 'to direct' and *rūkṣa-* 'rough': *ruj-* 'to break', 'to harm', with the same underlying idea as in *ádrūkṣṇa-* (BR. connect it with *rūṣ-* 'to make dusty', which is not convincing, both as regards meaning and change of *-ṣ-* to *-k-*, cf. Wack. I. § 118. n.). As instances of the lengthening of *u* gives Wack., *loc. cit.*, *pratyavarūhya*: *pratyava-ruh-* (Aufrecht, AB. 427), *nirūhya*, AB. 7.5.1: *nir-uhya*, *tūṣṇīm* 'silent': *tuṣ-* 'to be silent', VS. *sūmná-*: elsewhere, *sumná-*, Up. *sūkṣma-*: VS. ŚB. *sukṣmá-*.

It will be seen in the above instances that the *i* or *u*

---

[1] Other instances from the RV. are: *dákṣat* 1.130.8, 2.4.7, *dakṣi* 2.1.10, *dakṣi* (voc.) 1.141.8, *dakṣúṣaḥ* (g.s.) 1.141.7, *dákṣoḥ* (g.s.) 2.4.4: *dah-* 'to burn'; *adukṣat* 1.33.10, *adukṣata* 1.160.3, *dukṣáḥ*, 7.4.7, *dukṣán* 1.121.8, *dúdukṣan* 10.61.10, 74.4, *dúdukṣat* 7.18.4: *duh-* 'to milk', etc. In all these cases the pada-text replaces *d* (the second one in reduplicated stems) by *dh* after the manner of later Sanskrit. Cf. Wack. I. § 160.

in each case is followed by a conjunct whose last member or the last two, when it consists of three, are continuatives. Such conjuncts are, of course, easier to be pronounced as one whole, whether at the beginning or in the middle of a word. There grew up thus a dialectical tendency, as testified by TPr. 21.7.9 (mentioned in Wack. I. § 240. b), to consider such a conjunct in the middle of a word as belonging to the following vowel. The heaviness of the immediately preceding vowel, which is usual before a conjunct, being thereby shaken, there was occasion for a compensatory lengthening which is what we have in the above instances. The reason, then, why this phenomenon is not universal may possibly lie in the fact that the spelling was constantly corrected, where etymological connections were obvious.

Ádrūkṣṇa- would thus mean 'unharming' (cf. *druhila-* in Mān. Śr. 2.14.14,..*druhilam ahataṁ vāsaḥ paridhāya*.., 'putting on rough, new clothes') in the above passage: "That which is thy cloth for putting round, the waist-strip that thou makest; we make it auspicious for thy body, be it unharming in touch to thee."

ádroghāvitā

kṛṇutá dhūmáṁ vṛṣaṇaḥ sakhāyó 'droghāvitā vā́cam áccha: ayám Agníḥ pṛtanāṣā́ṭ suvī́ro yéna devā́ ásahanta dásyūn. 11.1.2=RV. 3.29.9, which has *kṛṇota..vṛṣaṇam* in **a**, *'sredhanta itana vā́jam áccha* in **b**, and *devā́so* in **d**.

V. l.: Wh.'s collation-book gives *-avitāḥ* in **b** as pada-reading without note of variant. SPP. gives *-avitā*, following one or two of his mss. and the commentator. Ppp. is corrupt, but has in **b**, *adroghā vitā vātam matsa.*

Previous Scholars: '*adrohakāriṇām sucaritrāṇām avitā rakṣitā vācam accha ...ṛgrūpāṁ vācam abhilakṣya*,'—Sāy. 'Adj. Wahrhaftigkeit liebend'—BR. Bloomfield, p. 611, thinks that the Śaunakīya text scarcely yields sense in **b**, and that the RV. and the Ppp. texts suggest the reading, *ádroghā vīta vā́jam áccha* or *ádroghā áveta* etc., on the basis of which he translates: 'unharmed by wiles go ye into the contest.' Henry translates **b**, 'dans la direction de la parole (sacrée) confiants dans la faveur du (Dieu) inoffensif.' "Make ye smoke, O ye bulls, companions, ye that are aided by the unhateful (?), unto speech: the Agni (is) fight-overpowering, having good heroes, by whom the gods overpowered the barbarians"—Wh.

Ádroghāvitā vācam áccha seems to be an exact paraphrase of *ásredhanta itana vājam áccha* in RV. *Ádroghāḥ* and *ásredhantaḥ* both mean 'unharming' or 'unharmed.' For double Sandhi between *ádroghāḥ* and *avitā*, see under *eru*. The meaning 'to move', 'to go', for *av-*, given in the Dhātupāṭha and quoted by BR., has to be assumed for several cases: for instance, *avatká-* in *adó yád avadhā́vaty avatkám ádhi párvatāt: tát te kṛṇomi bheṣajám súbheṣajaṁ yáthā́ 'sasi*, AV. 2.3.1, 'what runs down yonder, gliding off the mountain', etc.[1]; *ávani-*,[2] 'stream', 'river', or 'course of river', connected by some with *av-* 'to protect' and by others with *áva* 'down', both unsatisfactory: *ud-ávantau* in *ahám enāv údatiṣṭhipaṁ gā́vau śrāntasádāv iva: kurkurā́v iva kū́jantāv udávantau vṛ́kāv iva*, AV. 7.95(100). 2. 'I have made these two stand up like two weary-sitting cows: barking like dogs (du.) springing up like wolves (du.)'[3]; *pra-av-* in *marúdbhiḥ prácyutā meghā́ḥ prā́vantu pṛthivī́m ánu* AV. 4.15.9 **c, d,** 'let the clouds dropped forth by the Maruts glide along the earth'[4], etc. For the older form *avita* instead of *avata*, cf. RV. 7.59.6, *ā́ ca no barhíḥ sádatā 'vitā́ ca spā́rhā́ṇi dā́tave vásu*.

Vā́cam is a case of de-voicing, which, so common in the Ppp., is also found several times in the Śaunakīya text; cf., for instance, *áva-tiryatīḥ* (mss.) for *-dīrya-* (Wh.) in 19.9.8**d**, *śáṁ no bhū́mir vepyamānā́ śám ulkā́ nírhataṁ ca yát: śáṁ gā́vo lóhitakṣīrāḥ śáṁ bhū́mir ávatīryatīḥ; vitā́vati* for *vidhā-*

---

[1] Whitney renders "What runs down yonder, aiding (?) off the mountain," and remarks, "*Avatká* (*ava °tkám*: quoted in the comment to Prāt. i. 103: ii. 38, iv. 25) is obscure, but it is here translated as from the present participle of root *av* (like *ejatká*, v. 23.7. [cf. *abhimādayatká*, ÇB., *vikṣiṇatká*, VS.]); this the comm. favours (*vyādhiparihāreṇa rakṣakam*)."

[2] Johansson, IF. 2, 62, derives *ávani-* and *avatká-* (fn. 2) from an I.-E. root *eu̯e-* 'to be wet.' Cf. also Persson, *ib*. 35, 200.

[3] "....like (two) growling dogs, like (two) lurking (? *ud-av*) wolves,"—Whitney, noting, "The comm. explains *udávantau* by *goyūthamadhye vatsān udgṛhya gacchantau*: Henry renders, 'that watch one another' [He would reject *ud* in a]".

[4] Whitney renders **c, d**: "let the clouds, started forward by the Maruts, show favour (*pra-av*) along the earth."

(BR.) in **12.2.38d** (of which **c, d** are repeated as **c, d** of v. 52), *múhur gṛdhyaiḥ prá vadaty ā́rtiṁ mártyo nítya : kravyā́d yā́n agnír antikā́d anuvidvā́n vitā́vati ; priyā́sam* for *bhriyā́sam* (Sāy., Wh., Weber) in **3.5.4c**, *Sómasya parṇáḥ sáha ugrám ā́gann Índreṇa dattó Váruṇena śiṣṭáḥ : táṁ priyā́saṁ bahú rócamāno dīrghāyutvā́ya śatáśāradāya ; bhā́rcīkaḥ* (majority of SPP.'s and one of Wh.'s mss.) for *-ṛjīkaḥ* in **18.1.30c** ; *mathavyā́n* for *madhavyā́n* in **2.35.2c** ; *yáti* for *yádi* (Wh.) in **10.3.6b**, *svapnáṁ suptvā́ yádi páśyāsi pāpáṁ mṛgáḥ sṛtíṁ yáti dhā́vād ájuṣṭām : parikṣavā́c chakúneḥ pāpavādā́d ayáṁ maṇír varaṇó vārayiṣyate*, etc.

aparāparaṇáḥ

avāstúm enam ásvagam áprajasaṁ karoty aparāparaṇó bhavati kṣīyáte. **12.5.45. (12.11.7).** *yá eváṁ vidúṣo brāhmaṇásya kṣatríyo gā́m ādatté.* **v. 46.**

Previous Scholars : 'Adj. ohne Forsetzung, ohne Nachkommens-chaft',—BR. " Elle le prive de fortune, de patrimoine, de posterité : il n'a plus ni ancêtres ni descendants, il perit....,"—Henry. "Celui (*viz.*, sense) de *aparāparaṇó* paraît ressortir à la fois du contexte et de l'analyse du mot,"—*ibid.*, commentary, p. 259. "Without abode, without home, without progeny, she makes him ; he becomes without succession (?) ; he is destroyed : "—Whitney.

BR. and Henry evidently connect *aparāparaṇaḥ* with *parā-para-* which expresses the idea of relativity such as, 'far and near', 'prior and posterior', 'before and behind', etc. But how they explain the suffix *-na* is not clear. In its absence it would rather have meant 'without anything else to stand by, far or near, before or after, in future or in the past', 'all alone by himself', 'stranded in the world'. A change in accentuation would, however, enable us to see in it two words (with double Sandhi), ***áparāḥ* 'devoid of riches (: *raí-* 'riches') ' and **áparaṇaḥ* 'devoid of pleasure', cf. *ápavrata-*, *ápodaka* -etc. For the correspondence, *ā*-(before consonants) : *āy*-(before vowels), cf. Wack. I. § 91, Ved. Gr. § 362. Compare also *śatá-rā-* RV. 10. 106. 5, which, according to Grassmann and Macdonell (*loc. cit.*), has *raí-* for its second member.

arāṭakí-

é'yam agann óṣadhīnāṁ vīrúdhāṁ vīryā̀vatī : ajaśṛṅgy árāṭakī tīkṣṇaśṛṅgí vy ṛṣatu. 4. 37. 6.

Previous Scholars: "*arā adātāro hiṁsakāḥ tān asmāt sthānāt aṭayati uccāṭayatī'ti arāṭakī; tīkṣṇaśṛṅgī tīkṣṇe ugragandhe śṛṅgākṛti phale yasyāḥ evaṁguṇaviśiṣṭā,*"——Sāyaṇa. "N. der Pflanze Aǵaçṛṅgī oder Beiw. derselben........Vielleicht verwandt mit *arāla.*"——BR. "Hither hath come this mighty one (*vīryávant*) of the herbs, of the plants; let the goat-horned *arāṭakī*, the sharp-horned, push out".——Wh. Ludwig and Bloomfield also do not translate *arāṭakī*, nor *ajaśṛṅgī*, and they consider *tīkṣṇaśṛṅgī* as if in the instrumental ('with its sharp horns').

Arāṭa- in *arāṭakī* is evidently the same word as *arāḍa-* [1] in MS. 2. 5. 9, p. 59. 17, *aruṇás tūparáś caitreyó devā́nām āsīn (?) śyétó 'yaḥśṛṅgaḥ 'śaineyó 'surā́ṇāṁ, té 'surā utkrodíno 'carann, arā́ḍo 'smā́kaṁ tūpa 3 ro 'mīṣām iti*, and *arāḍí-* in Ś.Br. 4. 5. 5. 5, *atha yad upāṁśu ℔, hutvā ūrdhvam anumārṣṭi tasmād imā ajā arāḍītarā ākramamāṇā iva yanti*, and in TS. 5. 6. 21. 1, ... *vāruṇī kṛṣṇé vaśé arāḍyaù* [2] *divyā́v ṛṣabhaú parimaraú*. Sāyaṇa explains *arāḍyaù* in TS. as *ucchritaśṛṅgau* 'high-horned', but in view of the passage from MS. quoted above, where *arāḍa-* is contrasted with *tūpará-*'hornless', the meaning seems to be simply 'horned'. The first element in *arāṭa-*, viz., *ara-*, is most probably connected with *ará-* 'spokes', *ala-* 'sting of the scorpion (or, of an insect in general, cf. *alin-* 'bee')', *ā́rā-*'awl', etc., all denoting something pointed, considering how frequently the idea of piercing is associated with *śṛṅga-* 'horn', cf. *śíśīte śṛ́ṅge rákṣase viníkṣe* RV. 5. 2.9**d**, 'he sharpens his (two) horns in order to pierce the demon.' The second element is the suffix *-ṭa*, so frequently found in Apabhraṁśa. It is probably identical with the suffix *-ta*, [3] cerebralised through the influence of the neighbouring *r*-sound,

---

[1] Sans. *t*, between vowels, regularly becomes *-ḍ-* in Prākrit, and most of the modern Indo-Aryan vernaculars, cf Pischel, Prakr. Gramm. § 192; Geiger, Pali Gramm., § 38.

[2] Sāyaṇa (followed by others) connects *arāḍyaù* with *ṛṣabhaú* and accordingly takes *arāḍyà-* as the stem; but in view of the other two passages it seems preferable to take *arāḍí-* as the stem, the word qualifying *vaśé.*

[3] Suffix *-ta* is found in *án-ap-ta-* RV. 9. 16. 3 'not watery': *ap-* 'water', *ántita-* AV.6.4.2, 8.5.11 'near at hand': *ánti-* 'near', *ámanyuta-* AV. 12. 3. 31 'not wrathful': *manyú-* 'wrath', *avatá-* 'well': *áva* 'down', *párvata-* 'mountain' (lit.,'rugged'): *párvan*-joint, *śrómata-* :* *śroman-* (Grassmann), etc. It appears as *-ita* in *puṣpita, phalita,* etc.

although not immediately preceding.[1] For lengthening of the stem-vowel next preceding the suffix and a similar cerebralisation, cf. *kṛkāṭa-* 'neck-joint': *kṛka-* 'throat', *śṛṅgāṭa-* '*Trapa bispinosa*': *śṛṅga-* 'horn'.

Later Sanskrit *arāla-* 'bent', 'curved', 'crooked', must be a further development of the same word. From 'horned' to 'bent like a horn' seems to be an easy step. Intervocalic ṭ > ḍ > l (ḷ) is a common phenomenon in middle Indian, cf. Pischel, Prak. Grammar, § 238 ; Geiger, Pali Grammar, § 386.

As is clear from the quotation from Sāyaṇa above and from the synonyms *viṣāṇikā-* and *meṣaśṛṅgī-* given in the Dhanvantarinighaṇṭu, p. 23, the names and various epithets of this plant (*Odina pinnata*) are due to the hornlike shape of its fruit. The last two pādas of the above verse may be translated: "Let the horned *ajaśṛṅgī* ('goat-horned'), the sharp-horned, (or, with its sharp horns), pierce (the Gandharvas and Apsarases, mentioned above)." Cf. *arāyyàṁ brahmaṇaspate tīkṣṇaśṛṅgo 'dṛṣann ihi* RV. 10. 155. 2, *śṛṅgābhyāṁ rákṣa ṛṣaty ávartiṁ hanti cákṣuṣā* AV. 9. 4. 17, etc.

alají-

visalpásya vidradhásya vātīkārásya vālajéḥ: yákṣmāṇāṁ sárveṣāṁ viṣáṁ níravocam aháṁ tvát. 9. 8. 20.

Previous Scholars: *Alají-* has been rightly identified by BR. and others with *alajī-* of the medical Śāstras, but the meaning of the latter has unfortunately been narrowed down, doubtless through an oversight, to 'a disease of the eye', and Bloomfield goes so far as to render it with 'inflammation of the eyes'. Henry reads *bālají-* instead. Whitney does not translate it.

As a matter of fact, *alají-* appears to be a kind of boil which may be formed in any part of the body. BR. were misled by the occurrence of the word among diseases of the eye in Suśruta, Uttara. Chap. 2, and thought they found support in the word *andhālajī-* (*ghanām avaktrāṁ piḍakām unnatāṁ parimaṇḍalām: andhālajīm alpapūyāṃ tāṁ vidyāt kaphavātajām*, Suśr., Nidāna. Ch. 13, 6) which is simply a boil without a

---

[1] Cf. Pā. *paṭi*: *prati*, Pā. *paṭhama-*: *prathama-*, Saṁh. *dārvāghāṭa-* class. *cārvāghāṭa-*: *āghāta-*, *garuḍá-*: *garutmant-*, class. *asṛpāṭa-* 'bleeding' (lex.): *asṛk-pāta-*,—Wack. I. § 146 (a), para 5.

mouth. Bhelasaṁhitā, p. 91, considers the fifth layer of skin (of which it counts six layers) as the base of *alajī-* and *vidradhi-*, and Suśruta, Sūtra. Ch. 2. 7, 9, considers it as due to the morbidity of the flesh, along with various kinds of tumours and swellings (*adhimāṁsā-'rvudā-'rśo- 'dhijihvo-'pajihvo-'pakuśa-gala-śuṇḍikā-'lajī- māṁsasaṁghātau-'ṣṭhaprakopa-gala* [*gaṇḍa*]- *gaṇḍa-mālā-prabhṛtayo māṁsadoṣajāḥ*). Vāgbhaṭa counts it among boils due to Gonorrhœa (*prameha*), *dahati tvacam utthāne bhṛśaṁ kaṣṭā visarpiṇī : raktakṛṣṇātitṛṭ-sphoṭa-dāha-moha-jvarālajī*, Aṣṭāṅgahṛdaya, Nidāna. 10, 39 (cf. Suśruta, Nid. 6.14, 18), '*alaji* burns the skin, while rising, is very troublesome, expansive, reddish black, and attended with severe thirst, eruption, inflammation, fainting, and high temperature'; among diseases of the face, *gaṇḍālajī sthiraḥ śopho gaṇḍe dāhajvarānvitaḥ*, ib. Uttara. 21. 12, 'a *gaṇḍālajī* is a firm tumour on the cheek, attended with inflammation and high temperature'; among diseases of the eye, *kanīnasyā'ntar alajī śopho ruk-toda-dāhavān*, ib. Uttara. 10. 9 (cf. Suśruta, Uttara 2. 8.), '*alajī* is a tumour in the pupil with pain, pricking sensation, and inflammation'; and elsewhere. A comparison of the above passages would point to its being a boil or tumour similar to *vidradhi* (abscess), but much smaller.

álpaśayu-

yé mā krodháyanti lapitā hastínaṁ maśákā iva : tā́n ahám manye dúrhitān jáne álpaśayūn iva. 4.36.9.

V. l.—Sāyaṇa has *lipitaḥ* (=*upadigdhāḥ, saṁkrāntāḥ*) in **a**, and *durhatān* (=*duṣṭahananena viṣayīkṛtān*) in **c**. The pada- mss. read *lapitā́*, which SPP. emends to *-tāḥ*. Whitney suggests emendation to *lapitvā́*.

Previous Scholars : '. . . . *jane janasaṁghe tatsaṁcārasthale avastithān alpaśayūn, parimāṇataḥ, alpakāyāḥ śayanasvabhāvāḥ saṁcārakṣamāḥ tān alpaśayavaḥ, te yathā prāṇisaṁcāreṇa hanyante tadvad aham anāyāsena apunarbhavaṁ hanmī'tyarthaḥ.*'—Sāyaṇa. 'Ein bestimmtes lästiges Insekt oder dgl.'—PW. (V. 1055), and others have followed ('Ungeziefer' —Grill, 'small vermin'—Bloomfield, 'mites (?)'—Whitney), except Ludwig, who translates: 'die mich. erzürnen, zum sprechen gebracht (wie fliegen den elefanten) | mein ich, sind sie unglücklich, nur kurze zeit im volk verweilend.||' Grill ('durch Gesumm') and Bloomfield ('with their jabber') seem to consider *lapitā* as if in the instrumental.

The redundant syllable in the first pāda and the two obscure words *lapitā* (or *lipitāḥ*) and *álpaśayu-*, which can hardly be reconciled with the context in a satisfactory manner, make it obvious that the passage is corrupt. The meaning of *álpaśayu-* as given by Sāyaṇa and hesitatingly followed by others is a mere guess. The word does not appear to be found anywhere else. *Śayu-* is found elsewhere in the sense of 'the sleepy one', especially the snake called *ajagara*, or of 'couch' as in *śayutrā* (RV.). Neither of these meanings would suit *alpaśayu-*, which, as a Bahuvrīhi, would mean 'one having few *śayus*'. On the other hand, the adjective *dúrhitān*, which means 'miserable' as in RV. 8. 19. 26 (*ná tva rāsīyā 'bhíśastaye vaso ná pāpatvā́ya santya: ná me stotā́ 'matīvā́ ná dúrhitaḥ syā́d Agne na pāpáyā*), suggests that *álpaśayūn* is probably a corruption for *álpapaśūn* (so also Grill, p. 139). Compare, AV. 12. 4. 25, *anapatyám álpapaśuṁ vaśā́ kṛṇoti pū́ruṣam*, and 4. 17. 6, *kṣudhāmārám tṛṣṇāmārám agótām anapatyátām*, where, as in many other places, want of cattle is considered equivalent to misery. The process might have been this: by an unconscious metathesis in the mind of the copyist *álpaśapūn* was written in place of *-paśūn*, which then was easily simplified to *-śayūn*, helped by the similarity of the letters *p* (प) and *y* (य)[1] as well as by the comparative intelligibility of *-śayu-* as against *-śapu-*.

The first hemistich seems to have originally read, *yé me dháyanti lohitā́* (or *-tám*) *hastíno maśákā iva*. The first step seems to have been probably the intrusion of the root *krudh-* from the following verse, after which *lohitā́* (or *-tám*) might have been

---

[1] Another curious instance of confusion of these two letters, followed by a syncopation of the preceding vowel, appears to be *abhíśastyā-* in 6. 120. 2, *bhūmir mātā́ 'ditir no janítraṁ bhrā́tā 'ntárikṣam abhíśastyā naḥ : dyaúr naḥ pitā pítryāc cháṁ bhavāti jāmím ṛtvā́ mā́ ' va patsi lokā́t*, which is of such an obscuring character that Whitney is forced to remark ; 'the variants are of the kind that seem to show that the text was unintelligible to the text-makers, and that we are excusable in finding the text extremely obscure'. If, however, we see *abhíśastyā(ḥ)* < *-śastiyāḥ* < *- śastipāḥ*, the meaning is quite clear : "The earth our mother, Aditi our birthplace, the atmosphere our brother, are our protectors against imprecation; may heaven our father be weal to us from paternal (guilt); having harmed my relatives, may I not fall down from the wished-for-world". The reading in a, *ábhiśasta énaḥ*, in TA. 2. 6. 29 is due to a different kind of confusion, that between *p* (प) and *e* (ए) ; thus, *ábhiśasta énaḥ* < *-śasti panaḥ* < *-śastipā naḥ*. For other examples, see *eru*.

consciously changed to *lapitā* ('jabbering' ?) in order somehow to agree with it and, of course, the genetives *me* and *hastíno* to the corresponding accusatives. Sucking of blood being what is expected of the *piśācas*, the eaters of raw flesh (cf. AV. 5. 29. 9, *kravyā́dam Agne rudhiráṁ piśācám*), against whom the whole hymn is directed, the verse may be translated (with these emendations): "Those who suck my blood as mosquitoes that of the elephant; them I consider wretched, as, among the people, those who have few cattle".

ávarjuṣīṇām

turā́ṇām áturāṇāṁ viśā́m ávarjuṣīṇām: samaítu viśváto bhágo antarhastáṁ kṛtáṁ máma. 7. 50(52). 2.

tváṁ no vāvav eṣām ápūrvyaḥ sómānāṁ prathamáḥ pītím arhasi sutā́nāṁ pītím arhasi: utó vihúnmatīnāṁ viśā́ṁ vavarjúṣīṇām: viśvā́ ít te dhenávo duhra āśíraṁ ghṛtáṁ duhrata āśíram. RV. 1. 134. 6.

Previous Scholars: '*dyūtakriyām aparityajantīnām*',—Sāyaṇa on AV. "Ob reich sie sind oder nicht, die Leute helf kein Widerstand; ......"——Grill. "Of the quick, of the slow, of the people that cannot avoid it (?), let the fortune come together from all sides, my winnings in hand".— Whitney. "The meaning of *ávarjuṣīṇām* in **b** is extremely problematical; the translators "wehrloss" etc. Comparison with *viśā́ṁ vavarjúṣīṇām* RV. 1. 134. 6. and the irregularity of the unreduplicated form, make the reading very suspicious; Ppp. has instead *devayatīm*.... " —*ibid.*, notes. Grassmann and the RV. translators in general consider *vavarjúṣīṇām* as containing *vṛj-* 'to spread', thus meaning 'those who have spread the kuśa-grass'.

The meaning given to *vavarjúṣīṇām* in RV. may suit the context quite well, but *viśā́ṁ vavarjúṣīṇām* and *viśā́m ávarjuṣīṇām* are so much alike that one cannot help thinking that they probably express the same idiom and contain essentially the same words. Both *vavarjúṣīṇām* (: *vṛj-*' 'to spread') and *ávarjuṣīṇām* (: *vṛj-* 'to give up') are irregular if they are really perfect participles with *-vas*, the former because there is scarcely another example in Sanskrit of *-vas* with the strong stem of the perfect,[1] and the latter because of the want of reduplication. The Ppp. reading *devayatī(nā)m* 'worshipping the gods' in the

[1] Cf. Ved. Gr. § 491-92: Brugmann, Grundriss § 136. para. 4, "die Wurzel silbe erscheint meist in Tiefstufengestalt, regelmässig im Arischen.... " The latter, *loc. cit.*, notes some exceptions from Gr. and Goth.

corresponding passage seems to be a paraphrase of *ávarjuṣīṇām* in the Śaunakīya text. For the phrase, cf. RV. 1. 36. 1 (*viśāṁ devayatīnām*), 1. 77. 3, 3. 6. 3, 7. 69. 3 (*devayántīr viśáḥ*). Now, *ávarjuṣīṇām*, if containing *ávas-* 'help, protection (of the gods)' and root *juṣ-* 'to enjoy', 'to relish', with suffix *-i*, would give almost the same idea. The Rigvedic passage might in that case be considered as containing *viśām u avarjúṣīṇam*, which would first became *viśām v avar-*, as in VS. 23. 44, *śám v astu tanvè táva*, or AV. 6. 56.3, *sám v āsnā́ 'ha āsyàm*, and later on, when the meaning had become obscure with the consequence that *vavarjúṣīṇām* was considered one word, *-m* would naturally be changed to Anusvāra. Change of *-as* to *-ar* is not regular, but there are instances. Cf. *ánar-viś-*. RV. 1. 121. 7: *ánas-* and Wack. I. § 28 (γ). Or else, which is more likely, *ávar-* may be a parallel stem with *ávas-*, just as *amnar-: amnas-* (Pāṇ. 8. 2. 20), *usár-: usás-*, *ū́dhar-*: *ū́dhan-: ū́dhas-; áhar-: áhan-; ratharyati: rátha-, vádhar-: vadhá-, vanar-* in *vanargú-*, *vanárṣád-: vána-*, *saparyati-: sap-* 'to worship', etc.

Avár- in *avár mahá Indra dādṛhí śrudhī́ naḥ śuśóca hí dyauḥ kṣā́ ná bhīṣā́ adrivo ghṛṇā́n ná bhīṣā́ adrivaḥ* ......RV. 1. 133. 6, in the hymn just preceding the one considered above and attributed to the same Parucchepa Ṛṣi, may also be the same word. It has been so far considered an instance of *avás-* 'downwards', —the only instance of its ending in *r*. But its identification with *ávas-* gives a much better meaning, when *dādṛhi* (which has been tabulated by Grassmann under *dar-*, *dir-*, 'to burst', 'to split up', with a query) is, at the same time, considered a form of the root *dṛ-* 'to take notice of', 'to regard', which would be quite regular: "Take notice of our great cordial (Grassmann, s.v. *ávas-*, meaning ii), O Indra, (and) listen to us: for the heaven has burnt like the earth (?) for fear, for fear of heat, O you carrying stone ...." If that be the true meaning, the explanation of the present accentuation lies in the confusion of *dādṛhi* as above noticed.

aśvakṣabhā́-

iṣirā́ yóṣā yuvatír dámūnā rā́trī devásya Savitúr Bhágasya: aśvakṣabhā́ suhávā sáṁbhṛtaśrīr ā́ paprau dyā́vāpṛthivī́ mahitvā́, 19. 49. 1.

Previous Scholars: "*aśūni āśūni svaviṣaye śīghra-pravṛttīni akṣāṇi cakṣurādīndriyāṇi abhibhavati tiraskarotī'ti aśvakṣabhā, cakṣurādīnirodhike 'ti yāvat. .... yad vā 'aśvasya budhnaṁ puruṣasya māyum 'ity uttaratra vakṣyamāṇatvād ayam arthaḥ: aśvān kṣāpayati kṣapayatī 'ti aśvakṣā, aśvakṣā bhā dīptir yasyāḥ sā.*" — Sāyaṇa. "The lively woman, household maiden, night, of god Savitar, of Bhaga, all-expanded, of easy invocation, of assembled fortune (?-*çrī*), hath filled heaven-and-earth with greatness". —Whitney. "In **c**, all the mss., with the comm. and SPP., read *açvakṣabhā́* (*açvā̀ kṣabhā́*), which, as being unintelligible, our edition emends at a venture to *viçvá-vyacās*, and the translation follows the latter, for lack of anything better........ Ppp. reads *açvakṣarā.*" — *Ibid.*, notes.

The correct reading may probably be *aśvakṣubhā* 'restless or swift like a horse': *kṣubh-* 'to put in motion,' 'make restless,' cf. *kṣubhā* (Grassmann, "*kṣubh*, f., schnelle Bewegung") in RV. 5. 41. 13, *vidā́ cin nú mahā̄nto yé va évā brávāmo dasmā vā́ryaṁ dádhānāḥ: váyaś caná subhvà ā́'va yanti kṣubhā́ mártam ánuyataṁ vadhasnaíḥ.* If this be the true reading and meaning, it would lend the idea of swiftness to the verbs *ā́ paprau* in **d**, and *áti aruhat* in v. 2 **a**.

asaṁsūktagilá-

Rudrásyai 'labakārébhyo 'saṁsūktagilébhyaḥ: idáṁ mahā́syebhyaḥ śvábhyo akaraṁ námaḥ. 11. 2. 30.

Previous Scholars: "To Rudra's howlmaking, unhymned-swallowing (?), greatmouthed dogs I have said this homage."—Whitney, who notes, "The obscure *asaṁsūktagilá* (Ppp. *-girebhyas*) is paraphrased by the comm. with *asamīcīnam açobhamāna-vacanaṁ gṛṇatti bhāṣante.* How *asaṁsūkta* should come to mean 'unmasticated' as given in the Pet. Lexx. does not appear. The translation given above conjectures 'not having a hymn with it'". "Aux hurleurs de Rudra, | qui dévorent ceux qui n'ont point d'hymnes [à leur chanter]. . . . . " —Henry, who remarks in the commentary, "Je lis *asūkta* 'dépourvu d'hymnes,' le sens implicite étant: 'par conséquent, ils ne nous dévorent pas, nous qui avons un hymne à te chanter'".

The correct reading appears to be *asaṁsūtta-gilébhyaḥ* 'swallowing what is not properly cooked (or not cooked at all)'; *sūtta-*, past participle of *svād-* (alternating with *sūd-*, cf. *sūda-* 'cook' and Wack. I. § 20 and § 79 b) 'to make tasteful', 'to cook', formed in the same way as *nuttá-: nud-*, *vittá-: vid-*, *sattá-: sad-*, etc. The mistake may be due to one of the following reasons: (i) *tt* (त्त) and *kt* (क्त) are very easily confused: (ii) *kt*>*tt* in Pāli, Prāk. and the vernaculars, this being known to the reader or writer, a mistaken attempt to re-Sanskritise it is conceivable; and (iii) *sūkta-* being in much more general use than *sūtta-*, an emendation of the latter, if it is not understood, to the former is also conceivable. It will be seen that 'uncooked-swallowing' is a much happier epithet for dogs than any other that could come from *asaṁ-sūkta-*.

áharjāta-

sáṁ vo goṣṭhéna suṣádā sáṁ rayyā́ sáṁ súbhūtyā: áhar-jātasya yán nā́ma ténā vaḥ sáṁ sṛjāmasi. 3. 14. 1.

ā́ tvā cṛtatv Aryamā́ Pūṣā́ Bṛ́haspátiḥ: áharjātasya yán nā́ma téna tvā́ 'ti cṛtāmasi. 5. 28. 12.

Previous Scholars: '*ahany ahani jāyata ity aharjātaḥ prāṇiviśeṣaḥ, tasya yan nāma aharjāta iti tena nāmnā.*'—Sāyaṇa on 3.14.1. Whitney renders *áharjātasya yán nā́ma* in both the places with 'that which is the name of the dayborn one' and comments (under 3.14.1), "The obscure third pāda is found again below as V. 28. 12.c; it is altogether diversely rendered (conjecturally) by the translators (Weber, "with the blessing of favourable birth"; Ludwig, "with all that which one calls day-born"; Grill, "with whatever a day of luck brings forth"); R. suggests 'with all (of good things) that the day brings, or that is under heaven': none of these suits the other occurrence." "...... 'auspicious' comes very near its sense. Its opposite is anahar-*g*âta, *S*âṅkh. *S*r. XIV, 51, 2–5 'born on an unlucky day'=pâpa-nakṣatre *g*âtaḥ, Kau*s*, 46, 26 and elsewhere......Either it is 'born on a good (pu*n*ya) day' or 'born by day in distinction from night' (cf. naktaṁ*g*âta I. 23. 1.).... 'with the name' might mean 'with kind or species', cf. V, 4, 8."—Bloomfield, p. 351.

It seems that *áharjāta-* here probably refers to the god Bhaga and that there is a pun upon the word, as it also means 'luck'.[1] Cf. AV. 19.45.9, *Bhágo mā bhágenā'vatu*: 3.16.5, *Bhágo evá bhágavā̃ astu devás ténā vayáṁ bhágavantaḥ syāma;* 14.1.34, *sáṁ Bhágena sám Aryamṇā́ sáṁ Dhātā́ sṛjatu várcasā*, etc. Bhaga is frequently mentioned together with Aryaman, Pūṣan, Bṛhaspati, etc. (cf. AV. 3.20.3, 6.4.2, 6.74.1, 14.1.50, etc.),

---

[1] Cf. Macdonell, Ved. Myth., p. 45, "The word *bhaga* also occurs about twenty times in the RV. with the sense of 'bounty, wealth, fortune', and the ambiguity is sometimes played upon."

and might naturally be expected in 5.28.12 as well as in **3.14.1** (the latter immediately followed by, *sáṁ vaḥ sṛjatv Aryamā́ sáṁ Pūṣā́ sáṁ Bṛhaspátiḥ : sáṁ Índro yó dhanañjayáḥ. . . .*). In RV. **1.123.5,** Uṣas is called sister of Bhaga, which suggests that the latter was a morning deity, probably a particular aspect of the sun.[1] AV. 3.16. (=RV. 7.41.), devoted to Bhaga, is composed as if to be chanted in the morning. This supports the above contention and makes it plausible that ***prātarjitam*** in v. 2, which is generally translated as 'early-rising' and which Sāyaṇa (on RV.) takes as two separate words, is probably a corruption of *prātarjātám* 'born in the morning', essentially the same as our *áharjāta-*.

āṇḍika-

eṣá yajñā́nāṁ vítato báhiṣṭho viṣṭāríṇaṁ paktvā́ divám ā́ viveśa : āṇḍī́kaṁ kúmudaṁ sáṁtanoti bísaṁ śālū́kaṁ śáphako mulālí : etā́s tvā dhā́rā úpa yantu sárvāḥ svargé loké mádhumat pínvamānā úpa tvā tiṣṭhantu puṣkaríṇīḥ sámantāḥ. 4.34.5.

nā́'sya kṣétre puṣkaríṇī nā́'ṇḍī́kaṁ jāyate bísam : yásmin rāṣṭré nirudhyáte brahmajāyā́ 'cityā́. 5.17.16.

Previous Scholars: "This extended, is of sacrifices the best carrier; having cooked the *viṣṭārín*, one has entered the sky; the bulb-bearing lotus spreads (*sam-tan*), the *bísa*, *çalū́ka*, *çáphaka*, *mulālí* : let all the streams (*dhā́rā*) come unto thee swelling honeyedly in the heavenly (*svargá*) world; let complete (*sámanta*) lotus-ponds approach thee."—Whitney (4.34.5). "Not in his field is a lotus-pond, the bulb (?*bísa*) of the bulb-bearing lotus is not produced (*jan*), in whose etc., etc."—*ibid.* (5.17.16). Under 4.34.5 he notes, "The mss. (with the exception, doubtless accidental, of our P.K.) all read *báhiṣṭhas* at the end of **a**, and this SPP. retains, while our text makes the obviously called for emendation to *váh-*. The things mentioned in **c, d** appear to be edible parts of water-lilies; the bulbous roots, leaf-stems, and radical fibres, which in some species, as the *Nymphaea esculenta*, are savory, and which are eaten somewhat like asparagus. . . . The *kumuda* is the *N. esculenta* (*kairava*, comm.); and the comm. explains *bísa* (he reads *viśa*) as the root-bulb of the *padma*

---

[1] Cf. Ved. Myth., p. 44, "In the aggregate sense they (*i.e.*, the Ādityas) are the gods of celestial light, without representing any particular manifestation of that light, such as sun, moon, stars, or dawn", and p. 45 "Dawn is Bhaga's sister (1.123.5). Bhaga's eye is adorned with rays (1.136.2), and hymns rise up to Viṣṇu as on Bhaga's path (3.54.14). Yāska describes Bhaga as presiding over the forenoon (Nir. 12.13)".

(*Nelumbium speciosum*) [cf. Lanman, JAOS. XIX. 2d. half, p. 151f.], *çālūka* as that of *utpala* (a *Nymphaea*), *çaphaka* as a hoof-(*çapha*) shaped water-plant, and *mulālī* as=*mṛṇālī*. *Çaphaka* occurs also at Āp. Çs. IX. 14.14., where it seems to signify an edible plant or fruit, perhaps a water-nut".

Of the six names given in 4.34.5**c**, **d**, the meanings of three are definitely known: *kúmuda*-is the water-lily, *śālū̂ka*-is its root, and *mulālí* is the root of the lotus (Pāli has exactly the the same form), of which the latter two are edible. *Bisa*-, in later literature, is often confused with *mṛṇāla*-(*mulālī*-); it is, however, distinct from the latter (cf. *mṛṇālaṁ ca bisānvitam*, Caraka, Cikitsā. 11, 78; *bisāni ca mṛṇālaṁ ca*...., ibid. v. 82; *bisa-mṛṇāla-kaśeruka-sṛṅgāṭaka*......, Suśruta, Sūtra. Ch. 21.) and must originally have meant the stem of plants like water-lily, lotus, etc. The water-lily grows a bulbous (egg-shaped) container of seeds and the lotus, one which looks like a horse's hoof with a circular flat top gradually tapering downwards until it joins the stem; both of these are edible (*i.e.*, only the seeds). The former [1] may be the *āṇḍīka*- and the latter the *śaphaka*-[2]. The three pairs of words in the above verse stand in such a way that one in each pair seems to be the subject of *sáṁ tanoti* and the other its object, thus: "The water-lily spreads the 'egg-like' (at the top), the (lily)-stem—the lily-root (down), (and) the lotus-root—the 'hoof-like' (at the top)". This would imply emendation of *śáphako* to *-kaṁ*. A similar emendation seems to be required also for *vítato* and *váhiṣṭho* (as emended by Wh.) in **a**, which would then agree with *viṣṭāríṇam* and thus leave *eṣáḥ* free to be the subject of *paktvā́* and *ā́ viveśa*.

āśuṅgá-

nír balā́se 'táḥ prá patā́ 'śuṅgáḥ śiśukó yathā: átho íṭa iva hāyanó 'pa drā́hy ávīrahā. 6.14.3.

Previous Scholars: '*he balāsa*........*yathā yena prakāreṇa āśuṅgaḥ aśugāmī śuśukaḥ etatsaṁjño mṛgo dūraṁ dhāvati tadvat gaccha*'.—Sāyaṇa.

[1] It is interesting to note that it is called *bhẽṭ* in Bengali, while what is known as 'egg-fruit' in English is called *bhā̃ṭā* in Hindi.

[2] *Śaphaka* in Āp. Śr. 9. 14. 14, *kṛṣṇājinaṁ kūṭo vā karṇo vā gardabho hariṇo vā harinapṛṇākā va śyāmāka-pātro vā śaphako ve'ti vijñāyate*, is explained by the commentator as 'a deer that has lost a hoof' and Caland follows him in his translation.

"M. wohl so v. als *āśuga*, N.eines Thieres, vielleicht eines Vogels...... Möglich ist die Auffassung (in AV.): wie ein Füllen, das zum Rosse (*āśu*) läuft."—BR. "Fly forth from here, O balâsa, as a swift foal (after the mare). And even, as the reed in every year, pass away without slaying men".—Bloomfield. "Fly forth, O *balāsa*, like a young *açuṁgá*,"—Whitney.

In the present reading it is doubtful whether we have to take *áśuṅgáḥ* or *śiśukáḥ* as the substantive. If following BR. and Whitney we take the former as a noun, denoting some bird, and *śiśukáḥ* as its adjective, the comparison falls flat, since a young bird can hardly fly. On the other hand, if *āśuṁgá-* is an adjective, the formation causes difficulty. As a rule, when, in a compound word, a nominal stem has a nasal just before the verbal root following it, it is simply the sign of the accusative of that stem. *Āśu-* being an adverb can only have *āśu* in the accusative. The only other apparent exception to this rule is *makṣuṁgamá-* in *makṣuṁgamābhir ūtíbhiḥ* RV.8.22.16 [cf. Wack. 2.1.§86 (e). n: Ved. Gr. §. 276 (p. 164. fn. 5.)]. But *makṣuṁgamá-* may be explained as meaning 'going to the quick (in sacrifice)', not 'quickly-going'.

Śiśu (*ká*)- means 'the young of an animal or man' and it often stands for the calf as in RV. 2.34.8, *dhenúr ná śíśve*: the latter may be its meaning also here, its running away (at the approach of man, owing to nervousness), which is the point of comparison, being well-known. In view of this *-tā' śuṅgáḥ* may be considered a corruption for *-ta aśṛṅgáḥ*, helped by the pronunciation of *ṛ* as *ru* in some parts of Southern India, cf. *tā́bhi ṣṭuptó*, *sruptó*, or *stutó* for-*bhis-tṛptó* in AV. 19.4.1d (Wh.'s notes). *Aśṛṅgáḥ* 'hornless' would imply that the calf is very young and would thereby support the point of comparison

āsrāvá-

yáthā dyā́ṁ ca pṛthivī́ṁ cā́'ntás tíṣṭhati téjanam: evā́ rógaṁ cā 'srāvā́ṁ cā 'ntás tiṣṭhatu múñja ít. 1. 2. 4.

ā́d aṅgā́ kuvíd aṅgā́ śatáṁ yā́ bheṣajā́ni te: téṣām asi tvám uttamám anāsrāvám árogaṇam 2. 3. 2. *nīcaíḥ khananty ásurā arusrā́ṇam idáṁ mahát: tád āsrāvásya bheṣajáṁ tád u rógam anīnaśat.* v. 3. (of which **c** and **d** are repeated as **c** and **d** of vs. 4 and 5).

śatáṁ yā́ bheṣajā́ni te sahásraṁ sáṁgatāni ca: śréṣṭham āsrāva-bheṣajáṁ vásiṣṭhaṁ roganā́śanam. 6. 44. 2.

Previous Scholars: Sāyaṇa explains *āsrāvá-* as *mūtrātisāra-*(diabetes) in 1.2.4, *atīsārā-'timūtra-nāḍīvraṇādayaḥ* (diarrhœa, diabetes, ulcer, etc.) in 2.3.2, and *raktasrāva-* (bleeding) in 6.44.2. "Ein Körperschaden, Gebrechen",—BR. 'Diarrhœa',—Bloomfield and Grill. The latter remarks (p.80): "2.b. *âsrâvá* nicht: Fluss, eiternde Wunde,....sondern... Durchfall (Dârila: *atisára*). Die dreimalige Zusammen-stellung mit *róga* lässt für letztres die Bedeutung: Leibweh (cf. *rúj* f.) annehmen (so ist z.B, *çiroroga=çîrśakti* Kopfweh bei Dâr)." "*Āsrāvá* is rendered by the indefinite term 'flux', its specific meaning being uncertain;" —Whitney, under 2.3.2.

It seems to me that the specific meaning 'bleeding' is required in all the above occurrences of *āsrāvá*. The following are the reasons: (1) AV. 1. 2. is about the defiance (v. 2) and avoidance (v. 3) of the arrows of the enemy. V. 4. would fit in with the other verses only if it relates to a wound already made and its cure; otherwise, as Whitney suggests, it would seem unconnected. See Kauś., 14. 7 and 12, and Whitney's introduction to the hymn. (2) Hymn 2. 3. contains the word *arusrā́ṇa-* 'wound-healer' twice (vs. 2 and 5), and appears to be directed only against the healing of wounds and stoppage of bleeding. (3) *Róga-*, found in every case with *āsrāvá-*, seems to have a special meaning here, probably a derivative and archaic one, 'wound', lit. 'breach (in the body)' : *ruj-* 'to break'. This would help to clear the obscurity of the second half of the first verse quoted above, showing at the same time its special connection with *āsrāvá-*, and would also give a point to 6. 44. 1: "The heaven has stopped, the earth has stopped, this whole world has stopped: the erect sleeping trees have stopped, may this thy wound (*i.e.*, its bleeding) stop." And lastly (4), 6. 44. 3 contains the word *vātī́kṛta-nā́śanī* which as shown by Zimmer, Altindisches Leben, p. 389, means 'healer of the wound'. Thus all the three hymns in which *āsrāvá-* is found are solely directed towards the healing of wounds.[1]

[1] *Vātīkṛta-* is found again at 6. 109. 3 together with *kṣiptá-* ('bruised', Wh.) and *atividdhá-* ('pierced'), and *vātīkā́ra-* at 9.8(13).20 together with *visalpá-*, *vidradhá-* and *alají-*, all referring to an abcess or boil of some kind. Zimmer identifies *vāta-* with Germ. 'Wunde'. It

uttaradraú

meṣá iva vaí sáṁ ca ví co'rv àcyase yád uttaradrā́v úparaś ca khā́dataḥ: śīrṣṇā́ śíró 'psasā́ 'pso ardáyann aṁśū́n babhasti háritebhir āsábhiḥ. 6. 49. 2.

Previous Scholars: Sāyaṇa, following Kauś. 46. 14, considers all the three verses in the hymn as addressed to Agni by the pupil on the occasion of his preceptor's cremation. His reading is slightly different, having *ucyase* (< *uc samavāye*) for *acyase* in **a**, *aparaḥ* for *uparaḥ* in **b** and *bibhasti*(=*bhakṣayati*) in **d**. He explains *uttaradraú* either as *uparyavasthita-kāṣṭha-yukte dāhyaśarīre* or *utkṛṣṭataradrume mahāvṛkṣabhūyiṣṭhe vane* and supplies *Agniḥ* as subject of *babhasti* in **d**. "wie ein beutel [blasbalg] ziehst du zusammen weit dann auszeinander dich, wenn der oben laufende [uttara-drâh ?] stein und untere freszen, | drängend kopf an kopf, wange an wange friszt er die stängel mit grünem maul."—Ludwig, p. 432. "Like a ram, thou art bent together and wide apart, when in the upper wood the upper and the lower stone devour; exciting (*ard*) head with head, breast (*ápsas*) with breast, he gnaws the soma-stalks with green mouths."—Whitney.

The verse is one of three forming a hymn, which seem to have been originally unconnected (see Whitney, introduction to the hymn). As it stands it hardly gives any connected sense, and the text (given by Wh. in the notes) as found in Ppp., KS., or Āp. Śr. is still worse. The correct reading seems to be : *meṣá iva vaí sáṁ ca ví co 'rv àcyase yád uttara dvā́v úparaś ca khā́dathaḥ: śīrṣṇā́ śíró 'psasā́ 'pso ardáyann aṁśū́n babhatsi háritebhir āsábhiḥ*. "Like a ram, thou art bent together and wide apart, when, O upper stone, thou and the lower one, the two, devour; pressing head with head, breast with breast, thou gnawest the soma-stalks with green mouths."

As Whitney also has suggested alternatively, the action of the stones here is compared to that of the rams, butting and drawing back, in a ram-fight, a favourite pastime even now in India. The corruption would be explained by a graphic confusion in the change from *dvā-* (द्वा) to *drā-* (द्रा), followed by an emendation of *khādathaḥ* to *-taḥ*, and a metathesis in *babhatsi*

---

seems to contain a root *van-* 'to cut' which is probably to be traced also in *van- vána-* 'wood', *vaṁśá-* 'bamboo' (cf. *vṛkṣa-* 'tree' : *vraśc-* 'to cut') *vā́śī-* 'axe' etc. If this is identical with *van-* 'to like', 'to enjoy', the development of meaning may be traced thus: 'to cut'>'to divide'> to share'>'to enjoy'.

to *-sti*, the former being the second person, singular, present of root *bhas-*, viz., **babhas-si* (for change of *s* to *t*, cf. Wack. I. 153).

Similar must be the case with *babhasti* in v. 1 of the same hymn, *nahí te Agne tanvàḥ krūrám ānáṁśa mártyaḥ: kapír babhasti téjanaṁ sváṁ jarā́yu gaúr iva*, which Whitney translates, "Surely no mortal, O Agni, hath attained the cruelty of thy self (*tanú*). The ape gnaws (*bhas*) the shaft (*téjana*) as a cow her own after-birth." Here the second half-verse as it stands, presents no traceable connection with the first, and as nothing is known about the ape's gnawing a shaft, the comparison is obscure. But an emendation of *babhasti* to *-tsi* and *téjanam* to *te jánam* not only brings out a good sense, but also supports Kauśika's injunctions: "The tawny one, thou gnawest thine own man (*i.e.*, worshipper, namely, my preceptor), like a cow her after-birth." For *kapí-* in the sense of 'tawny', cf. Abhidhāna-Rājendra, s.v. *kavi*, and also *kapila-* and *kapiśa-*.

ṛdantu

Índra jahí púmāṁsam yātudhā́nam utá stríyaṁ māyáyā śā́śadānām: vígrīvāso mū́radevā ṛdantu mā́ té dṛśant sū́ryam uccárantam. 8. 4. 24.=RV. 7. 104. 24.

Previous Scholars: *ṛdantu*=*naśyantu*, *śā́śadānām*=*hiṁsantīm*.—Sāyaṇa, RV. and AV. BR., followed by Grassmann, consider it a form of √*ard-* and give the meaning 'in Bewegung (der Theile) gerathen, zerstieben, sich auflösen'. "O Indra, frappe le sorcier mâle | et la femelle qui s'enorguillét de sa magic: || que le démons au col tors soient anéantis: | qu'ils ne voient pas le soleil se lever."—Henry. "O Indra, smite the man sorcerer, likewise the woman who is prevailing with magic (*māyā́*); let the neckless false-worshippers vanish (*ṛd*); let them not see the sun moving upwards."—Whitney, with the remark, "The obscure *ṛdantu* is glossed by the comm. with *naçyantu*".

Besides here the root *ṛd-* is found in the following typical instances: (*a*) *ārdrá-* RV. 1. 116. 4, 2. 13. 6, AV. 1. 32. 8, and in the compounds °*dānu-* AV. 16. 3. 4, VS. 18. 45, °*pavi-* AV. 16. 3. 4, °*pavitra-* AV. 9. 6. 27, °*hasta-* AV. 12. 3. 13; (*b*) *ṛdu-* in *ṛdūdára-*, epithet of Rudra RV. 2. 33. 5, of Mitra, Varuṇa, and the Ādityas *ib.* 3. 54. 10, of Soma *ib.* 8. 48. 10, and *ṛdūpé* (p. *ṛdu° pé*) and *ṛdūvṛ́dhā* (p. *ṛdu° vṛ́dhā*) RV. 8. 77. 11;

(c) *ārdan dhánvāni* RV. 4. 17. 2; (d) *kāṭám ardati* AV. 12. 4. 3; (e) *ardati* 'to pray,' *ardanā-* 'prayer,' later Sans.; (f) *prārdayo nīcīr apásaḥ samudrám* RV. 6. 17. 12; (g) *udadhím ardáya* AV. 4. 15. 6,—*ardayāti* ib. v. 11; (h) *párāñcaṁ śúṣmam ardaya* AV. 6. 65. 1, (i) *vṛtrám ardáy-* RV. 1. 187. 1, 10. 142. 2, *Āyúm Kútsam, Atithigvám*....8.53.2 *ví parirāpáḥ*....2.23.14; (j) *śīrṣṇā śiró 'psasā 'pso ardáyan* AV. 6. 49. 2 and later Sans.

Outside Sanskrit it is found in the Gr. verb ἄρδω, ἀρδεύω 'to sprinkle, to water' and in the derivatives, ἀρδμός 'water for sprinkling,' ἀρδάνιον 'vase of water'; also in Av. *arədvī* 'goddess of the waters.'—Boisacq, Greek Dictionary, s.v. ἄρδω.

All facts considered, the original meaning appears to be, (1) 'to be or make wet or watery,' from which, through association of ideas, must have developed the following meanings: (2) from the impression of running water or rainfall, (i) 'to glide,' (ii) 'to fall'; (3) from moistening one's heart through prayer, 'to pray, to ask for'; (4) in the causatives, (i) 'to make something, such as water, glide,' (ii) 'to make fall,' 'to send down rain,' etc., (iii) 'to make an enemy fall,' *i.e.*, 'to defeat or kill'; (5) from 4 (iii) 'to press or oppress."[1]

We shall now see how these meanings fit in with the above typical instances.

To begin with, (a) *ārdrá-* not only means 'wet' (*i.e.*, soaked with water) as in RV. 2. 13. 6, *yó bhójanaṁ ca dáyase ca várdhanam ārdrād ā śúṣkaṁ mádhumad dudóhitha*, but also 'watery' (*i.e.*, composed wholly of water) as in RV. 1. 116. 4, *tisráḥ kṣápas trír áhā 'tivrajadbhir Nāsatyā Bhujyúm ūhathuḥ pataṅgaíḥ: samudrásya dhánvann ārdrásya pāré tribhí ráthaiḥ*

---

[1] Prof. Sieg thinks there are probably two different roots, (1) *ṛd-* 'to water' contained in the Gr. and Av. instances, in *ārdrá-*, and probably in *ṛdu-*, and (2) *ṛd-* 'to fall' contained in the other instances. But considering the relationship of *dru-* 'to melt,' and *dru-* 'to glide,' 'to run fast,' of *gal-* 'to melt' and *gal-* 'to slip or fall,' H. *girnā* 'to fall,' and of Eng. verbs *drip* and *drop*, it seems not unlikely that they are one and the same root in different stages of development of meanings. Walde, s.v. *erd-* "(zer)fliessen, Feuchtigheit," also connects *ardati, ṛdáti* 'flows, etc.', *ardayati* 'kills, etc.', *ārdrá-* 'wet,' *ṛduḥ-* 'moisture', and Av. *arədvī-*, although he separates Gr. ἄρδω etc., from this group.

śatápadbhiḥ ṣáḷaśvaih, and in *ārdrádānu-* 'having watery drops,' cf. VS. 18. 45, *samudró 'si nábhasvān ārdrádānuḥ*.

(*b*) Yāska, Nir. 6. 8, equates *ṛdūdára-* with *mṛdūdara-* and is followed by Sāyaṇa and BR., the latter giving the meaning 'mild, sanft, gnädig.' Following the traditional accentuation Grassmann splits up the word into *ṛdu°dára-* (suggested also by BR.); the pada-text does not divide it. As there is hardly another instance of loss of an initial *m*, Grassmann is evidently right in holding that an element *ṛdu-*[1] (which has nothing to do with *mṛdu-*) is to be seen in the three words *ṛdūdára-*, *ṛdūpé*, and *ṛdūvṛ́dhā*. *Ṛdūdára-* probably has the same meaning as *vapódara-* in RV. 8. 17. 8, *tuvigrī́vo vapódaraḥ subāhúr ándhaso máde : índro vṛtrā́ṇi jighnate*, which does not appear to mean 'obese' as taken by Grassmann, but rather 'one having fat (here a special variety of it, namely, ghee) in his stomach' (like *vā́jajaṭhara-*, epithet of *gharmá-*, 5. 19. 4); cf. the epithets, *ghṛtā́nnau* RV. 6. 67. 8, *ghṛtā́sutī* 1. 136. 1, 2. 41. 6, and *ghṛtáyonī* 5. 62. 2 of *Mitrā́-Váruṇā*, *ghṛtā́sutī* 6. 69. 6 of *Índrā-Víṣṇū*, and *ghṛtaśrī́* 10. 65. 2, *ghṛtásnu-* 9. 88. 5, of Soma. Compare also *vapā́vant-*, epithet of Agni RV. 6. 1. 3, with *ghṛtávantaṁ yónim* of Agni RV. 10. 91. 4. Thus *ṛdu-*= *vapā́-* or *ghṛtá-* (: *ṛd* with meaning 2. i.), and the second element is *udára-*, not *dára-*.

This meaning of *ṛdu-* suits also RV. 8. 77. 11, *tuvikṣáṁ te súkṛtaṁ sūmáyaṁ dhánuḥ sādhúr bundó hiraṇyáyaḥ : ubhā́ te bāhū́ ráṇyā súsaṁskṛtā ṛdūpé cid ṛdūvṛ́dhā*, of which the fourth pāda seems to have presented a difficulty ever since the time of Yāska. Sāyaṇa simply quotes Yāska, Nir. 6. 8, '*eṣā nirukte ekam api padaṁ vihāya Yāskena vyākhyātā, tad eva likhyate. tuvikṣaṁ bahuvikṣepaṁ mahāvikṣepaṁ te sukṛtaṁ sūmayaṁ susukhaṁ dhanuḥ sādhayitā te bundo hiraṇyaṇyaḥ : ubhā te bāhū raṇyau ramaṇīyau sāṁgrāmyau va' rdupe ardana-pātinau marmaṇy ardanavedhinau vā.*' How the form *ṛdupé* (not, however, considered a *pragṛhya* in the pada) can qualify, as an adjective, a masculine noun *bāhū́* does not appear. BR. and Grassmann take it to mean 'Biene oder ein anderes süssigkeit suchendes Thier, f.'; but even then the force of *cid* 'even'

---

[1] For this word, see also IF 2, 27.

is lost and we have to assume it here as equivalent to *iva*. It is probably the locative singular of *ṛdupá-*, 'in the sucking of butter,' used in a verbal sense like *avaghraḥ* (=*avaghrāṇam* 'smelling') in Āp. Śr. 8. 16. 3, 12; 13. 17. 9; 15. 11. 14. The adj. *súsaṁskṛta-* 'well-polished' seems also to imply the rubbing of Indra's arms with ghee (or some other oily substance), which would afterwards shine and thus give out all the more the gloss due to it (*ṛdūvṛ́dh-*). Thus we may translate: "Many-killing, well-made, well-finished is thy bow, magnificent, golden is (thy) arrow: both thy arms are fit for the fight (*rányа-* <*ráṇa-* 'fight'), well-polished, which, even in sucking butter, are butter-increasing."

(c) *Árdan dhánvāni* in RV. 4. 17. 2, *táva tviṣó jániman rejata dyaúr éjad bhū́mir bhiyásā svásya manyóḥ: ṛghāyánta subhvàḥ párvatāsa ā́rdan dhánvāni saráyanta ā́paḥ*, probably means 'the dry lands became wet' (1),[1] cf. the contrast between the wet sea and the dry land in RV. 1. 116. 4, quoted above, and *dhánvant srótaḥ kṛṇute* ib. 1. 95. 10a or *íre 'va dhánvan ní jajāsa te viṣám* AV. 5. 13. 1.

(d) *Kāṭám ardati* in AV. 12. 4. 3, *kūṭáyā 'sya sáṁ śīryante sloṇáyā kāṭám ardati: baṇḍáyā dahyante gṛhāḥ kāṇáyā dīyate svám*, definitely means 'falls into a pit'.

(e) *Ardati* in the sense of 'requesting, praying (3)' is found only in classical Sanskrit, as in Raghuvaṁśa 5. 17, ... *nirgalitāmbugarbhaṁ śaradghanaṁ nā 'rdati cātako 'pi.*

(f) In the instance quoted above it means 'thou madest (the waters) glide forward (4. i.)'.

---

[1] Prof. Sieg thinks that here too, as in (*d*), the root *ṛd-* means 'to fall', the imagery, according to him, being that the mountains dropped down stones on to the dry land and water below, and made the latter move. He, together with several other authorities, considers that the passage refers to the violent movements on the earth's surface during a volcanic eruption or earthquake. This, however, is not sufficiently clear from the context, which seems rather to indulge in a glorification of Indra by stating that fixed states of things alter when he is angry, cf. in particular v. 13. Another objection is that the construction of the verse is such as to imply that *dhánvāni* and *ā́paḥ* are as much subjects to the verbs attached to them as *dyaúḥ, bhū́miḥ* and *párvatāsaḥ* to those attached to them.

(*g*) In the AV. instances quoted above it means 'send down (the cloud) (4. ii)'.

(*h*) *Áva manyúr ávā́ 'yatā́ 'va bāhū́ manoyújā : párāśara tvám téṣām párāñcaṁ śúṣmam ardayā́ 'dhā no rayím ā́ kṛdhi*, AV. 6. 65. 1, is translated by Whitney: "Down (*áva*) be the fury, down the drawn [arrow], down the mind-yoked arms. O demolisher (*parāçara*), do thou vex (*ard*) away the vehemence (*çúṣma*) of them; then get us wealth." I think **d** rather means, 'do thou make their vehemence fall far away (4. ii)'.

(*i*) In the defeating or killing of enemies the idea of making them fall (4. iii) is prominent.

(*j*) *śīrṣṇā́ śiró 'psasā́ 'pso ardáyan aṁśū́n babhasti háritebhir āsábhiḥ*, 6. 49. 2. Whitney has 'exciting (*ard*) head with head, breast (*ápsas*) with breast', etc. It rather means 'pressing (5) head with head', etc. *Ardati* in this sense is common in later Sanskrit.

Ṛdantu in the verse under discussion appears to contain the root-aorist stem and to mean 'fall' (2. ii). Accordingly our verse may be translated: "O Indra, slay the male sorcerer and the female, shining forth with magic; let the root-devotees fall neckless (on the ground); may they not see the rising sun."[1]

éru-

udaprúto Marútas tā́ iyarta vṛṣṭír yā́ víśvā nivátas pṛṇā́ti : éjāti gláhā kanyè 'va tunnái 'ruṁ túndānā pátye 'va jāyā́. 6. 22. 3.=TS. 3. 1. 11[8], with variants:........*Marutas*...... *vṛ́ṣṭiṁ yé víśve Marúto junánti : króśāti gárdā*......*pérum tuñjānā́*........

V. l.: Ppp., with the majority of SPP.'s authorities and some of Wh.'s (P.M.), reads *udaplútas*. One of Wh.'s (W.) mss., three of SPP.'s, and apparently also the commentator's text have *gálhā* for *gláhā*.—See Wh.'s notes.

---

[1] The meaning 'to shine forth, to become prominent', given by Grassmann as the first meaning of √*śád-*, seems to suit all the Rigvedic occurrences. *Mū́ardevāḥ* are those who are devoted to the roots, as means of sorcery, as the Ṛṣis to the gods. It does not necessarily imply literally worshipping the roots, but simply expecting everything through their help, as others do through that of the gods. For Fuller discussion, see *s.v.* below.

Pada........*tā́n*......*yā́ḥ víśvāḥ*....:........*pátyā iva*....

Previous Scholars: Sāyaṇa on AV: "*he Marutaḥ udaprutaḥ udaksya prerakān tān meghān iyarta prerayata*........*yā yadīyā yeṣāṁ meghānāṁ saṁbandhinī vṛṣṭiḥ viśvā viśvāni vrīhiyavādīni nivataḥ nimnagāminīr nadīś ca pṛṇāti pūrayati*:...... *gahlayati kutsayati bhītim utpādayatīti gahlā stanayitnurūpā mādhyamikā vāk*:........ *yathā tunnā dāridryādi-bhiḥ pīḍita kanyā mātāpitrādīn kampayati tadvat*........*erum gantāraṁ meghaṁ prāpya tuñjānā ābhāṣamāṇā dhvanantī*....*patyā sahitā jāyeva*...." The commentary on the TS. is essentially the same except for slight modifications required by the text. Pischel, Ved. Stud., I. 81-85, has a long discussion on this verse, and after trying to show, — *tā́*=*tā́m*; *gárda*- synonymous with *gláha*-, both adj. meaning 'lascivious'; *péru*-<√*pī* and *éru*-<√*īr*, both synonymous, meaning 'penis', and *tuñjānā́* or *túndānā*, passive— he translates: "O ihr Maruts, im Wasser schwimmend, sendet solchen Regen herab, dass er alle Thäler Anfülle. Er möge herab-stürzen wie ein geiles Mädchen (sich heftig bewegt), wenn sie gebraucht wird (*tunnā́*), wie eine Frau, wenn ihr von dem Manne der penis eingestos-sen wird." Whitney renders,— "Water-swimming are the Maruts; send ye that rain which shall fill all the hollows; the *gláhā* shall bestir itself, like a girl that is thrust, thrusting the *éru*, like wife with husband," and remarks, "The text of this verse is hopelessly corrupt, and all attempts to make connected sense of the second half must apparently be (like that of Pischel in Ved Stud. I. 81. ff.) forced and unsuccessful". See his elaborate notes.

It seems necessary first of all to try to reconstruct the original text and to find out the value, grammatical or otherwise, of the obscure words. *Udaprúto Marutas* of TS. may be accepted, the first qualifying *nivátas* and the second being a vocative. *Tā́* stands for *tā́ḥ*, qualifying *nivátas*, the Anunāsika standing merely to prevent a hiatus, cf. *aminantā́ évaiḥ* RV. 1. 79. 2, *kṣā́ ná bhīṣā́ adrivaḥ* ib. 1. 133. 6, *stríyaḥ satís tā̃* (p. *tā*) *u me puṁsá āhuḥ* ib. 1. 164. 16, etc., and Wack. I. §267. γ. The **b** of TS. is simply a substitution, due to reminiscence, of **b** of RV. 5. 58. 3. *Gláhā* is a simplification to a better known word of *gálhā* (see *v.l.* above), which must have come out of *gáldā*, a variant of *gárdā*, through a confusion of *d* (द) and **h** (ह) cf. *hāsyán áhāsyan* in some mss. for *dāsyán ádāsyan* AV. 6. 71. 3 (in Wh.'s collation book), *āhuta*, variant of *ād uta* AV. 19. 2. 5 (Wh.'s notes), etc. *Éru*- in AV. must be a corruption for *péru*, occasioned through a confusion of *e* (ए) and *p* (प), cf. *v.l.* to Pariśiṣṭas of the AV., XLVIII. 116, where mss. A.E.T.V. read *pelava* for *ailava*; Ch. 8. चंद्र। पनान for चंद्र। एनान्

AV. 8. 8. 3, and footnote to *álpaśayu*. *Krόśāti* in TS. is due to a remembrance of Nigh. 1. 11, where *galdā́-* is considered a synonym of *vāc-*. *Pátyeva* is for *pátya iva* < *pátye iva*, an instance of double Sandhi, cf. *vándaneva* for *vándanaḥ iva* AV. 7. 115. 2, *kṛtyéti* for *kṛtye íti* 10. 1. 15, *vā́teva* for *vā́taḥ iva*, *úcchiṣaiṣām* for *úcchiṣaḥ eṣām* (as shown by meter) AV. 10. 1. 17, etc. *Jāyéva pátye* is a favourite Vedic expression, here inverted for the sake of meter, cf. *jāyéva pátye tanvàṁ riricyām* RV. 10. 10. 7, which contains the same idea as here, and also RV. 1. 124. 7, 10. 71. 4. Or, probably *va* is to be read here instead of *iva* as in a number of instances in the RV., cf. Grassmann, Wört., s.v. *iva*. *Tuñjānā́* as read by the commentator and the TS. will be found a better reading than *túndānā*.

Thus the reconstructed text would be (in pada-pāṭha): *udaprútaḥ Marutaḥ tā́ḥ iyarta vṛṣṭíḥ yā́ḥ víśvāḥ nivátaḥ pṛṇā́ti: éjāti gáldā kanyā̀ iva tunnā́ pérum tuñjānā́ pátye iva jāyā́.*

We have now to find out the meanings of *gáldā-* and *péru-*. Keśavasvāmin, a very careful and well-read lexicographer (see Introduction to Kalpadrukośa, GOS. XLII, vol. I, p. xxxviiif.), gives the meaning 'stream or current' to *gardā*: *gardā strī dravadhārāyāṁ dhamanīṣu ca vāci nā.* The other two meanings, *viz.*, 'veins' and 'speech', must have come out of a metaphorical use of the word,—'veins' and 'speech' considered as streams. This is apparently supported by the Nighaṇṭu, which, besides counting *galdā́-* among the homonymous words at 4. 3, has at 1. 11: *ślokaḥ* | *dhā́rā* | ...... *dhamánī* | *nā́ḷīḥ* | .... *galdā́* | *sáraḥ* | *suparṇí* | *bekure 'ti saptapañcāśad vāṅnāmāni.* Even a cursory glance at the Nighaṇṭu will suffice to show that the words given there as 'names' of a certain thing are not to be taken literally as synonyms. They are in almost every case a motley collection of synonyms as well as of words adjectively or metaphorically used in reference to the object in question. The same must be the case here, as the selected words given above will show. Nir. 1. 6. 24 has, "*galdā dhamanayo bhavanti galanam āsu dhīyate*: '*ā́ tvā viśantv índava ā́ galdā́ dhamánīnām*' (found in M. Śr., and elsewhere with variants: see Ved. Concord.); *nānā-*

vibhakty ete bhavataḥ, āgalanā dhamanīnām ity atrā 'rthaḥ." As a matter of fact, the meaning 'stream' is what is required here, —'let the drops (of soma) enter thee, enter the streams of thy veins'. The other known occurrence of the word is in RV. 8. 1. 20=SV. I.4.1.2.5: *mā́* (*ā́*, SV.)*tvā́ sómasya gáldayā sádā yā́cann aháṁ girā́* (*jyā́*, SV.)*: bhū́rṇiṁ mṛgáṁ ná sávaneṣu cukrudhaṁ ká ī́śānaṁ ná yācisat.* "May I not, asking always (for something) with streams of soma, (and) with prayer, anger thee in the libations, like a (wild) beast; who would not beg of the lord?" Cf. *sómasya dhā́rā* RV. 9. 80. 1, and many other instances where *dhā́rā-* stands for the stream of soma, Grassmann, Wört., s.v. *dhā́rā.* The above two will, I think, explain why the Nigh. grouped *dhamánī-* and *gáldā-* among the names of speech. H. *gād* f. 'impure liquor from an indigo vat', Beng. *gād* 'foamy dirt on the surface of a liquid, such as treacles', are probably the same word as *gáldā-*, the meaning having conceivably been transferred from the foamy surface of a stream, when full.

Péru- appears to be only a bye-form of *pera-* or *pela-* 'testicles'. For alternaces of *a* and *u*, see above under *ákṣu*. As a matter of fact Vj. 178, 126 has *pheluka-, astriyo muṣkakośāṇḍāḥ pheluko vṛṣaṇo 'ṇḍukaḥ*. Here it stands for the female generating organ; cf. *muṣká* 'testicles' used in the same sense, *amúṣyā ádhi muṣkáyoḥ* AV. 6. 138. 5, *arā́yān asyā́ muṣkā́bhyāṁ bháṁsasó 'pa hanmasi* 8. 6. 5. Transference of meaning from 'testicles' to the 'generating organ' is also found in Hindi *ā̃ṛ*, Beng. *ẽṛ* 'penis' < *āṇḍa-* 'testicles'. For use of singular instead of dual, cf. *ū́rum* in AV. 14. 2. 39, *ā́ rohó 'rum úpa dhatsva hástam*, etc. Kautsavya Nighaṇṭu, Pariśiṣṭas of the AV., p. 315, 124, has [*paraṃgatuvilike* (v.l., *°tilike, paraṃgati vilīke, paraṃgatī°*)] *iti strīprajananasya*, which, as it stands, does not give any sense. As this Nigh. professes to be particularly attached to the AV., we may expect to find these words in the latter. The correct reading may probably be *perv-aṅga-tauvilikā iti*, etc., of which *péru-* is found here, referring to the female organ (*strīprajanana-*), *áṅgena* in *evā́ te śépaḥ sáhasā 'yám arkó 'ṅgenā́ 'ṅgaṁ sáṁsamakaṁ kṛṇotu* 6. 72. 1, and *taúvilikā* in *taúvilikḗ 've 'layā́ 'vā 'yám ailabá ailayīt* 6. 16. 3, whose meaning is not certain, but may possibly be the same.

Thus we may translate: "O Maruts, impel those hollows (*viz.*, rivers, lakes, etc.), over-flowing with water, all of which the rain fills up: may the current heave like a maiden, struck, (or) a wife offering (lit., thrusting forth) her member for the husband."

The comparison is between the undulation of water, stirred by the wind, and the rising and falling of the breast of a girl, sobbing when she is beaten, or of a wife, due to the agitation in *coitus*. For *tunnā́*, cf. *grā́vnā tunnó abhíṣṭutaḥ pavítraṁ soma gacchasi* RV. 9. 67. 17, and for *tuñjānā́*, cf. *áthā́ 'bhara śyena-bhṛta práyāṁsi rayíṁ túñjāno abhí vā́jam arṣa* RV. 9. 87. 6. For a similar idea as in **d**, cf. RV. 5. 61. 3, 10. 10. 8, 10. 86. 6, etc.

kákutsala-

asaú hā́ ihá te mánaḥ kákutsalam iva jāmáyaḥ : abhy ènaṁ bhūma ūrṇuhi. 18. 4. 66.

Previous Scholars: The commentator reads *kákutsthala-*, explaining it either as the head or the part of body just below the neck. "Dieser [N.] du hast deinem geist gelaszen [kakutsalam ? kutsalâm es ist um eine silbe zuvil; jâmayaḥ kann nicht richtig sein, wenn es von jâmi stammen soll. Villeicht ist es jâ-mayaḥ] als erdegebildeter den im haupte wandelnden [kakut-sala] |, bedeck ihn rings, o erde||".—Ludwig, p. 492. "Thou yonder, ho! hither thy mind; as sisters (*jāmí*) a *kákutsala*, do thou cover him, O earth".—Whitney. "The translation implies the evidently necessary emendation to *ásau* in **a**; both editions give *asaú* because this is read by all mss. The comm. understands the word as vocative......The Pet. Lexx. conjecture *kákutsala* to be a pet word for a little child".—*ib.*, notes.

The correct reading seems to be *kákutsthala* as read by the commentator, the *th* having been dropped by manuscript corruption. Such dropping of the last of three consonants coming together is found elsewhere, cf., for instance, *ārśá-* for *ārśyá-* at 4. 4. 5, and *krámasvárśa* for *-rśya* at v. 5, *kṣiṅkaḥ* for *kṣvi-* in two of Wh.'s mss. at 8. 3. 7, *dhukṣa* for *-kṣva* in several mss. at 10. 9. 13d., *budhnāt* for *-dhnyāt* in three of Wh.'s at 4. 1. 5, etc. *Kakút-*, usually 'the hump of a bull', also signifies any raised place or prominence, and in *kákutsthala-* it may stand for 'the buttocks of a woman', as it certainly does in *kakudmatī-* 'waist', lit., 'having a hump'. The difference in accent is undoubtedly due to the unintelligibility of the word. This meaning would give a point to the comparison, suggesting a complete and careful covering of the bone-relics to which they refer: " ....like women their buttocks, do thou cover him round, O earth ".

kanáknaka-

yád agnaú sū́rye viṣám pṛthivyā́m óṣadhīṣu yát : kā̆ndāviṣám kanáknam niraítv aítu te viṣám. 10. 4. 22.

Previous Scholars: The commentary is wanting. BR. consider each of *kāndāviṣá-* and *kanáknaka-* a different variety of poison. Ludwig, Henry and Whitney do not translate the two words. Bloomfield, who agrees with them in not translating, remarks at p. 608, " Kândâvisham and kanaknakam are ἅπ. λεγ.; it is not even certain that the latter refers to a particular substance: the word may be an adjective qualifying kândâvisham. It seems to be an intensive formation from root Kan. "

As suggested by Bloomfield, *kanáknaka-* appears to contain an intensive stem of root *kan* ' to be bright '. The last *-ka* is, of course, a diminutive suffix. The *a-* vowel, instead of *i*, between the two parts of the reduplicated root is as in *carācará-*, *calācalá-*, *ghanāghaná-*, etc., while its lengthening is prevented by the following conjunct, just as in the case of the *i*-vowel, cf. Whitney, Sans. Gram. §1002. IIIf; Brugmann, Grund. § 467. The syncope in the second part is just like that in *pánipnat-* : *pan-*. Thus *kanáknaka-* would mean ' bright ', ' glistening ', while *kāndāviṣá-* evidently means ' root-poison ' (: *kanda-* ' root ', for length of the second vowel cf. *sahásrāmagha-*, *áśvāmagha-*, etc.). I should think from the first hemistich that the former refers to the poison (of a serpent) that is in the fire or in the sun, which would, of course, be bright, while the latter to that on the earth, among the herbs.

kamála-

yáḥ kṛṇóti mṛtávatsām ávatokām imā́m stríyam : tám oṣadhe tvám nāśayā 'syāḥ kamálam añjivám. 8. 6. 9.

Previous Scholars: The last pada has been understood variously: '*asyāḥ kamalam garbhadvāram añjivam abhivyaktimat mlakṣaṇopetaṁ vā.*'—Sāyaṇa; ' und ihre scheide sei glatt,'—Ludwig, p. 524; 'l'être lubrique et glissant qui la convoite,'—Henry; "Whoever makes this woman having a dead child (*-vatsā*) or a miscarriage, him, O herb, do thou make disappear, lustful [accusative] for her, slippery."—Whitney.

Kamála here appears to be the same word as *śamara-*[1] in GBr. I. 2. 18, *tasya ha snātasyā 'śvasyā 'bhyukṣitasya romaśamarebhyo* (cf. *romakūpa-*) *'ṅgārā āśīryanta*, and I. 5. 5, *etāvanta eva puruṣasya peśaśamarāḥ*, where it evidently means 'hole', 'pit', or 'cavity'. It is apparently also identical with Gr. καμάρη 'vault', 'ear-hole', etc., Lat. *camero* 'bent', old Pers. *kamara* 'girdle'—Meyer, Handbuch d. Griech. Etymologie,—Goth. *himins*, old H. Germ. old Sax. *himil*, 'heaven', originally 'vault'—Boisacq, Greek Dictionary, s.v. καμάρη.

As words denoting 'cavity' or 'hole' such as *bhedá-* (RV.), *kuhara-*, *vivara-* (later Sans.) are often used to denote also the 'pudenda' or 'womb', the commentator is apparently right in his conjecture, as the context also shows. *Añjí-* in *añjivám* and in VS. 23. 21, *útsakthyā áva gudáṁ dhehi sám añjíṁ cārayā vṛṣan : yá strīṇā́ṁ jīvabhójanaḥ*, seems to stand for 'the seminal fluid', not 'penis' as given in the dictionaries.

kalmalí-

śraddhā́ puṁścalī́ Mitró māgadhó vijñā́naṁ vā́só 'har uṣṇī́ṣaṁ rā́trī kéśā háritau pravartaú kalmalír maṇíḥ. 15.2.1(5).

[1] Alternances of *ś* and *k*, of which the definite conditions are unknown, are found in a number of cases. Wack. I. § 201. a. gives the following instances : *rúśant-* 'bright' : *ruc-* 'to light'; *śru-* 'hear' : *kárṇa-* 'ear'; *śram-* 'to be tired' : *klam-*, *klānta-*; *lopāśá-* 'jackal' : *lopāka-*; *śṝ-* 'to crush,' *śṛṇāti*, *śīrṇa-* : Dhp. *kṛṇāti*, *kīrṇa-* 'to harm,' 'to kill'. To these may be added: *krakaśa* : *krakaca-* 'saw'; *yuvaśá-* : *yuvaka-* 'young man,' and, in general, suff. *-śa* (*étaśa-*, *babhluśá-* etc.) : suff. *-ka*; *śábala-*: *kabara-*, Māgha 5. 19, Halāyudha 4. 56, 'variegated'; *śambara-*: *kambala-* 'a kind of deer'; *śambu-*, *śambūka* 'snail', 'rice dust' : *kambu-*, *kambūka-*, 'conch,' 'rice dust' (Vj.); element *śar-* in *śarvarī-* 'night', *śāra-*, *sā(śā?)raṅga-* 'variegated', element *kar-* in *karvara-*, *karvura-*, *kalmāṣa-*, 'variegated', *karvarī* 'night,' Ujjvala, Uṇādi. 2. 123, and *śir-* in *śilpá-* 'variegated', *śíriṇā-* 'night' : *kir-* in *kirmira-* 'variegated,' (all : √*śrai-*, I.-E. k̑erā* (Walde) 'to mix,' 'to cook' ?); *śarabha-* : *karabha* 'young elephant', 'camel'; *śarkarā-* : *karkara-* 'gravel'; *śāla-* : *kāla-* 'resin,' Kalpadrukośa, 66, 415; *śrāṇa-* : *kāṇa-* 'one-eyed', *ib.* 51, 279; *kanthā-* 'quilt' : *śnath-* 'to pierce' (?); *kárūḍatin-* 'having broken teeth' : **śarus-dat*, root *śṝ-* 'to crush' (?); *śampā-* 'lightning' : *kamp-* 'to quake' ?, cf. *capalā-*. As *variae lectiones*, *kokā-* for *kośā-* 'name of a river', *vikīrṇa-* for *viśīrṇa-*, BR. s.v. *śar+vi*, etc.

uṣā́ḥ puṁścalī́ mántro māgadhó vijñā́nam, etc., v. 2(14). *irā́ puṁścalī́ háso māgadhó vijñā́nam*, etc., v. 3(19). *vidyút puṁścalī́ stanayitnúr māgadhó vijñā́nam*, etc., v. 4 (25).

prá babhráve vṛṣabhā́ya śvitīcé mahó mahī́ṁ suṣṭutím īrayāmi : namasyā́ kalmalīkínaṁ námobhir gṛṇīmási tveṣáṁ Rudrásya nā́ma. RV. 2. 33. 8.

tvám Indra śarmáriṇā havyám pā́rāvatebhyaḥ : víprāya stuvaté vasuvániṁ Duraśravasé vaha. AV. 20. 135. 11. (*śarmá riṇaḥ*, RV., GB., ĀŚ., ŚŚ., AB., KS., of which only ŚŚ. has the whole verse, others only the first pāda.—Ved. Concord.).

Previous Scholars : Sāyaṇa on RV. : '*jvalato nāmadheyam etat* (Naigh. 1. 17) : *jvalantam : kalayaty apa gamayati malam iti kalmalīkam tejaḥ : tadvantam.*' Grassmann, 'etwa bunter, funkelnder Glanz.' Whitney,—"....faith is the harlot, Mitra the *māgadhá* (bard ?), discernment the garment, day the turban, night the hair, yellow the two *pravartás, kalmalí* the jewel (*maṇí*) ", etc.

In form *śarmári-* in AV. 20. 135. 11 appears to be identical with *kalmalí-*, see discussion under *kamála-*. Now, *śarmári-* is used as an instrument of Indra and *kalmalí-* in the RV. verse as something possessed by Rudra. Both these gods have the weapon *vájra* 'thunderbolt' in common. The first group of verses from the AV. relate to the paraphernalia of Vrātya as those of a king. As all the rest of these refer figuratively either to abstract qualities or to natural objects or phenomena, *háritau* and *kalmalí-* should be expected to do so too. *Harít-* f.du. in RV. 3. 44. 3, *dyā́m índro háridhāyasaṁ pṛthivī́ṁ hárivarpasam : ádhārayad harítor bhū́ri bhójanaṁ yáyor antár háriś cárat*, probably refers to the two worlds (so also Grassmann). The same may be the case here, as *pravartaú* (found also in Āp. Śr. 19. 23. 11, 13. 21. 2) means 'ear-rings' (Sāyaṇa on TS. 2. 3. 11[4], quoting Āp. Śr.). 'Thunderbolt' for *kalmalí-* (or *śarmari-*) would suit here as in the other two passages and Whitney's translation may be modified, "......the two worlds the ear-rings, the thunderbolt the jewel." AV. 20. 135. 11, with the obviously required emendation of *vaha* to *-has* and *Duraśravasé* to *Dūra-*, may be translated : "Thou, O Indra, with the thunderbolt, broughtest from the Pārāvatas the desired (*havyá-*) acquisition of wealth for the wise, singing, Dūraśravas."

Kalmalí- is probably connected with the group of words containing the element, *śar-*, *śir-*, *kar-*, *kir-* (such as *śarvarī-*, *kalmāṣa-* etc., see footnote under *kamála-*), all meaning 'variegated' and its original meaning might well have been 'many-coloured', 'shining' (cf. the epithets, *darśatá-*, *dyumánt-*, *śubhrá-*, *hári-*, *hárita-*, *hiraṇyáya-*, of *vájra*, Grassmann, s.v. *vájra*).

kúmba- —*kurī́ra-* —*opaśá-*

tvám vīrúdhām śréṣṭhatamā 'bhiśrutā́ 'sy oṣadhe: imám me adyá pū́ruṣaṁ klībám opaśínaṁ kr̥dhi. 6. 138. 1. *klībáṁ kr̥dhy opaśínam átho kurīríṇaṁ kr̥dhi: áthā 'syé 'ndro grā́vabhyām ubhé bhinattv āṇḍyaù.* v.2. *klība klībáṁ tvā 'karaṁ vádhre vádhriṁ tvā 'karam árasā 'rasáṁ tvā 'karam: kurī́ram asya śīrṣáṇi kúmbaṁ cā ' dhinídadhmasi.* v.3.

stómā āsan pratidháyaḥ kurī́raṁ chánda opaśáḥ: Sūryā́yā Aśvínā varā́ 'gnír āsīt purogaváḥ. 14. 1. 8.=RV. 10. 85. 8.

Sinīvālī́ sukapardā́ sukurīrā́ svaupaśā́. TS. 4. 1. 5³.=VS. 11. 56.

Kúmba- and *kurī́ra-* are also found in ĀP. Śr. 10. 9. 5, 6, 7 (and in the corresponding sūtras in Baudh. Śr. 6.1 : 6. 4, 5; 15. 15; 25. 4) : *atha patnīśirasi kumbakurīram adhyūhate. kr̥ṣṇaṁ jīvorṇānām iti Vājasaneyakam. jālaṁ kumbakurīram ity ācakṣate. Kúmba-* alone is found also in ĀP. Śr. 1. 21. 3, *udīcīnakumbāṁ śamyām*, where it has a development of the original meaning. *Kurī́ra-* is found also at AV. 5. 31. 2, *yā́ṁ te cakrúḥ kr̥kavākāv ajé vā yā́ṁ kurīríṇi: ávyāṁ te kr̥tyā́ṁ yā́ṁ cakrúḥ púnaḥ práti harāmi tā́m*, where it has a different but not wholly unconnected meaning. *Opaśá-* is found also in AV. 9. 3. 8, discussed under *ákṣu*: and in RV. 1. 173. 6, *prá yád itthā́ mahinā́ nŕ̥bhyo ásty áraṁ ródasī kakṣyè nā́ 'smai: sáṁ vivya Índro vr̥jánaṁ ná bhū́mā bhárti svadhā́vā opaśám iva dyā́m*; ib. 8. 14. 5, *yajñá Índram avardhayad yád bhū́miṁ vy ávartayat: cakrāṇá opośáṁ diví*; ib. 9. 71. 1, *ā́ dákṣiṇā sr̥jyate śuṣmy āsadaṁ véti druhó rakṣásaḥ pāti jā́gr̥viḥ: hárir opaśáṁ kr̥ṇute nábhas páya upastíre camvòr bráhma nirṇíje*; Tāṇḍ. Br. 4. 1. 1, *gāvo vā etat satram āsata tāsāṁ daśasu māssu sr̥ṅgāṇy ajāyanta tā avadann arāsmo 'ttiṣṭhāmo 'paśā no 'jñate 'ti tā udatiṣṭhata*, and 13. 4. 3, *dvyopaśāḥ saṁstutā bhavanti tasmād dvyopaśāḥ paśavaḥ*; and in *gó-opaśā-*, epithet of *áṣṭrā-*, RV. 6. 53. 9 and *hṛdayaupaśá-* VS. 25. 8, in all of which it has a slight modification of the original meaning.

Previous Scholars: Sāyaṇa on AV: '*upaśete asmin puruṣa iti opaśaḥ strīvyañjanam*', 6. 138. 1; '*kurīrāḥ keśāḥ*', v.2; '*kurīraṁ keśajālaṁ kumbaṁ tadābharaṇaṁ ca strīṇam asādhāraṇam*', v.3. In explaining the passages in RV. he seeks the help of etymology and arrives at a different meaning of *opaśá-* in each case, thus: *sṛṅgam* or *lokadvayam* 1. 173. 6; *upetya śayānam* or *vīryaviśeṣaḥ* 8. 14. 5; *sarvasya dhārakam* 9. 71. 1; *upaśerat ity opaśāḥ, gāva opaśā yasyās tādṛsī, ata eva paśu-sādhanī*, 6. 53. 9; and goes farther at 10. 85. 8, by stating that there is a metre called *kurī́ra-*, '*sūryāyā rathasya stomās trivṛdādayaḥ pratidhaya āsan : pratidhīyata iti pratidhaya īṣātiryagāyatakāṣṭhādayaḥ : tathā kurīraṁ chandaḥ kurīra-nāmakaṁ chando 'nasa opaśo 'bhavat : yeno 'paśerate sa opaśaḥ*'. BR: *kúmba*= 'eine Art weiblicher Kopfputz', *kurī́ra*= 'eine Art Kopfschmuck der weiber', *opaśá-* = 'ein Kopfutz—: Büschel, Locke, cirrus; oder viell. Zoff' and 'Flechte' at AV. 9. 3. 8. Geldner, Ved. Stud. I, 130—137. basing his arguments on AV. 5. 31. 2, Tāṇḍ. Br. 4. 1. 1, 13. 4. 3, and Āp. Śr. 1. 21. 3 (where he wrongly interprets *kumba-* as the 'pointed end'), concludes that all the three words mean in the first place 'horn' and then a 'horn-shaped head-ornament' or 'diadem'. Caland alone, having had access to Baudh. Śr. and the commentaries, has given the right interpretation to *kúmba-* and *kurī́ra-* in his translation of Āp. Śr. 10. 9. 5.

Baudh. Śr. 25. 4 (p. 232, 1.1.) has, *vidalam u ha kumbaṁ bhavati jālam u kurīram*, and thereupon the commentator adds *vaṁśavidalaṁ jālasya nemibhūtam* as *kúmba-*. The commentator to Āp. Śr. 10. 9. 7 also has, *jālam ānāyaḥ, tac ca vaidale valaye syūtam*, and quotes Baudh. for his support. Thus *kúmba-* is a circular rim made of sliced bamboo and *kurī́ra-*, a net of sheep's wool (Āp. Śr. 10. 9. 6, above), of which the *kúmba-* formed the edge. The two together formed a dome-shaped female head-dress (that is, when put on) and are often referred to as one, cf *kumbakurīram* Āp. Śr. 10. 9. 5, 7 above and Baudh. Śr. 6. 5, 15. 15.

Kumbā- 'sacrificial enclosure' must be the same word as *kúmba-* with an extended meaning. It seems to contain a root *kum-* 'to bend', probably to be traced in *komyā́-* RV. 1. 171. 3, *stutā́so no Marúto mṛḷayantū 'tá stutó maghávā śámbhaviṣṭhaḥ : ūrdhvā́ naḥ santu komyā́ vánāny áhāni víśvā Maruto jigīṣā́*, which Sāyaṇa explains as *kamanīyāni* 'pretty' and others have hesitatingly followed without being able to find a satisfactory derivation. If, however, *komyā́-* contains this root, it would mean 'bending', 'pliant', which as applied to trees, desired to be saved from the wrath of the storm-gods, would be most appropriate (the third pāda giving the sense, 'let our pliant trees remain erect'). The root is probably also to be seen in *kumbha-* 'pitcher', Gr. κύμβη, κύμβος (for formation cf. *kamba-*, *kambha-*: *kam-*, Pāṇ. 5. 2. 138); in *kumāra-*, 'the bending, crawling, baby', in *komala-* 'bending' > 'yielding' > 'soft', etc.; and in the root *kuñc-* 'to bend', which may be an enlargement of *kum-*. In view of Lith. *kum̃pti* 'to bend oneself', *kum̃pas* 'bent', Lett. *kùmpt* 'to be bent', old Pruss. *etkūmps* adv. 'round about' (Walde, s.v. *qam-*, *qamp-* 'to bend'), Gr. κύμβος 'pitcher', κύμβαχος 'upper part of a helmet' and of Gr. καμπτω 'to bend', Sans. *kamála-*, and its correspondences in the other languages given under it, there seems to have been a duplicate root **kam* or **kum-* in the original language, which gave rise to the various enlargements and derivatives.

From looking upon *kumba-kurīra-* as one thing *kúmba-*, and probably also *kurī́ra-*, came to denote the whole thing, which as we have already remarked looked like a dome or vault when put on. Thence came the use of *kúmba-* as the 'knob' of a stick or peg of a yoke in Āp. Śr. 1. 21. 3, *udīcīnakumbāṁ śamyām*, the commentator explaining *kumba-* here as the thick end of a *śamyā-*. As already in the time of Baudhāyana and Āpastamba the use of this form of female head-dress had become obsolete (judging from their manner of describing it, of course,) it may well have been Indo-European and Gr. κύμβαχος 'the upper part of a helmet' may have the same source.

Kurī́ra-, which as we have seen was made of sheep's wool, meant also 'blanket', cf. *kurīras tu pumān mālāviśeṣe kambale 'pi ca: klībaṁ tu maithune padme jāle ca munibhāṣitam*, Keśavasvāmin's Nānārthārṇavasaṁkṣepa, Triv. Sans. Ser. It might well have originally meant 'wool' and in AV. 5. 31. 2, quoted above, *kurīrín-* wedged, as it is, in between *ajé* 'goat' (loc.) and *ávyām* 'ewe' (loc.), may possibly stand for 'sheep'. As a matter of fact we find *kurarī-* (for *kurīrī ?*) and *jālakinī-* (lit., 'furnished with a net') as names of an ewe, see Vaijayantī 70, 129. But the case is doubtful, and *kurīriṇi* may be an adjective to *ajé*, *kuríra-* referring to its horns as 'head-ornaments'. This last remark applies with greater force and more certainty to *opaśá-* in Tāṇḍ. Br. 4. 1. 1 and 13. 4. 3, quoted above.

A comparison of AV. 6. 138. 1, 2, 3, RV. 10. 85. 8 = AV. 14. 1. 8, and TS. 4. 1. 5³ = VS. 11. 56 will show that either *kuríra-* and *kúmba-* or *kuríra-* and *opaśá-* are found together, but nowhere *kúmba-* and *opaśá-*. This, as referring to a particular female head-dress, is sufficient to give us *kúmba-* = *opaśá-*, 'the circular sliced-bamboo rim'. This, as we have seen under *ákṣu-*, is its meaning also at AV. 9. 3. 8. In AV. 14. 1. 8= RV. 10. 85. 8, *pratidhí-* probably means 'ornament' as 'something put on' (compare also Wh.'s remark under AV. 14. 1. 8) cf. *práti yád asya vájraṁ bāhvór dhúḥ* RV. 2. 20. 8c, and the verse may be rendered, "The ornaments were the laudations, the net and the rim, the metre", etc. *Opaśá-* in RV. 1. 173. 6, 8. 14. 5 and 9. 71. 1 refers to the whole head-dress, and with this modification the translations of Geldner in Ved. Stud., I.131f., may be accepted. *Gó-opaśā-* probably means 'with the knob made of cow's bone (or covered with cow's hide)' and *hṛdayaupaśá-* 'that which covers the heart'.

kurūṭínī-

ayáṁ pánthāḥ kṛtyéti tvā nayāmo 'bhipráhitāṁ práti tvā prá hiṇmaḥ; ténā 'bhí yāhi bhañjaty ánasvatī 'va vāhínī viśvárūpā kurūṭínī. 10. 1. 15.

Previous Scholars: The commentary is wanting. BR. think that it is probably = *kiríṭinī-*. Ludwig: "......auf diesem wege geh brechend los zum angriff, wie ein vollständig heer mit wagen und mit rossen [?]." Bloomfield: "...... go this way like a crushing army, with heavy carts, thou that art multiform, and crowned with a crest (?)," and at p. 604, "Kurûṭínî translated by 'crowned with a crest' is in truth a ἅπ. λεγ. of unknown value......Hemakandra also reports a word kuruṭin 'horse', and Ludwig apparently, on this basis, translates 'mit rossen'". Henry: "par ce chemin marche en te le frayant, comme montée sur un chariot, montée sur un char, revêtue de toutes les formes, coiffée d'une mitre", and in the commentary, "*vāhínī* synonyme de *ánasvatī*, et, quant à *kurūṭínī*, cf. l'usuel *kiríṭin* et l'épithéte *tirīṭínas* AV. VIII. 6. 7." Whitney: ".......breaking, like a draft-cow with a cart, all-formed, wearing a wreath (? *kurūṭín*)".

Kurūṭa- in *kurūṭínī* seems to be identical with later Sanskrit *kurula-* or *-rala-*[1] 'curls on the forehead (*bhramarālaka-*)', found also in Prāk. (for correspondence of Sans. ṭ>ḍ>l in middle Indian see references under *arāṭakī-*). *Kurūṭínī* would thus mean 'having curls on the forehead', and this would fit in with *kr̥tyā́-* 'witchcraft', which has been described several times in the same hymn as a woman[2] with head, ears, nose, etc., cf. v. 1, *yā́ṁ kalpáyanti vahataú vadhū́m iva viśvárūpāṁ hástakr̥tāṁ cikitsávaḥ: sā́ 'rā́d etv ápa nudāma enām;* v. 2, *śīrṣaṇvátī nasvátī karṇínī kr̥tyākŕ̥tā sáṁbhr̥tā viśvárūpā*, etc.

For *kuruṭin-* 'horse' in Böhtlingk's edition of Hemacandra's Śeṣanāmamālā, v. 176, the Bhavanagar edition of Abhidhānacintāmaṇi gives *kuṭara-*. If the former reading is correct, it may signify a 'horse with a tuft on the forehead.'

Pādas **c** and **d**, which have been diversely translated, seem to compare the retreat of *kr̥tyā́-* to that of an invading army (cf. *bhagna-*, 'vanquished': *bhañjatí*). *Ánasvatī*, 'furnished with chariots', epithet of *vāhínī* 'army', is probably due to a reminiscence of *vahataú vadhū́m iva* in v. 1.

khaḍū́ra-

khaḍū́re 'dhicaṅkramā́ṁ khárvikā́ṁ kharvavāsínīm: yá udārā́ antárhitā gandharvāpsarásaś ca yé: sarpā́ itarajanā́ rákṣāṁsi. 11. 9 (11). 16.

Previous Scholars: Sāyaṇa: '*dūrabhūtaṁ khaṁ khadūram ākāśe dūradeśe.*' Ludwig. p. 531: "die über den khaḍûra [das schwert] taumelt die verstümmelte, bei verstümmelten [auf dem schlachtfeld] wonet", etc. Henry: "Celle qui monte sur le brancard mortuaire", etc., and in the commentary, "Il semble que *khaḍū́ra* doive necessairement s'interpreter par le posterieur *khaḍū*." Bloomfield, who renders with 'mist', remarks at p. 636, 'Our rendering of khaḍúre reflects simply our own and Sâyaṇa's perplexity.'

Khaḍū́ra- appears to be identical with later Sanskrit *khalūra-* in *khalūrikā-* 'place of exercise for soldiers'. This meaning suits the context here: the whole hymn has reference to battle, soldiers, and weapons, and a spectre haunting the

---

[1] The long *ū* in *kurūṭínī* may be due to the exigencies of metre.

[2] Cf. *Kurulālikulāvalikhyamānabhrūlatāntahr̥dayaṅgamaṁ*, epithet of a *priyatamājana*,—Somadeva's Yaśastilaka I, 526, 2.

place of exercise may be expected to be mentioned amidst a host of other different kinds of spectres. *Ḍ* is regularly represented by ḷ in RV., and for *ḍ*>ḷ (1), in Pāli and Prāk., see references given under *arāṭakī*.

khṛ́gala-

piśáṅge sū́tre khṛ́galaṁ tád ā́ badhnanti vedhásaḥ : śravasyúṁ śúṣmaṁ kābavám vádhriṁ kṛṇvantu vandhúraḥ. 3. 9. 3.

nāvé 'va naḥ pārayataṁ yugé 'va nábhye 'va na upadhī́va pradhī́va : śvā́ne 'va no áriṣaṇyā tanū́nāṁ khṛ́gale'va visrásaḥ pātam asmā́n. RV. 2. 39. 4.

Previous Scholars: Sāyaṇa on both the passages explains *khṛgala-* as 'armour'. BR., 'viell. Stab, Krücke'. Bloomfield, 'talisman', but agrees with BR. in the meaning 'crutches' for RV. Whitney does not translate the word.

Kauśika, 43. 1, has concerning this hymn (AV. 3. 9.), *karśaphasyeti piśaṅgasūtram araludaṇḍaṁ yadāyudham*, which, when compared with the verse quoted above, gives us *khṛgala-*= *daṇḍa-* 'stick'. This is supported by the RV. verse quoted above, its fourth pāda meaning, 'like two sticks save us from fall'. *Khṛgalya-* in MS. 2. 7. 12 (=Āp. Śr. 16. 18. 4), *udyojannam antaryāmam īṣāṁ khṛgalyaṁ* (Āp. *kha-* or *khaḍga-*) *śavam* (Āp. *śapham*) *: aṣṭrāṁ tāḍam* (Āp. *-la-*) *pratīnāhā ubhe maṇḍūkyau yuje*, apparently means the same thing.

galuntáḥ

asū́tikā rāmā́yaṇy àpacít prá patiṣyati : glaúr itáḥ prá patiṣyati sá galuntó naśiṣyati. 6. 83. 3.

Previous Scholars: Sāyaṇa: '*glauḥ vraṇajanito harṣakṣayaḥ itaḥ asmād aṅgāt prapatiṣyati yadvā glauḥ candramāḥ....[illegible].... sa candramāḥ. galuntaḥ. gaṇḍamālodbhavavikāreṇa tatra tatra hastapādādisandhiṣu udbhūtan gaḍūn tasyati upakṣayatīti gaḍuntaḥ*', etc. Ludwig: "....fort von hier die eule [glaûḥ] fliegen, und der vogel wird verschwinden." Bloomfield, p. 17: "....the boil will fly away from here, the galunta (swelling) will perish". "Barren shall the *apacít*, daughter of the black one, fly forth; the boil (*glaú*) shall fly forth from here; it shall disappear from the neck (? *galuntás*)".—Whitney, who remarks, "the translation here given of *galuntás* is the purest conjecture, as if the word were a corruption of some form of *gala* (our W.O.D. read *galantás*), with ablative suffix *tas* ".

If *galantás*, the reading of three of Whitney's mss., be correct, its relation to root *gal-* 'to ooze' would be just like that of *jīvantá-* 'living one', AV.: *jīv-* 'to live', *tarantá-* n. pr.: *tṝ* 'to conquer', *pāntá-* 'drink': *pā-* 'to drink', *vasantá-* 'spring': *vas-* 'to be bright', *veśantá-* 'pool': *viś-* 'to enter (*e.g.*, running water)' (?), *hemantá-* 'winter': *hím*, *himá-* 'cold', 'frost', etc. Being thus presumably a substantive like the others, it would mean in this connection 'the oozing one', viz., 'the pus'. If Sāyaṇa's explanation of *asū́tikā-* as 'not giving out pus' be correct, an emendation of *sá galantás* to *ságalantas* would give a good sense: "The barren *apacít*,[1] daughter of the black one will fly forth: the boil shall fly forth from here, (and) disappear together with the pus."

ghṛtastā́vas-

yásmin devā́ ámṛjata yásmin manuṣyā́ utá: tásmin ghṛtastā́vo mṛṣṭvā́ tvám Agne dívaṁ ruha. 12. 2. 17.

Previous Scholars: 'von Schmalze triepfend'—BR., who take *-stāva-* to be the stem. Ludwig, p. 480: 'an dem wisch dich ab und ghṛta-triepfend [?], steig empor zum himmel'. Henry: 'puisque tu dégouttes de beurre, essui-toi sur lui, | Ô Agni, et monte au ciel'. "......on that having wiped off the drops of ghee (?), O Agni do thou mount the sky"—Whitney, who remarks, "Our mss. seem to read *-stā́-* very plainly [and SPP. reports no variant], but need not prevent our understanding instead *-snā́-*, if more acceptable".

BR. assume a root *stu-* 'to drop', 'to come together' in order to explain *stuta-* (v.l., *sruta*) in Hemacandra, *-stā́va-*, *stúkā-* 'tuft or knot of hair', and *stoká-* 'drops'. Of these, *stuta-* is only a corruption of *sruta-* and *stoká-* has been explained by Wackernagel, I. 239. c., as a methathesis of **skota-*: *ścut-*

---

[1] *Apacít-* is rightly identified by Bloomfield, p. 504, with *apacī-* of the medical works. The latter seems to be a Prakritisation of the former. The commentators of Kauś. and AV. also identify it with *gaṇḍamālā*. BR. give 'scrofulous swelling of the glands of the neck' for *gaṇḍamālā*, which is misleading, as the following extract from Vāgbhaṭa (Aṣṭāṅgahṛdaya, Uttara. 29, 18) will show: *medaḥsthāḥ kaṇṭhamanyākṣakakṣāvāṁkṣāṇajā malāḥ: savarṇān kaṭhinān snigdhān vārtākāmalakākṛtīn: avagāḍhān bahūn gaṇḍāṁś cirapākāṁś ca kurvate: pacyante 'lparujas tvanye sravanty anye 'tikaṇḍurāḥ: násyanty anye bhavanty anye dīrghakālānubandhinaḥ: gaṇḍamālā 'pacī seyam dūrveva kṣayavṛddhibhāk.*

'to drip'. The remaining *stúkā-* or *stú-*, as well as *stū́pa-* 'tuft or knot of hair', *stavaka-* 'bunch', Beng. *thokā* 'bunch', contains an element *stu-* which gives the idea of a 'bunch' or 'bundle'. This, however, would not apply to *ghṛta*.

On the other hand, if, following Whitney's recommendation, we read *-snā́vas*[1], we find *-snā́vas-: snu-* 'to drip' as *vā́sas-* 'covering': *vas-* 'to clothe', *-vā́cas-* in *suvā́cas-* etc.: *vac-* 'to speak', *vā́has-* 'offering': *vah-* 'to carry', *pā́jas-* 'brilliance': *pajrá-*, etc., Ved. Gr. § 126. Then *ghṛtasnā́vas-* would mean 'drippings of ghee', object of *mṛṣṭvā́*, cf. *ghṛtasnú-* 'dripping with ghee'.

cītí-

devā́s te cītím avidan brahmā́ṇa utá vīrúdhaḥ: cītíṁ te víśve devā́ ávidan bhū́myām ádhi. 2. 9. 4.

Previous Scholars: Sāyaṇa: '*grahavikārād rogiṇa ādānaṁ grahādeḥ saṁvaraṇaṁ chādanam abhistaraṇaṁ vā*'. BR. and Weber: 'Sammeln. Ludwig, 'pflückung'. Grill: "Den Göttern und Brāhmanen ward's, wie man dich Holz zusammenlegt, Die Götter all ersahn, wie man zur Erde dich zusammenlegt". Bloomfield, p. 292: "The word *kîtím* is found only here and is very problematic......we are connecting the word with *kinoti* in the sense of 'arrange', 'build up', having in mind the peculiar amulet or remedy dasavriksha 'consisting of ten woods', in st. 7." Whitney, who renders, 'gathering (?)', remarks, "If it comes from *ci*, there is hardly any other example".

Cītí- appears to be connected with *cāy-* 'to fear', 'to be in awe of',[2] thus meaning 'apprehension' and thence 'trouble' or 'disease', just like *ātaṅka-* which means both 'fear' and 'disease'. The hymn is about curing one of a dangerous kind of seizure of the joints, said to be caused by demons, and the meaning suits quite well: "The gods have noticed thy trouble, the priests, and the plants: all the gods on earth have noticed thy trouble". That the diseased, and not the amulet, is addressed is clear from the following verse.

---

[1] Mss. often confuse *st* (स्त) and *sn* (स्न) and, in general, *t* and *n*, cf. *stāvā* or *stāva* in two mss. for *snāvā*, Gaastra's ed. of GBr., p. 120, n. 2.

[2] Cf. Wack., I. § 79. a.: "So von *cāy-*,, Scheuen" AV. *cīti- cíkīhi* kl. *ceki-yate*: v. *cā́yamāna-*, *-cā́yya cāy-ú*, sp. weiteres, vgl. gr. τῑ-μή."

For formation, cf. *gīti-*: *gāyati*, *pīti-*: *pā-*, *pāyayti* (caus.), *sphīti-*: *sphāyate*, etc., Wack. I. §79. (a). α, β.

jabhya- —*tardá-* —*vághā-*

hatáṁ tardáṁ samaṅkám ākhúm Áśvinā chintáṁ śíro ápi pṛṣṭīḥ śṛṇītam : yávān néd ádān ápi nahyataṁ múkham áthā 'bhayaṁ kṛṇutaṁ dhānyā̀ya. 6. 50. 1.

tárda haí pátaṅga haí jábhya hā́ úpakvasa : brahmé 'vā́ 'saṁsthitaṁ havír ánadanta imā́n yávān áhiṁsanto apódita. v. 2.

tárdāpate vághāpate tṛṣṭajambhā ā́ śṛṇota me : yá āraṇyā́ vyàdvarā́ yé ké ca sthá vyàdvarā́s tā́nt sárvān jambhayāmasi. v. 3.

yā́vatīr bhṛ́ṅgā jatvàḥ kurū́ravo yā́vatīr vághā vṛkṣasarpyò bábhūvuḥ : tátas tvám asi jyā́yān, etc. 9. 2. 22.

Previous Scholars : Sāyaṇa : *tardaḥ= hiṁsakaḥ* (*ākhuḥ*), *jabhya= upadravakāritvād asmābhir hiṁsya, vaghāḥ=avaghnanti avabādhanta iti vaghāḥ pataṅgādayaḥ*. Bloomfield and Whitney render *tardá-* and *jabhya-* as 'borer' and 'grinder' respectively. *Samaṅkám* and *úpakvasa* have been left out as doubtful by everybody. Sāyaṇa explains the former as *samañcanaṁ bilaṁ sampraviśya gacchantam*, adj. of *ākhum*, and for the latter he reads *apakvasaḥ* (=*adagdhāḥ santaḥ*).

Keśava on Kauś. 51. 22 (dealing with AV. 6. 50) has *samāptam mūṣaka-śalabhapataṅga-ṭiṭṭibha-kīṭaka-kīṭikā-hariṇa-ruru-śalyaka-goṣedhā-gokṛmyādi-svastyayanam ;* similar is Sāyaṇa's remarks in the introduction to this hymn, which is directed against the pests to crops. In the well-known verse, *ativṛṣṭir anavṛṣṭiḥ śalabhā mūṣikāḥśukāḥ; pratyāsannāś ca rājānaḥ ṣaḍ ete ītayaḥ smṛtāḥ*, the most harmful to crops, among animals, are 'locusts', 'rats', and 'parrots'. These three must be intended in vs. 2 and 3 by the words, *tárda : tárdā-pate*, 'borer' ='rat', *pátaṅga : vághāpate*='locust', cf. Beng. (dial. of Mānbhūm) *bāghḍulu* 'a kind of moth', Sindhi *bagh(g)äi* 'a kind of fly that sticks to dogs and horses', and *jábhya : tṛṣṭajambhāḥ*, 'grinder' or 'having sharp grinders' ='parrot', which cuts anything by grinding with its beak.

The remaining animals in Sāyaṇa's and Keśava's enumerations are included in the words *āraṇyā́ vyàdvarā́ḥ* and *yé ké ca sthá vyàdvarā́ḥ* in v. 3.

The construction suggests that *samaṅkám* in v. 1 is probably a verb, second, du., imp., like *hatám, chintám* and *śr̥ṇītam.* A loss (by ms. corruption) of *t*, the third member of the conjunct (see under *kákutsala-*) is probably to be seen after *-ṅk-*, *samaṅkám* thus standing for *samaṅktám*. Now, *sám-añj-* has a meaning 'to consume', 'to devour' (BR., RV. 10. 45. 4 ; 52. 3 ; 87. 16) which would quite suit the context.

Úpakvasa, taken by others as a substantive of doubtful significance, also appears to be a verb, probably a corruption for *-krasa* (for a reverse process in the confusion of *v* and *r*, see *uttaradraú*). The form **kras-* not known to be found elsewhere, may be an enlargement of *kram-* 'to step' through the intermediate *kraṁs-* which is frequently used. Compare the relations of, *tam-* 'to be exhausted', 'to perish': *tas-*, *nam-* in *evéd yū́ne yuvatáyo namanta yád īm uśánn uśatī́r éty áccha*, RV. 10. 30. 6 : *naṁs-* in *ní te naṁsai pīpyānéʼva yóṣā máryāye 'va kanyā̀ śaśvacaí te*, RV. 3. 33. 10 : *nas-* 'to approach with lust', *śam-* 'to kill': *śas-*, etc., and alternate presence or absence of nasal in *danś-*: *daś-* 'to bite,' *dans-* 'to be worth seeing': *das-* in *dasmá-* etc., *nanś-*: *naś-* 'to disappear', *bhranś-*: *bhraś-* 'to fall', *srans-*: *sras-* 'to fall', etc. If that be the true reading and meaning, **úpakrasa* would mean 'step nearer' (that is, in order to listen), and would correspond even in this respect (as in the names) to *ā́ śr̥ṇota me* in v. 3.

tāyādarám—párasvant-

yáthā pásas tāyādaráṁ vā́tena sthūlabháṁ kr̥tám: yā́vat párasvataḥ pásas tā́vat te vardhatāṁ pásaḥ. 6. 72. 2. *yā́vad aṅgī́naṁ pā́rasvataṁ hā́stinaṁ gā́rdabhaṁ ca yát: yā́vad áśvasya vājínas tā́vat te vardhatāṁ pásaḥ.* v. 3.

ayám Indra Vr̥ṣā́kapiḥ párasvantaṁ hatáṁ vidat: asíṁ sūnā́ṁ návaṁ carúm ā́d édhasyā́ 'na ā́citaṁ víśvasmād Índra úttaraḥ. RV. 10. 86. 18.

Ī́śānāya párasvata ā́labhate Mitrā́ya gaurā́n Váruṇāya máhiṣān, Bŕ̥haspátaye gavayā́s Tvástra úṣṭrān. VS. 24. 28.

suparṇaḥ pārjanyo haṁso vr̥ko vr̥ṣadaṁśas te aindrā apām udro 'ryamṇo lopāśas siṁho nakulo vyāghras te Mahendrāya Kāmāya parasvān. KS. V, 7, 11= TS. 5. 5. 21.

sa iha kīṭo vā pataṅgo vā matsyo vā śakunir vā siṁho vā varāho vā paraśvān (v. l., *-śvā*) *vā śārdūlo vā puruṣo vā 'nyo vā teṣu teṣu sthāneṣu pratyājāyate.*—Śāṅkh. Āraṇ. 3. 2.

Previous Scholars: The commentator simply calls *tāyādará-* (which he reads *tāyodara-*) 'a kind of animal' and no one has yet any suggestion as to what it is; he has nothing to say about *párasvant-* either. Sāyaṇa on RV. has: '*he Indra ayaṁ Vṛṣākapiḥ parasvantaṁ parasvam ātmano viṣaye 'vartamānaṁ hataṁ hiṁsitaṁ vidat'*. On TS. he explains it as *mahiṣa*, with which may be compared Vj. 65, 21, *gavalaś ca parasvāṁś ca mahiṣaḥ syād araṇyajaḥ*. The commentary to Śāṅkh. Āraṇ. calls it 'a kind of snake'. BR. suggest that it is probably the 'wild ass'.

Tāyādarám is probably to be read *tā́yād áram*, the former being the subjunctive of *tāya-*, passive stem of *tan-* 'to extend.' Cf. Whitney, Sans. Gr. § 774, "Examples of the transfer of stems from the **yá**- or passive class to the **ya**- or intransitive class were given above (761 b.); and it was also pointed out that active instead of middle endings are occasionally, even in the earlier language, assumed by forms properly passive: examples are *ā́ dhmāyati* and *vy àpruṣyat* (ÇB.), *Bhūyati* (Māi. U.)." Or, *tā*, itself, found in *atāyi* (aor.), *tāyitā* (fut.), *-tāya* (ger.), *tāyitṛ-* etc., may be the stem. The verse would then mean, 'so that the member may extend sufficiently, made big by the wind', etc.

From the passages from KS. and Śāṅkh. Āraṇ., quoted above, *párasvant-* appears to be a wild animal like the jackal, the lion, the tiger, and the boar, and from AV. it is known to have a large member like the elephant, the ass, and the horse. Both these features are satisfied in its identification by Bühler, ZDMG. 48, 63, with Pāli *palasata-*, Aśoka. Delhi—Topra V. 6, Jātaka VI, p. 277, v. 1205 and *palāsāda-*, Jātaka, V, p. 406, v. 267,[1] which the commentator to Jātaka explains as *khagga* 'rhinoceros'. Bühler thinks that the intermediate steps were **parassanto*, **parasato*, and Trenckner, Pāli Miscellany, p. 58, n. 6 (cited by Hultzsch, Aśoka Inscrip., p. 127, n. 8) considers *palasato* to be the original of *palāsādo*

---

1 Compare with the above passages: *tathā pānāya- -m- āyanti nānā-migagaṇā bahu: sihā vyagghā varāhā ca acchakokataracchayo. palāsādā* (v. l. *palāsājā, palasādā, pallasadā*) *ca gavayā mahiṣā rohitā rurū: eneyyā varāhā c'eva gaṇino nikasūkarā*, etc.

and the latter, which literally means 'eating leaves', to be an etymologizing corruption of the former.

If this be the true meaning, the proper form is probably *páraśvant-*, literally, 'having an axe (*paraśu-*)', the reading of Śāṅkh. Āraṇ. Compare, *khaḍga-*, *-ḍgin-*, *vārdhrīṇasa-*, Germ. *Nasehorn*, etc. For syncope of *u*, cf. *paraśvadha-* 'axe' (*paraśu-vadha?*), *parśvadha-* (*parśu-vadha?*) 'axe': *paraśu-*, *parśu-*, *vánanvat-*: **vanana-vat-* (Grassmann), *indhanvat-*: *indhana-* (Ved. Gr. § 234), *hiraṇmaya-*, *hiraṇín-*: *híraṇya*, etc.

tirīṭín-

yás tvā svápne nipádyate bhrā́tā bhūtvā́ pité'va ca: bajás tā́n sahatām itáḥ klībárūpāṁs tirīṭínaḥ. 8. 6. 7.

Previous Scholars: Sāyaṇa: '*tirīṭinaḥ, antardhānena aṭataḥ.*' BR.: *tirīṭa*=' *eine Art Kopfputz, Turban, Diadem* Aruṇadatta bei Uǵǵvala, die Erklärer zu AK. (3. 6. 3, 30).' Others have followed BR.

It appears that the meaning 'head-ornament' or 'tiara' (Wh.) for *tirīṭa-* depends solely on a quotation from Aruṇadatta and statements of commentators later than him; it is not given in any of the old Kośas, nor do the modern dictionaries quote any occurrence of its actual use in literature. It might have arisen from a false reading of *kirīṭa-*, just as *bālatanaya-*, a synonym of *khadira-*, in Amara from that of *bālapatra-* (see Kṣīrasvāmin's comment).

The PTS's Pali Dictionary gives two meanings to this word, (1) 'the tree Symplocos racemosa' (*lodhra*) and (2) 'a garment made of its bark.' This second meaning suits the passage in question admirably well, for the *arā́yas* ('niggards') spoken of in this hymn, although vested with spectral qualities, are conceived by the poet to have been like a sort of wild folk who clad themselves in barks, skins, and tattered clothes. There seems to be no point in describing them as wearing a head-ornament. Puggalapaññatti, p. 51, '*so sāṇāni pi dhāreti masāṇāni pi dhāreti chava-dussāni pi dhāreti paṁsukulāni pi dhāreti tirīṭāni pi dhāreti ajināni pi dhāreti*', read together with v. 11 of this hymn, *yé kukúndhāḥ kukū́rabhāḥ kṛ́ttīr dū́rśāni bíbhrati; klībā́ iva pranṛ́tyanto váne yé kurváte ghóṣaṁ tā́n itó nāśayāmasi* (especially the words *chava-dussāni*, *tirīṭāni* and *ajināni* in the one and *kṛttīḥ* and *dūrśāni* in the other, together with *tirīṭínaḥ* in v. 7), makes it abundantly clear that *tirīṭa-* has the same meaning in both.

turmiśam

citrā́ṇi sākáṁ diví rocanā́ni sarīsṛpā́ṇi bhúvane javā́ni: turmiśaṁ sumatím icchámāno áhāni gīrbhíḥ saparyā́mi nā́kam. 19. 7. 1.

Previous Scholars: The commentator explains *turmiśam* either as *turmayo hiṁsakāḥ hiṁsākāriṇaḥ tān śyati tanūkarotīti turmiśā* or as *turo hiṁsakān miṣati hinastīti turmiśā: miṣa spardhāyām....mūrdhanyasya tālavyopajanaś chāndasaḥ.* "Seeking favour of the twenty-eightfold (?) wondrous ones, shining in the sky together, hasting in the creation (*bhúvana*), I worship (*sapary*) with songs the days, the firmament (*nā́ka*)."—Whitney, after emendation of *turmiśam* to *aṣṭāviṁśám* (or *-śā́*).

Turmiśam seems to be a corruption for * *turviśam* 'settlement of the stars' (cf. *tārāpatha-*, *nakṣatraloka-*, etc., for the 'sky') the first member (*tur*) being the genetive singular of *tṛ-* 'star' and the second *viś-* 'settlement.' For interchange of *m* and *v*, cf. *anarmáṇām* AV. 7. 7. 1: *anarváṇām* RV.; *amāmasī-: amāvasī-* 'new-moon', Vj. 160, 35; *ávradanta* in *áśrathnan dṛḷhā́ ávradanta vīḷitā́-* RV. 2. 24. 3 prob. =*ámradanta* (: *mṛdú-*) 'the firm became loose, the hard became soft' (for it Grassmann supposes a root *vrad-*, *vrand-* 'to become weak'); *āmataḥ, parāmataḥ* (mss.) for *-vataḥ*, Gaastra's GBr. p. 2, fn. 1; *vaṅgāvagadhāḥ*, Ait. Āraṇ 2. 1. 1 prob. = *-magadhāḥ* (Keith); and Wack. I. § 177. n. For singular giving a plural sense in an *aluksamāsa*, cf. Ved. Gr. § 275,—"A singular case-ending (the acc. or inst.) may here indicate a plural sense; *e.g.*, *áśvamiṣṭi-* 'seeking horses', *puram-dará-* 'destroyer of forts', *śúneṣita-* 'driven by dogs' (*śúnā-*)".

Áhāni in **d** is probably elliptical for *víśvā áhāni*. Thus the third and fourth pāda may be translated: "Desiring good-will of the settlement of stars, every day with songs I worship the firmament."

taimātá-

asitásya taimātásya babhrór ápodakasya ca: sātrāsāhasyā́ 'háṁ manyór áva jyā́m iva dhánvano ví muñcāmi ráthā̃ iva. 5. 13. 6.

nír vaí kṣatrám̐ náyati hánti várco 'gnír ivā́ 'rabdho ví dunoti sárvam ; yó brāhmaṇám̐ mányate ánnam eva sá viṣásya pibati taimātásya. 5. 18. 4.

Previous Scholars : BR. and others consider *taimātá-* to be the name of a kind of snake. Whitney translates 5. 13. 6, "Of the Timatan (?) black serpent, of the brown, and of the waterless, of the altogether powerful (?)· I relax the fury, as the bow ; I release as it were chariots". To this Lanman remarks : "Whitney would doubtless have revised this carefully. The divergences of the translators reflect the uncertainties of the exegesis. 'I slacken as it were the cars of the wrath of' etc.—Griffith. 'I release (thee) from the fury of' etc.— Bloomfield. 'Des Asita...... des Manyu Streitwagen gleichsam spanne [ich] mir ab' or 'die Streitwagen des Grimmes des Asita' etc. — Weber. For **d**, 'as the string from off (*áva*) the bow'".

There seems to be a contrast in 5. 13. 6 between *taimātá-* and *ápodaka-*. The word *ápodaka-* 'out of water' means either 'not in water' as in RV. 1. 116. 3,.... *naúbhir ātmanvátībhir antarikṣaprúdbhir ápodakābhiḥ*, or 'not containing water', 'dry', as in AV. 5. 16. 11, where it is obviously used as equivalent to *árasá-* 'sapless'. *Taimātá-* also appears to mean 'wet', but modified into 'living in water' at 5. 13. 6 and 'liquid' (*e.g.*, the poison of a snake) in 5. 18. 3. It is probably a derivative of *tema-* 'moisture' with suffix *-ta*, for which and for length of the vowel before the suffix, see under *arāṭakī́-*; for superfluous Vṛddhi in the first syllable, cf. *praiṇāná-* 5. 27. 3 and *sauprajāstvám* 2, 29. 3, for which other texts, including Ppp., have *prīṇ-* and *suprajās-*. The first member of *sātrāsāhasya* is obviously the same as *satrā́*, which means 'together', 'altogether', 'all at once', 'always', etc., and may here mean 'everywhere'; thus the word would mean 'prevailing everywhere, *i.e.*, both on land and water'. *Dhánvan* in **d** appears to be elliptically used in both senses, 'bow' with *jyā́m* and 'sandy wasteland' with *ráthān*, the comparison in the latter case being with the extrication of the wheels of a chariot stuck in a sandy piece of land.

Thus we may translate 5. 13. 4 : "I release (thee) from the fury of the wet black snake, the dry tawny snake, and of the all-prevailing one, like the string from the bow or chariots (from a sandy tract)."

taulá-

ā́jyasya parameṣṭhiñ jā́tavedas tánūvaśin: Ágne taulásya prā́śāna yātudhā́nān vílāpaya. 1. 7. 2.

Previous Scholars: The commentator derives it from *tulā-* 'balance', here standing for the sacrificial ladle. Roth and Whitney emend it in their edition to *tailásya* 'of sesame oil' against all authorities and Ppp., which has *tūlasya.*

Taulásya is evidently an adjective of *ā́jyasya*, and is probably from *tū́la-* 'a tuft of grass, etc. (here *kuśa-*).' Cf. *pavitra-*, with which ghee was sprinkled. *Tū́la-* is used with reference to *darbhá-* at 19. 32. 3.

duradabhnā́-

vilohitó adhiṣṭhā́nāc chaknó vindati gópatim: táthā vaśā́yāḥ sáṁvidyaṁ duradabhnā́ hy ùcyáse. 12. 4. 4. *duradabhnaí 'nam ā́ śaye yācitā́ṁ ca ná dítsati: nā́ 'smai kā́māḥ sámṛdhyante yā́m ádatvā cíkīrṣati.* v. 19.

Previous Scholars: BR: 'Thore täuschend d.h. durch Schloss und Riegel nicht zu halten'. Ludwig: 'unbetrieglich' at v. 4, but leaves the word without rendering at v. 19. Henry, p. 250, sees no reason for, or suitability of, the meaning given by BR. and Ludwig; he suggests *durdaghnā-* or *dur-adaghnā-* 'killing those who do not give' as the correct reading. "Anæmia (*vilohitá*) from the station of the dung visits (*vid*) the master of kine; so is the agreement of the cow; for door-damaging (?) art thou called."—Whitney (v. 4), who remarks, "Nearly everything in the second half verse is doubtful...... *sáṁvidya* (given by four of his mss.) seems a much more probable form of stem........ The second person *ucyáse* is quite unexpected", and at v. 19, "That the conjectural rendering ('Door-damaging lies she on him' etc.) is extremely unsatisfactory is plain".

The correct reading is probably *durādabhnā́-* 'hard to deceive (or harm)', paralleled by *ádabdhāḥ* 'unharmed' RV. 1. 173. 1 and *durādhárṣā-* 'hard to be dared against' AV. 12. 5. 17, both epithets of the cow, and *ná tā́ naśanti ná dabhāti táskaro nā́sām āmitró vyathír ā́ dadharṣati* AV. 4. 21. 3 (=RV. 6. 28. 3), about the cows. The suffix *-na* is also found in *mathná-* 'shaking vehemently' RV. 1. 181. 5 (cf. also *mathnāti* and *dabhnoti*) and after roots like *bhañj-*, *bhug-*, *ruj-*, *pṛ-*, etc., as forming the past participle.

Sā́ṁvidyaṁ, as suggested by Whitney, is a better reading in c of v. 4 and in view of the second person *ucyáse* in **d**, *vaśā́yāḥ sáṁvidyaṁ* seems to be a corruption for *vaśe 'yāḥ sáṁvidyaṁ*, 'O cow, thou camest to recognition'. Thus we may translate the verse: "Anæmia visits the lord of kine for taking possession of the dung; thus, O cow, thou comest to recognition, for thou art called 'hard-to-deceive' ".

In v. 19 *ā śī-* is used in the sense of 'to enter into' for the purpose of doing something evil as in RV. 10. 162. 1, *bráhmaṇā 'gníḥ saṁvidānó rakṣohā́ bādhatām itáḥ : ámīvā yás te gárbhaṁ durṇā́mā yónim āśáye*, and elsewhere. Thus: "The 'hard-to-deceive' gets into him, if he does not wish to give her, when asked", etc.

dūrśá-

pavástais tvā páry akrīṇan dūrśébhir ajínair utá ; prakrír asi tvám oṣadhé 'bhrikhāte ná rūrupaḥ. 4. 7. 6.

yé kukúndhāḥ kukū́rabhāḥ kŕttīr dūrśā́ni bíbhrati ; klībā́ iva pranŕtyanto váne yé kurváte ghóṣaṁ tā́n itó nāśayamasi. 8. 6. 11.

Previous Scholars: Sāyaṇa takes *dūrśébhiḥ* as adjective of *ajinaiḥ* (=*duṣṭa-ṛśyasambandhibhiḥ*) at 4. 7. 6 and reads *kŕtyair dūṣyāṇi* for *kŕttīr dūrśā́ni* at 8. 6. 11. 'Eine Art Gewebe oder Gewand', —BR. Weber on 4. 7. 6, Ind. Stud. 18. 29, follows BR. and remarks," zu d û r ç a, Pet. W., ist ausser d û ç y a, d û s h y a vielleicht auch t û s h a zu vergleichen ", but renders it with 'Häute' at 8. 6. 11. (*ib.*, 5, 255). Ludwig leaves the word untranslated. Grill (4. 7. 6): 'Für Decken tauschten sie dich ein, Gewebe, Felle gab man her', etc. Henry (8. 6. 11): 'Les kukundhas, les kukûrabhas qui portent des peaux en guise de vetêments', etc. Bloomfield (4. 7. 6): 'with broomstraw (?), garments' etc. Whitney renders the first *dūrśá-* with 'garments' and the second with 'pelts', each followed by a query-mark.

Dūrśá is found at least three times in the Kauśika Sūtra; (i) *jihvāyā utsādyam akṣyoḥ paristaraṇam astṛhaṇaṁ hṛdayaṁ dūrśa upanahya tisro rātrīḥ palpūlane vāsayati* 11, 16, where the tongue and several other parts of a cow are prescribed to be tied up in a *dūrśa-* and soaked in cowdung for three nights; (ii) *kṛmukaśakalaṁ saṁkṣudya dūrśajaradajināvakarajvālena*, 28, 2, where it is prescribed as an easily inflammable light fuel along with worn-out goatskin and broomstraws; and (iii) *vilumpantām agham iti pari cailam* (v.l., *śelam*, *śilam*, of which the latter seems to be the correct reading) *dūrśam vilumpati* 85, 22, where it is to be spread around (Keś.) a piece of stone (*pariśilam*). In all these instances Dārila and Keśava[1] render it with *jīrṇavastra-* 'old or tattered cloth'. It will be seen that this meaning suits also the two occurrences in the AV. In the first passage it is used together with hemp-textures (see *pavásta-*) and goatskins, both of which are inexpensive, as a means of exchange for a herb. (It may not be out of place to mention here that in India even to-day old clothes are very often exchanged for herbs from the forest-folk.) In the second a set of wild people (or spectres conceived as such, see *tirīṭín-*) are said to clothe themselves in skin and *dūrśá-*.

Prāk. *dūsa-* has two meanings 'cloth' and 'tent', in the first of which it must be the same as Sans. *dūrśá-* and in the second as Sans. *dūṣya-* 'a tent'. Pāli *dussa-* is also to be similarly assigned. It would appear that in these two languages *dūrśá-* has developed a wider meaning, from 'old cloth' to 'cloth in general'. In Pāli *chavadussa-* 'a miserable garment' it seems to have retained its original meaning.

Beng. *dhūs*, Nep. *dhusā*, Punj. *dhussā*, and corresponding words in other modern Indian vernaculars, all meaning 'a kind of woollen covering', may be connected with it, but the aspiration is unexplained.

nyá- —*ánya-*

dṛḍhó dṛṁhasthiró nyó bráhma viśvasṛ́jo dáśa : nā́bhim iva sarvátaś cakrám úcchiṣṭe devátāḥ śritā́ḥ. 11. 7 (9). 4.

---

[1] It may be mentioned here that Keśava appears to have flourished in the time of King Bhoja of Malwa (c. 1018–1060 A.C.), when the Muhammadans were terrorising the country. Speaking about the importance of *abhicāra* at the end of Kāṇḍika 49, he remarks, *pṛthivyām duṣṭa utpannaḥ sarvadā ca vināśayet : adharmasambhavo duṣṭo prajāhiṁsanatatparah : Turuṣkā nāmnā pāpiṣṭhā devabrāhmaṇa-hiṁsakāḥ : pṛthivyāṁ Śrī-Bhojadeva dharmasaṁrakṣaṇāya ca : deśe tu Mālavake utpannaḥ śrīrājagṛheṣu ca ;* again under 47, 22, *idam ahaṁ Mahmadasya Turuṣkasya Mūtikarṇaputrasya prāṇāpānāv apayacchāmi.* He was thus a contemporary of Uvaṭa, commentator of the VS., and preceded Sāyaṇa by nearly three centuries. Dārila, whose work forms the basis of Keśava's Paddhati, must have flourished much earlier.

ā́ tv àdyá sabardúghā̃m huve gāyatrávepasam : índram dhenúm sudúghām ányām íṣam urúdhārām araṁkṛ́tam. **RV. 8. 1. 10.**

idā́ hí va úpastutim idā́ vāmásya bhaktáye : úpa vo viśvavedaso namasyúr ā́ āsṛkṣy ányām iva. **RV. 8. 27. 11.**

yó asyá viśvájanmana ī́śe víśvasya céṣṭataḥ : ányeṣu kṣiprádhanvane tásmai prāṇa námo'stu te. AV. 11. 4 (6). 23.

yásyāś cátasraḥ pradíśaḥ pṛthivyā́ yásyām ánnaṁ kṛṣṭáyaḥ saṁbabhūvúḥ : yā́ bíbharti bahudhā́ prāṇád éjat sā́ no bhū́mir góṣv ápy ánye dadhātu. **12. 1. 4.**

ányebhyas tvā púruṣebhyo góbhyo áśvebhyas tvā : níḥ kravyā́daṁ nudāmasi yó agnír jīvitayópanaḥ. **12. 2. 16.**

púruṣa evé'dáṁ sárvaṁ yád bhūtáṁ yác ca bhāvyàm : utā́ 'mṛtatvásye 'śvaró yád ányenā́ 'bhavat sahá. **19. 6. 4.**

Previous Scholars: (1) *nyá.*—Sāyaṇa: '*dṛṁha-sthiraḥ dṛṁhanena sthirīkṛto lokaḥ, nyaḥ netāras tatratyāḥ prāṇinaḥ*'. BR., 'wohl adj. von unbekannter Bed.' Grassmann: '*niedersinkend* (?) [von ní], enthalten in ánia.' Henry: 'Affermi et solide toi-même, affirmis', etc. He thinks (p. 158) that *nyá-* may be an artificial formation from *anyá-* as *sura-* from *asura-*, thus meaning 'no other', 'himself'. Bloomfield, who would read *dṛḍhadṛṁhá(ḥ)* and consider *nyáḥ* 'leader' (sing.): *nī-* 'to lead': 'He who fastens what is firm, the strong, the leader,' etc. Whitney, who considers *dṛṁha* a verb: 'Being fixed, fix thou, being staunch, *nyá*', etc. (2) *ánya-*. —Sāyaṇa on RV. and AV. 11. 4(6). 23 sees no difference between it and *anyá-* 'other'. His commentary on the 12th book is wanting and at 19. 6. 4 he reads *ánnena* (SPP. reads *anyéna*, other texts *ánnena*). BR: '*ányā*, (3. *a+nyā*, zusammengezogen aus *ni-yā*, wie auch zu sprechen ist) f. adj. *nicht versiegend*'. Henry gives a number of substitutes for *góṣv ápy ánye* such as *go-ṣṭhāpátye*, * *go-śvadhā́nye*, etc. and renders 12. 1. 4d: 'daigne cette Terre nous accorder la possession des vaches.' At 12. 2. 16 he as well as Ludwig considers *ányebhyaḥ* as equivalent to *anyé-* and in the dative. Whitney: 'to thee being such, O breath, having a quick bow among the unexhausted (?*ánya*), be homage', 11. 4. 23c,d; 'let that earth (*bhū́mi*) set us among kine, also in inexhaustibleness (?*ánya*), 12. 1. 4d; 'Thee from inexhaustible (?*ánya*) men, kine, horses' etc. 12. 2. 16.

The correct reading in 11. 7. 4a appears to be *dṛḍhó 'dṛṁhas sthiró nyáḥ*, the loss of a sibilant before a sibilant followed by an explosive (as between *-dṛṁhas sthiró*) being prescribed by the Prātiśākhyas and Kātyāyana (Wack. I. § 287. b) and widely followed in the Vedic texts. This gives us a pair of contrasted words, *dṛḍháḥ* 'firm': *ádṛṁhaḥ* 'not-firm' (cf. *bhūmidṛṁhá-* 5. 28. 14, 19. 33. 2), *sthiráḥ* 'stable': *nyáḥ*, which should therefore mean 'unstable', 'movable', 'perishable', or the like. *Nyá-* (to be read *niá*) may easily have this meaning, if its relation to root *nī-* in the sense, 'to take away', 'to remove', is considered to be the same as that of *priyá-* 'dear' to the root *prī-* 'to please'.

Ányа- would thus mean 'immoveable', 'imperishable', and thus be an exact equivalent of *amṛ́ta-*, which is sometimes an adjective, meaning 'imperishable', and sometimes a noun, meaning 'nectar', often applied to sacrificial butter or the soma-drink (see Grassmann, *s.v.*). At 12. 1. 4 and 12. 2. 16 *ánya-* is probably used in the sense of sacrificial butter; at RV. 8. 1. 10 and 8. 27. 11 it qualifies *íṣam* 'libation', understood in the second passage; and at AV. 19. 6. 4 it means 'nectar', thus giving a much better sense than the other texts which read *ánnena*. *Ányeṣu* at AV. 11. 4. 23 is probably a vocative of *ányeṣū*: 'O one of inexhaustible arrows, to thee of quick bow, O Prāṇa, be homage.'

paṭū(ṭau)rá-

pratighnānā́ḥ sáṁ dhā́vantū́ 'raḥ paṭūrā́v āghnānā́ḥ : aghāríṇīr vikeśyò rudatyàḥ púruṣe hatè raditè Arvude táva. 11. 9 (11). 14.

Previous Scholars: Sāyaṇa: '*uraḥ vakṣaḥsthalam paṭūrau tatpradeśau ca*'. Böhtlingk: 'ein bestimmter Körperteil'. Bloomfield who renders with 'thigh', remarks [Reprint of A.J.P. XI. 3 (pp. 319-356), p. 22]: "Our translation of the obscure word is based upon Kauç. 84, 10, *triḥ prasavyaṃ prakirṇakeçyaḥ pariyanti dakṣiṇam ūrum āghnānāḥ*. The word seems to contain *ūru* with some modifying adjective, perhaps *pṛthu* in a Prākṛtic form." Henry suggests emendation to **paṭair avaghnānā́ḥ* and renders: 'Qu'elles accourent, celles qui se meurtrissent de coups, | arrachant les voiles qui couvrent leurs seins,' etc. Whitney notes: "I follow both translators in rendering *paṭaurá* by 'thigh', although it is not too acceptable, considering the familiarity of *ūru* as name for 'thigh'".

Paṭūrá- or *-ṭaurá-* is evidently identical with *pāṭora-* in KS. V. 13, 11-12, *Agneḥ pakṣatiḥ Sarasvatyā nipakṣatiḥ Somasya tṛtīyā.......devānāṁ dvādaśī dyāvāpṛthivyoḥ pārśvaṁ Yamasya pāṭoraḥ*, and *pāṭūra-* in a corresponding passage in TS. 5. 7. 21-22. This is about the ribs of a horse. VS. 25, 4-5 and MS. 3. 15. 21-22 in the corresponding passages count thirteen ribs and leave out *pāṭūra-*. Caraka, Śārīra. 7, 5, counts only twelve ribs on each side, while GBr. I. 5. 3, thirteen. It thus appears that there have been two views about the exact number of ribs, and in any case *pāṭūra-* seems to be outside, but just following, them on each side. It is most probably the bone, on each side, just about the thigh-joint and below the waist. Vaijayantī, p. 22, gives *pāṭūra-* as a name for the fourteenth lunar night.... *pratipat tv ekapakṣatiḥ: pakṣatiś cā 'tha pāṭūro bhūteṣṭā ca caturdaśī: ni-pakṣatir dvitīyā syāt.* This also supports the above contention, the two fortnights in a month being considered its two sides (*pakṣa*).

In the above passage *paṭūraú* evidently stands not actually for these bones, but for the two sides of the belly just near them, referring to the common phenomenon of the striking of the breast and the belly by women in grief.

paruṣá-

darbháḥ śocís tarū́ṇakam áśvasya vā́raḥ paruṣásya vā́raḥ: ráthasya bándhuram. 10. 4. 2.

Previous Scholars: Ludwig: "das junge darbhagras ist flamme [der schlange], der pferdes scheif, des paruša schweif [ist flamme für die schlange], | [ebenso] des wagens sitz." Henry: "Ardeur brûlante [contre le venin] est le brin de darbha, ainsi que le jeune brin [d'orge ?], | le crin de cheval, le poil d'homme||......le caisson du char........" Bloomfield renders *paruṣá-* with 'the shaggy one', but remarks (p. 607), "For the unintelligible parusháysa we are tempted to substitute arusháysa relying upon the oft-emphasised whiteness (svetá) of Pedu's horse". Whitney: "*Darbha*-grass, brightness, young shoot (? *tarū́ṇaka*); horse's tail-tuft, rough one's tail-tuft; chariot's seat (? *bándhura*)."

Paruṣá- here probably refers to the bull. It is used as an epithet of *ukṣán* 'bull' in RV. 5. 27. 5, *yásya mā paruṣā́ḥ śatám uddharṣáyanty ukṣáṇaḥ*, and of *gaú* 'bull' or 'cow' in RV. 6. 27. 5, *utā́daḥ paruṣé gávi sū́raś cakrám hiraṇyáyam: ny aìrayad rathī́tamaḥ*, and 8. 93. 13, *tvám etád adhārayaḥ kṛṣṇā́su róhiṇīṣu ca: páruṣṇīṣu rúśat páyaḥ.* This epithet is due probably to its shagginess (of the tail ? Cf. *puruvāra-* 'having an ample tail-tuft', another epithet, RV. 1. 139. 10), as it is applied elsewhere also to *ū́rṇā-* 'wool' (RV. 4. 22. 2, see Grassmann, s.v. *paruṣá-*).

Paruṣa- seems to be the correct reading for *púruṣa-* (note that two of Wh.'s and one of SPP.'s mss. read *puruṣa-* for *puruṣa-* in the above passage) in AV. 6. 38. 4, *rājanyè dundubhā́v ā́yatāyām áśvasya vā́je púruṣasya māyaú: Índraṁ yā́ devī́ subhágā jajā́na sā́ na aítu várcasā saṁvidānā́*, and 19. 49. 4, *siṁhásya rā́try uśatī pīṁṣásya vyāghrásya dvīpíno várca ā́dade: áśvasya vradhnáṁ púruṣaṣya māyúṁ purú rūpā́ṇi kr̥ṇuṣe vibhātī́*, as *māyú-* 'bellowing', 'lowing', etc., is usually applied to an animal such as the cow or the sheep, cf. Whitney's remark at 6. 38. 4, "*Māyú* is not properly used of *púruṣa* 'man', and the expression is obscure and doubtful".

párśāna-

Índrā-Somā vartáyataṁ divás páry agnitáptebhir yuváṁ áśmahanmabhiḥ: tápurvadhebhir ajárebhir atríṇo ní párśāne vidhyataṁ yántu nisvarám. 8. 4. 5=RV. 7. 104. 5.

giráyaś cin ní jihate párśānāso mányamānāḥ: párvatāś cin ní yemire. RV. 8. 7. 34.

yád vīḷā́v Indra yát sthiré yát párśāne párābhr̥tam: vásu spārháṁ tád ā́ bhara. RV. 8. 45. 41.

Previous Scholars: Sāyaṇa: *pārśvāsthipradeśe*, AV. =*pārśvasthāne* at RV. 7. 104. 5, *pīḍyamānāḥ* or *spr̥śyamānāḥ* at RV. 8. 7. 34; and *vimarśana-kṣame* at 8. 45. 41. BR.: 'm. Einsenkung, Abgrund, Kluft...... Nach Naigh. 1. 10. Wolke, wohl derselben ursprungs wie *parśu*.'

In RV. 8. 45. 41 *párśāna-* is contrasted with *vīḍú-* 'strong' and *sthirá-* 'firm', while AV. 8. 4. 5, when compared with 8. 4. 17**d**, *táṁ pratyáñcam arcíṣā vidhya mármaṇi*, and 8. 6. 24**d**, *hr̥dayé'dhi ní vidhyatam*, would point to some 'tender' part of the body as its meaning. The meaning 'soft', 'tender', not only suits these two passages but also the third.

The original meaning seems to have been what Sāyaṇa gives at RV. 8. 75. 41, viz., *vimarśanakṣama-* 'worthy of being touched or felt': *sparśa-* 'touch' with suffix *-āna*. This suffix *-āna*, used to form adjectives, is found in several words: *ápnav-āna-: *apnu(?)*, *ūrdhvas-āná-: ūrdhvá(s)-*, *jrayas-āná-: jráyas-*, *dhiyas-āná-: *dhiyas-*, *pŕ̥thav-āna-: pr̥thu-* (see under *suśíma-*), *mandas-āná-: *mandas-*, *rabhas-āná-: rábhas-*, *vasáv-āna-: vásu-*, *vr̥dhas-āná-: vr̥dhás-*, *śavas-āná-: śávas-*, *sahas-āná-: sahás-*, etc. Grassmann and Macdonell (in Vedic Grammar) consider it identical with the participial suffix, but added to a double stem of the root, in the case of *jrayasāná-*, *dhiyasāná-*, *mandasāná-*, *rabhasāná-* etc. It seems however more likely to be a secondary suffix in view of the above examples, placed side by side with the corresponding nouns.

pavásta-

pavástais tvā páry akrīṇan dūrśébhir ajínair utá : prakrír asi tvám oṣadhé 'bhrikhāte ná rūrupaḥ. 4. 7. 6.

ábhūr v aúkṣīr vyù āyur ānaḍ dárṣan nú pūrvo áparo nú darṣat : dvé pavásta pári tám ná bhūto yó asyá pāré rájaso vivéṣa. RV. 10. 27. 7.

Previous Scholars: Sāyaṇa: '*pavastaiḥ pavanāya astaiḥ sammārjanītṛṇaiḥ*,' on AV. and '*pavaste pavatir gatikarmā..........mahatvena sarvasyābhibhavanāya gacchantyau (dyāvāpṛthivyau)*,' on RV. BR.: '*Zeltdecke* oder dergl. AV. 4. 7. 6. du. bildlich von *Himmel und Erde* RV. 10. 27. 7.' Oldenberg, RV. II. p. 227, remarks: "*Pavásta* dunkel. Ungewissheit der auf kombination von AV. IV. 7. 6. und Kauś. 28. 2. beruhenden Gleichsetzung mit *avakara* hat schon Bloomfield S. B. E. 42. 377f. hervorgehoben; ebenso die Schwierigkeit, auf diesem Wege Verständniss unseres st. zu fördern. Unzutreffend Weber, Ind. Stud. 18. 29."

Pāli *potthaka-* ('a cloth made of makaci fibre', PTS's P.D.) is the regular representative of Sans. *pavasta(ka)* and, as we shall presently see, its meaning suits both the occurrences of the latter. In Jātaka IV, p. 251, *potthakam* is explained by *ghana-* or *saṇa-sāṭakam*. From the descriptions of *potthaka-* given in Aṅguttaranikāya p. 246 and Puggalapaññatti p. 33, *saṇasāṭaka-*, 'a texture made of hemp', appears to be the true reading. It is described there as having an indifferent colour (*dubbaṇṇo*), rough (*dukkhasaṁphasso*), and cheap (*appaggho*)[1] which are exactly the characteristics of a hemp-texture. It would appear that a rough texture of this kind was used as a wrapper just like a blanket, cf. Kauś. 57. 13, *sarveṣāṁ kṣaumaśāṇakambalavastram*, and Puggalapaññatti p. 51, *so sāṇāni pi dhāreti masāṇani pi dhāreti*, etc.

[1] *tayo potthakā:—navo pi potthako dubbaṇṇo c'eva hoti dukkhasaṁphasso ca appaggho ca, majjhimo pi potthako dubbaṇṇo c'eva hoti dukkhasaṁphasso ca appaggho ca, jiṇṇo pi potthako dubbaṇṇo c'eva hoti dukkhasaṁphasso ca appaggho ca: jiṇṇaṁ pi potthakaṁ ukkhaliparimajjanaṁ vā karenti saṅkarakuṭe vā naṁ chaḍḍenti.*—Pug. 33.

Accordingly, the RV. verse may be translated: "Thou becamest, thou grewest up, thou didst attain age; now the first one, now the other one has pierced. Two hemp-wrappers (*i.e.*, the heaven and the earth) wrap, as it were, him who has spread beyond this region." And the AV. one, "They bought thee for hemp-wrappers, for tattered cloth and for goat-skin", etc.

Av. *pāṣt-* 'skin of a man', Pers. *post* 'skin', later Sans. *pustaka-* and Pāli *potthaka-* 'a book', form quite a different group of words.

Bloomfield's (SBE. 42, 377 b.) and apparently Sāyaṇa's (AV. 4. 7. 6) identifications of *pavásta-* with *avakara-*, on the ground that the latter word is found with *dūrśa-* and *jarad-ajina-* in Kauś. 28. 2, is without any force, since the words are used in different contexts. *Pavásta-*, *dūrśá-*, and *ajína-* in AV. are referred to as inexpensive means of exchange, while *dūrśa-*, *jarad-ajina-*, and *avakara-* in Kauś. are prescribed as easily lighted fuels.

pṛṣṭí-

Previous Scholars: Sāyaṇa :=*parśu-* RV. 10. 87. 10, AV. 2. 7. 5, 4. 3. 5, =*pārśvāvayava-* AV. 2. 32. 2, =*pṛṣṭhavaṁśasya abhito vartamānāḥ parśūḥ* 11. 10. 14. BR.: 'rippe (=*párśu*)'. Grill, Henry, Whitney, and other scholars generally follow BR., except when *pṛṣṭí-* and *párśu-* come together in the same sentence and where they try to differentiate with 'side' ('flanks', Henry) and 'rib' ('côte', Henry) respectively. Uhlenbeck, Etym. Wört., has: "p ṛ ṣ ṭ í s f. rippe, vgl. afgh. *puštai* rippe and *parçus* rippe, sichel. AV. *parštis* np. *pušt* rücken gehören nicht hierher, sondern zu *pṛṣṭham.* "*Pṛṣṭi* denotes not 'rib', which is *parśu*, but a transverse process of a vertebra, and so the vertebra itself", —Ved. Ind., *s.v.* Śarīra. This last one will appear to be the right meaning.

It would appear from the above that scholars are often doubtful as to the precise meaning of *pṛṣṭí-*, especially when they have to distinguish between it and *párśu-*. *Pṛṣṭí-* is distinguished from *párśu-* in AV. 9. 7. 6, *devā́nām pátnīḥ pṛṣṭáya upasádaḥ párśavaḥ*, and 10. 9. 20, *yā́ḥ pṛṣṭír yā́śca párśavaḥ*; and from *pārśvá-* in 9. 1. 34, *yā́ḥ pārśvé uparṣánty anuníkṣanti pṛṣṭī́ḥ.* In 12. 1. 34, *uttānā́s tvā pratīcī́ṁ yát pṛṣṭíbhir adhi śémahe* (addressed to the earth), men are said to lie on the earth, facing upwards, with their *pṛṣṭís.* Whitney and Griffith here give a derivative meaning 'stretched out' to *uttāná-*, apparently in order to be consistent with the meaning 'rib'. But *uttāná-* usually means, not only in classical but also in Vedic Sanskrit, 'lying on one's back', 'facing upwards', cf. RV. 10.142.5, *bāhū́ yád Agne anumármr̥jāno nyàṅṅ uttānā́m anvéṣi bhū́mim*, and 10. 27. 13, etc., where *uttāná-* is contrasted with *nyàṅ* 'facing downwards'. In 18. 4. 10 horses are called *pr̥ṣṭivā́hah*, which Whitney renders 'back-carrying (?)'. These instances show that *pr̥ṣṭí-* is not the same as *párśu-*, but is either the back itself or some part of the body at the back. GBr. I. 5. 3, just after counting the *párśus*, analyses the spine (*anūka-*) thus: *anūkaṁ trayastriṁśo, dvātriṁśatir hy evai 'tasya pr̥ṣṭikuṇḍīlāni bhavanty, anūkaṁ trayastriṁśam, tasmād anūkaṁ trayastriṁśaḥ*, where it (*viz.*, the spine) is said to have thirty-two rings (?) of *pr̥ṣṭí-* [cf. Suśruta, Śārīra. ch. 5., *pr̥ṣṭhe triṁśat (asthīní)*]. The number and the description agree with those of the transverse processes of the vertebra.

From this the meaning was easily widened to indicate the spine or the back itself, as is seen in the case of *pr̥ṣṭivā́hah*. Hastyāyurveda of Pālakāpya, which seems to be a fairly ancient work, uses at 3. 9. 55 *pr̥ṣṭau* for *pr̥ṣṭhe*. A similar use is also found in Kalyāṇamandirastotra, Ind. Stud. 14, 386, and Siṁhāsanadvāttriṁśika and Pañcadaṇḍachatraprabandha, *ib.*, 15, 378.

In the light of the above Pāli *piṭṭhi* and *piṭṭhī* (f.), Prāk. *paṭṭhi*, *piṭṭhi*, and *puṭṭhi* (f.), Guj, *puṭh* (f.), Sindhi *puṭhi*, *puṭhī*, Mār. *puṭh*, and H. *pīṭh* (f.), all meaning 'back', are to be traced back to *pr̥ṣṭí-*. Cf. Turner, Dictionary of Nepali, s.v. *piṭh* and Bulletin of the School of Oriental Studies, vol. V. p. 124, s.v. *puštai*. It is also clear now that Av. *paršti-š* and nP. *pušt* do really belong to *pr̥ṣṭí-*, not to *pr̥ṣṭha-* as Uhlenbeck thought.

péṣṭra-

yát te riṣṭáṁ yát te dyuttám ásti péṣṭraṁ ta ātmáni : dhātā́ tád bhadráyā pūnaḥ sáṁ dadhat páruṣā páruḥ. 4. 12. 2.

yó naḥ śápād áśapataḥ śápato yáś ca naḥ śápāt : śúne péṣṭram ivā́ 'vakṣāmaṁ táṁ práty asyāmi mr̥tyáve. 6. 37. 3.

Previous Scholars : Sāyaṇa reads *preṣṭham* (=*priyatamam*) at 4. 12. 2 and *peṣṭam* (=*piṣṭam*) at 6. 37. 3. 'Knochen......vielleicht von 1. *piś*'.—BR., followed by Ludwig, Grill, and Griffith. Weber, Ind. Stud. 18, 47, renders with 'Quetschung', and Hillebrandt, Ved. Chrest., vocabulary, remarks: "Ich stelle das Wort zum Wurzel *piṣ*, zermalmen, und vermuthe: losgeschlagenes Stück Fleisch, Fleischfetzen". Bloomfield also renders with 'bone', although not satisfied. Whitney renders the two passages respectively: "What of thee is torn (*riç*), what of thee is inflamed (*?dyut*), is crushed (*?péṣṭra*) in thyself—may Dhātar excellently put that together again, joint with joint", and, "Whoever shall curse us not cursing and whoever shall curse us cursing, him, withered (?), I cast forth for death, as a bone (??) for a dog".

Bloomfield, SBE. 42, 385, has already suggested a connection of *péṣṭra-* with *piśitá-* and *peśí-*, and that, like the other two, it may also mean 'flesh'. In fact all these three words contain the same root *piś-* 'to prepare, make ready (especially meat, by cutting it up and carving it)', followed by different suffixes, *-tra* (Ved. Gr. § 152), *-ta* (ib. § 145), and *-i* (ib. § 131) respectively; cf. *janiḥ* and *ā-jāniḥ*, *jātám*, *janítram* RV. 7. 34. 2, 56. 2 (Sāy.), 'birth': *jan-* 'to be born', *nṛtíḥ*, *nṛttám* 'dance': *nṛt-* 'to dance', *vasitam*, *vastram* 'cloth': *vas-* to clothe', etc. For root *piś-* in this sense, cf. AV. 12. 5. 36, *Śarváḥ kruddáḥ piśyámānā śímidā piśitā́ (brahmagavī́)*. The word *piśitá-* itself occurs twice in the AV., at 5. 19. 5, *krūrám asyā āśásanaṁ tṛṣṭáṁ piśitám aśyate*, and at 6. 127. 1, *vidradhásya balā́sasya lóhitasya vanaspate : visálpakasyau 'ṣadhe mó'chiṣaḥ piśitáṁ caná*, where it seems to have a figurative meaning.

This meaning not only suits both the contexts but seems to be required by them. AV. 4. 12., where the first passage occurs, is all about the healing of fractured bones, torn and damaged flesh, etc., cf. v. 3, *sáṁ te māṁsásya vísrastaṁ sáṁ ásthy ápi rohatu*, and v. 4, *ásṛk te ásthi rohatu māṁsáṁ māṁséna rohatu*. In the second passage, a piece of meat offered to a dog would make a better simile than a bone for a man offered to death, for in the former case there is also the suggestion of being completely devoured.

prā́rtha-

anyakṣetré ná ramase vaśī́ sán mṛḍayāsi naḥ: ábhūd u prā́rthas takmā́ sá gamiṣyati bálhikā́n. 5. 22. 9.

Previous Scholars: "Lies *prá-arthas*, nach PW.: ≫Ausrüstung zur Reise≪; vielleicht aber praedic. zu *takmá*=fortstrebend (vgl. *arthay*+*pra*), Ludwig: ≫begierig nach der Ferne≪ Hillebrandt: ≫Bereitwillig≪".—

Grill. "The pada-reading in **c** is *pra-árthaḥ ; prá-ar-* would better suit the meaning given 'ready to set out', lit. 'having an object in front'".—Whitney.

Prārtha- seems to be a corruption for *prārthya-*, 'amenable to supplication', cf. RV. 1. 82. **1c,d**, *yadā naḥ sunṛtāvataḥ kára ād artháyāsa íd yójā nv Índra te hárī*, and Grassmann, s.v. *arthay-*, meaning (2). This (*prārthia-*) is required also by the metre and would save us an awkward resolution and a forced meaning. The loss of *y* is only another instance of the tendency of the AV. mss. to drop the last of a conjunct of three, see instances under *kákutsala-*, to which may be added *akṣ(y)aù* 4. 3. 3 (majority of Wh.'s mss.), *tálp(y)āni* 14. 2. 41**d**, *mekṣ(y)-āmi* 7. 102. 1, *rákṣ(y)amāṇaḥ* 18. 4. 70, etc.

bhṛmalá-

yás te sarpó vṛ́ścikas tṛṣṭádaṁśmā hemantájabdho bhṛmaló gúhā śáye : kṛ́mir jínvat pṛthivi yád yad éjati prāvṛ́ṣi tán naḥ sárpan mó'pasṛpad yác chiváṁ téna no mṛḍa. 12. 1. 46.

Previous Scholars : The commentary is wanting on this kāṇḍa. BR : 'adj. beläubt, torpidus'. Wackernagel, I. § 63.γ.: 'v.: *bhṛmá-* „Verirrung" *bhṛmí-*, *bhṛ́mi-*, AV. *bhṛmalá* : v. *bhramá-* „Lohe" sp. *bhramati* „schweifen"'. Ludwig, p. 548 : "der sarpa, der stechende, mit hartem zahn, der dir von winter erfroren, der sich hin und her schlagelnde im verborgen ligt". Bloomfield : 'The serpent, the scorpion with thirsty fangs, that hibernating torpidly lies upon thee' etc. Henry : 'Ton serpent. ton scorpion à l'âpre morsure, | qui englouti par l'hiver git assoupi dans sa cachette' etc. Whitney : "What stinging (*vṛ́ścika*) harshbiting serpent of thine lies in secret, winterharmed, torpid (*?bhṛ́malá*); whatever worm, O earth, becoming lively stirs in the early rainy season—let that crawling not crawl upon us ; be thou gracious to us with that which is propitious".

The Ppp. reading *bhramalo* suggests that our *bhṛmalá-* may be identical with *bhramara-* 'a humble bee'. Confusion of *ra* and *ṛ* in mss. is very common ; cf. for instance, *pṛṣṭi-* or *pṛṣṭhi-* in some mss. for *praṣṭi-* AV. 10. 8. 8, 13. 1. 21, recorded by Whitney in his translation ; *kramuka-*, *v. l.* for *kṛmuka-* Kauś. 28. 2 ; *praśnyam* for *pṛśnyam* in Dārila's comm. to Kauś. 11. 16 ; *drati-* for *dṛti-* Kauś. 38. 12 ; ms. Ech *hṛdam*, PBh *hṛdayam* for *hradam* ib. 52. 5, etc. Keśava commenting on *yuktayor mā no devā yas te sarpa* (the present verse) *iti śayanaśālorvarāḥ parilikhati*, Kauś. 51. 17, remarks, *atha sarpādisvastyayanam ucyate : sarpa-*

vṛścika-dvidaṁśamaśaka-bhramara-bhūmikīṭa-kṛmayah ; eteṣāṁ bhayaṁ na bhavati, and again under the following sūtra,........ *ahibhaye vṛścikabhaye maśakabhaye bhramarasaṁghe kṛmibhaye* etc. His enumerations, especially the second one, when equated in order of presentation with our verse, show that according to him *tṛṣṭádaṁśmā*= *dvidaṁśa-maśaka-* or *maśaka-* and *bhṛmalá-* = *bhramara-*. For *tṛṣṭádaṁśmā* cf. also AV. 7. 56. 3, *arbhásya tṛpradaṁśíno maśákasyā 'raṣáṁ viṣám*, and Sans. *daṁśa-*, Beng. etc. *ḍā̃ś* 'a gnat'. This makes it clear that in Keśava's time (c. 11th century) either the reading itself was *bhramará-* or *bhramalá-* instead of *bhṛmalá-*, or the latter was understood to be identical with the former. The above verse may accordingly be translated: "The serpent, the scorpion, the harsh-biting (mosquito), the bee of thee, that, pressed (lit., 'ground': *jabh-* 'to grind') by winter lie in concealment; whatever worm, being lively, O earth, stirs up in the early rainy season, let that crawling not crawl on to us, favour us with that which is propitious".

maṇ(n)aú

devā́ imáṁ mádhunā sáṁyutaṁ yávaṁ Sárasvatyām ádhi maṇā́v acarkṛṣuḥ: Índra āsīt sīrapatiḥ śatákratuḥ kīnā́śā āsan Marútaḥ sudā́navaḥ. 6. 30. 1[1].—V.l., *manā́v-*.

ní tigmám abhy àṁśúṁ sīdad dhótā maṇā́v ádhi: juṣāṇó asya sakhyám. RV. 8. 72. 2.

áyukta sū́ra étaśaṁ pávamāno maṇā́v ádhi: antárikṣeṇa yā́tave. ib. 9. 63. 8.

rā́jā medhā́bhir īyate pávamāno maṇā́v ádhi: antárikṣena yā́tave. ib. 9. 65. 16.

Previous Scholars: All have taken *maṇā́u* (or *-ṇaú*) as if identical with *mánau* 'man' or 'Manu' (loc.), although some, like Whitney, are not quite satisfied.

The accent indicates that *maṇ(n)aú* may be altogether different from *mánu-;* and *maṇ(n)ā́v ádhi* with verbs like *acarkṛṣuḥ* 'ploughed', *sīdat* 'sat', *pávamānaḥ* 'being purified', suggests

[1] "It occurs also in TB. (ii. 4. 87; exactly repeated in ĀP. ÇS. VI. 30. 20; PGS. iii. 6. 1.), MB. (ii. 1. 16), and K. (xiii. 15). The TB. version begins with *etám u tyám mádh-* (so MB. also), and it gives in **b** *sárasvatyās* and *manā́v*".—Whitney.

that it may refer to some place or plot of land on which these actions could be performed. Now, Beng. has a word *mānā* (< * *maṇyā* ?) which means 'a fertile piece of land on either side of a river' (so near that it is often flooded when the river is full). Cf. also *maṇi-rūḍhaka-*, synonym of *śimbidhānya-* (podded grain, such as pulses) Kalpadrukośa p. 142, 89, *śimbidhānyaṁ jalaklinnaṁ sāṅkuraṁ maṇirūḍhakam*. The application of such a meaning to the first verse, where the river Sarasvatī (cf. TB. reading *-svatyās*) is mentioned, is clear, while the other three verses relate to Soma, who is frequently connected with the river or river-bank; cf. in the same hymns, *duhánti saptaí 'kām úpa dvā́ páñca sr̥jataḥ : tīrthé síndhor ádhi svaré*, 8. 72. 7; *tám īṁ mr̥janty āyávo háriṁ nadī́ṣu vājínam : índum Índrāya matsarám*, 9. 63. 17; *yá ārjikéṣu kŕ̥tvasu yē mádhye pastyā́nām : yé vā jáneṣu pañcásu* (*sómāsaḥ sunviré*), 9. 65. 23; also 9. 76. 1, 8. 96. 14, 15, etc. [1]

madhyamaśír

yásyā 'ñjana prasárpasy áṅgam aṅgaṁ páruṣparuḥ : táto yákṣmaṁ ví bādhasa ugró madhyamaśír iva. 4. 9. 4 = RV. 10. 97. 12, VS. 12. 86 with v.l., *yásyau 'ṣadhīḥ prasárpatha* in **a**, and *bādhadhva* in **c**.

Previous Scholars: Sāyaṇa: '*madhyame antarikṣasthāne śete saṁcaratīti madhyamaśīḥ vāyuḥ*', or, '*arir mitram arer mitram iti nītiśāstroktarājamaṇḍalamadhyavartī rājā*' (AV.), and, '*madhyamasthāne vartamāno rājā*' (RV.). BR.: 'etwa *intercessor*'. Grassmann: 'wol; *der in der Mitte sich lagernde* als Bezeichnung etwa des Heer-führers'. Whitney: "*Madhyamaçī* is of obscure meaning; 'arbiter', as conjectured by BR. seems very implausible [BR. express their conjectural meaning by the Latin word *intercessor*; by which, I suspect, they intend, not 'mediator', but rather 'adversary' or 'preventor' of the disease, which would be plausible enough]; more probably 'midmost man', like *madhyameṣṭhā* or chief (see under iii. 8. 2.), and *madhyamaçī* used especially of the leader about whom his men encamp, for his greater safety, in the night".

In the simile in the second half we have on one side, 'thou drivest away disease'—a subject, an object, and a verb—, while on the other side apparently only the subject (*madhyamaśír*) and the verb (the same *vi-bādh-*). This suggests

---

[1] Cf. Punj. *maṇḍ* 'low moist ground on the bank of a river or stream', which cannot in the ordinary way come from the same source as Beng. *mānā*, and Telugu *manu* 'earth, soil'.

that we have probably to split up *madhyamaśír* into two words, *mádhyam*, acc. sing. of *mádhya-* 'the central part', and *aśír*, nom. sing. of **aśír* (for accent and gender cf. *vandhúr-*), probably 'a boring instrument' or 'awl' as will appear from the following correspondences. Walde, Idg. Wört., *s.v.* ak̑ (z. T. auch ak-) ,, scharf, spitz, kantig; Stein ", gives a detailed account of words formed with this element, of which those formed with *-l* (p. 29) seem to be identical (at least some of them) with our **aśír-*: "arm. *aseł̄n* ,, Nadel", aksl. *Os(ъ)la*, ,, Wetzstein", ags. *egle* pl. ,, Ährenspitzen, Grannen", engl. *ails* ,, Grannen", ahd. *ahil* m. ,, Ähren-spitze, Granne", nhd. (dial.) *agel, ägel* ,, festuca" und Achel; acymr. *ocolin* ,, cos", ncymr. *agalen*, und *(h)ogalen*, nbret. *higolen* ,, Wetzstein"; lat. *aculeus* ,, Stachel"; anord. *soð-āll* ,, Fleischgabel"; cymr. *ebill* ,, Bohrer" corn. *epill hoern* ,, clavus", mbret. *ebil* ,, Pflock, Stiff, Nagel"."

Assuming this modification of the text and meaning of **aśír-*, Whitney's translation may be modified: "Of whomsoever, O ointment, thou creepest over limb after limb, joint after joint, from thence thou drivest away the *yákṣma* 'as a sharp boring instrument the middle portion (of anything, by cutting a hole)'".

mū́ra- —mū́radeva-

1. *mū́ra-*

yā́ śaśā́pa śápanena yā́ 'gháṁ mū́ram ādadhé: yā́ rásasya háraṇāya jātám ārebhé tokám attu sā́. 1. 28. 3 = 4. 17. 3.

Mū́ra- has been rightly identified with *mū́la-* 'root', but the import of c seems to have been misunderstood. Thus the commentator takes *mū́ram* as adj. of *aghám*, meaning either *ādibhūtam* or *mūrchākaram*, and reads *ādade* (=*parijagrāha, kṛtavatī 'tyarthaḥ*) for *ā dadhé*; Grill, '....hat gift'ge Wurzel angewandt'; Whitney, '..that hath taken malignity as her root (? *mū́ra*).' As, however, *ā dhā-* usually means 'to lay', 'to deposit', 'to bury or impregnate', cf. RV. 9. 19. 5, *kuvíd vṛṣaṇyántībhyaḥ punānó gárbham ādádhat*, and roots are mentioned as having been used for sorcery, cf. *mūlakṛ́t-* in *yáḥ kṛtyākṛ́n mūlakṛ́d yātudhā́no* 4. 28. 6, and *mūlín-* in *kṛtyākṛ́taṁ valagínaṁ mūlínaṁ śapatheyyàm* 5. 18. 12, the rendering should rather be, 'that hath buried the wretched root'. Cf. 5. 18. 8, *yā́ṁ te kṛtyā́ṁ kū́pe 'vadadhúḥ śmaśānè vā nicakhnúḥ*, or 10. 1. 18, *yā́ṁ te barhíṣi yā́ṁ śmaśānè kṣetré kṛtyā́ṁ valagáṁ vā nicakhnúḥ*.

2. *mū́radeva-*

áyodaṁṣṭro arcíṣā yātudhā́nān úpa spṛśa jātavedaḥ sámiddhaḥ : ā́ jihváyā mū́radevān rabhasva kravyā́do vṛṣṭvā́ 'pi dhatsvā 'sán. 8. 3. 2=RV. 10. 87. 2.

párā śṛṇīhi tápasā yātudhā́nān párā 'gne rákṣo hárasā śṛṇīhi : párā 'rcíṣā mū́radevāñ chṛṇīhi párā 'sutṛ́po abhí śóśucānaḥ. 8. 3. 13 (=10. 5. 49)=RV. 10. 87. 14.

Índra jahí púmāṁsaṁ yātudhā́nam utá stríyaṁ māyáyā śā́śadānām : vígrīvāso mū́radevā ṛdantu mā́ té dṛśant sū́ryam uccárantam. 8. 4. 24=RV. 8. 104. 24.

Previous Scholars: Sāyaṇa: =*māraṇakrīḍā rākṣasāḥ* (8. 104. 24), *mūḍhadevān mārakavyāpārān* (10. 8. 2), *māravyāpārān* (ib. v. 24) on RV., and, *mūlena auṣadhena dīvyanti*, or *mūḍhāḥ santo dīvyanti te* (8. 3. 2), *māraṇena karmaṇā dīvyantīti* (v. 13), *māraṇakrīḍā mūlena viṣauṣadhyā dīvyantīti vā* (8. 4. 24) on AV. BR: '=*mūladeva* Kâç, zu P. 8, 2, 18, Vârtt. 2, Bez. *gewisser Unholde.*' Grassmann: 'Bezeichnung dämonischer Wesen oder ihrer Verehrer.' Whitney: 'falseworshippers.' Henry renders with 'demons' or 'impies', but remarks in his commentary to 8. 3. 2 that it is probably a possessive compound with *mū́ra-* 'root', and not *mūrá-* 'foolish', as the accent on the first member shows.

As Henry has already pointed out, the accentuation shows that the first member in *mū́radeva-* is *mū́ra-* 'root', thus the word meaning, 'having the roots as one's god'. In view of the importance of the use of roots in sorcery, as seen under *mū́ra-*, this implies simply that the sorcerers were so called because they were devoted to and expected everything from the roots just as much as the Ṛṣis did with regard to the gods. That roots were actually worshipped as fetish and their worshippers were later confused with demons, as Henry would suggest, does not seem to be a necessary implication.

vrā́-

Venás tát paśyat paramáṁ gúhā yád yátra víśvaṁ bhávaty ékarūpam : idáṁ pṛ́śnir aduhaj jā́yamānāḥ svarvído abhyànūṣata vrā́ḥ. 2. 1. 1.

sánn úchiṣṭe ásaṁś co 'bhaú mṛtyúr vā́jaḥ prajā́patiḥ: lokyā́ úcchiṣṭa ā́yattā vráś ca dráś cā́ 'pi śrī́r máyi. 11. 7 (9). 3.

stámbhīd dha dyā́ṁ sá dharúṇaṁ pruṣā́yád ṛbhúr vā́jāya dráviṇaṁ náro góḥ: ánu svajā́ṁ mahiṣáś cakṣata vrā́ṁ ménām áśvasya pári mātáraṁ góḥ. RV. 1. 121. 2.

svásā svásre jyā́yasyai yónim āraig ápaity asyāḥ praticákṣyèv: vyucchántī raśmíbhiḥ sū́ryasyā́ 'ñjy aṅkte samanagā́ iva vrā́ḥ. Ib. 1. 124. 8.

pū́rvām ánu práyatim ā́dade vas trī́n yuktā́ aṣṭā́v arídhāyaso gā́ḥ: subándhavo yé viśyā̀ iva vrā́ ánasvantaḥ śráva aiṣanta pajrā́ḥ. Ib. 1. 126. 5.

té manvata prathamáṁ nā́ma dhenós tríḥ saptá mātúḥ paramā́ṇi vindan: táj jānatī́r abhyànūṣata vrā́ āvírbhuvad aruṇī́r yaśásā góḥ. Ib. 4. 1. 16.

góbhir yád īm anyé asmán mṛgáṁ ná vrā́ mṛgáyante: abhitsáranti dhenúbhiḥ. Ib. 8. 2. 6.

samudrā́d ūrmím úd iyarti Venó nabhojā́ḥ pṛṣṭháṁ haryatásya darśi: ṛtásya sā́nāv ádhi viṣṭápi bhrā́ṭ samānáṁ yónim abhyànūṣata vrā́ḥ. Ib. 10. 123. 2

Previous Scholars: Sāyaṇa on RV. gives various meanings to this word: 'night' or 'dawn' (1. 121. 2), *samyagananahetava āpaḥ, samanāḥ, tā gaccantīti samanagā vidyutaḥ, vrā vrātāḥ, vidyutsaṁghā iva* (1. 124. 8), *vriyanta iti vrāḥ vrātāḥ takāralopaś chāndasaḥ* (1. 126. 5), *vrā ity uṣaso nāma* (4. 1. 16), and *vrā varitaro jālādibhir upāyair nirundhānā vyādhāḥ* (8. 2. 6). On AV. 2. 2. 1 he has *vrāḥ*= either *āvṛtātmānaḥ prajāḥ*, or, *vriyamāṇāḥ....apaḥ*, and on 11. 7 (9). 3, *vraḥ vārako varuṇaḥ draḥ drāvakaḥ amṛtamayaḥ somaḥ*. Geldner, Trans. of RV. p. 149. n., summarises the opinions of leading modern scholars and gives his own opinion: "*vrā́* nach Roth: Haufe, Schar, nach Pischel: Weib, nach Bergaigne (40. h. 14) femelle en rut oder femme amoureuse. Dies wohl richtig. *vrā́* ist das Lockweibchen. In 8. 2. 6. bezeichnet es die weiblichen Locktiere, mit denen Jäger das Wild einfangen wie die Sänger den Indra. 1. 124. 8 sind die Frauen gemeint, die auf die Hochzeit gehen um Männer einzufangen (vgl. AV. 6. 60); 1. 126. 5 mit dem Beiwort *viśyā́ḥ* die Hetären (δημόσιαι παιδίσαι); 4. 1. 16; 10. 123. 2; AV. 2. 1. 1. die Lockstimmen der Sänger, wobei das Bild der nach dem Stier brüllenden Kühe festgehalten wird. 1. 121. 2. ist das den Büffel lockende Weibchen, das Indra als der Büffel für sich selbst erzeugt hatte, gemeint, also eine *māyā*". Whitney renders with 'troops', although he refers to Pischel's interpretation.

Pischel's view (and evidently also that of Bergaigne and Geldner) that *vrā-* means 'a woman', Ved. Stud., II. 131 and 313–322, rests on the following: (1) corresponding to *samanagā́ iva vrāḥ* RV. 1. 124. 8. there are RV. 4. 58. 8, 6. 75. 4, 7. 2. 5, 10. 86. 10, 10. 168. 2, etc., where women are said to go to a *sámana*, which is shown to have been a kind of festive gathering; (2) in RV. 1. 121. 2, like *mé nām áśvasya* and *mātáraṁ góḥ*, *vrā́-* should also refer to a female animal, namely, that of the *mahiṣáḥ*; (3) in RV. 8. 2. 6 there may be a reference to capturing elephants with the help of a she-elephant, *vrā́ḥ* standing for *vrābhiḥ* (he refers to Bergaigne, Mélanges Renier p. 88ff.); (4) in 1. 126. 5 *viśyā́ḥ* 'belonging to the people (*víś-*)' qualifying *vrā́ḥ* may make it equivalent in sense to *veśyā-* 'courtesan'; and (5) in the phrase *abhy ànūṣata vrā́ḥ* the word may stand for the 'prayers', which are often compared to women.

Against this may be considered the following: (1) corresponding to *samanagā́ iva vrā́ḥ* RV. 1. 12. 48 and *viśyā́ iva vrā́ḥ* ib. 1. 126. 5, we have *samanagā́ aśucaj jātávedāḥ* ib. 7. 9. 4 (cf. Pischel, *loc. cit.*, p. 315) and *víśa ā́ kṣeti viśyó víśaṁ* ib. 10. 91. 2, the only other recorded instances of *samanagā́-* and *viśyā́-*, both referring to 'fire'; (2) the meaning of *vená-*, with which *vrā́ḥ* appears in AV. 2. 1. 1 and RV. 10. 123. 1 is uncertain; sometimes the word appears as an epithet (=*medhāvin-* 'wise' Naigh. 3. 15., 'eager', 'loving', BR.), at others as a particular deity. In the latter case it is particularly associated with the sun, cf. RV. 1. 83. 3, *tátaḥ sū́ryo vratapā́ vená ā́jani*, ib. 10. 123. and particularly v. 1, *ayáṁ Venáś codayat pṛ́śnigarbhā jyótirjarāyū rájaso vimā́ne: imám apā́ṁ saṅgamé sū́ryasya śíśuṁ ná víprā matíbhī rihanti*, and AV. 2. 1. 1 and 4. 1. 1 which seem clearly to refer to the rising of sun and the consequent unravelling of the universe, erstwhile immersed in darkness. Apparently on these rest the statements of Nir. 1. 7., ŚBr. 7. 4. 1. 14, etc., that it means the 'sun'. The root *ven-* 'to long for' seems identical with Av. *vaen-* 'to see' and in the latter sense *vená-* may certainly refer to the sun as the 'observer'; (3) *abhy ànūṣata* may as well be the 3rd aor. plur. of *uṣ-* 'to burn' (cf. *úṣ-*, *uṣás-* 'dawn' which would be intended by *vrā́ḥ* in this case) with *abhí* and *ánu*; and (4) *mṛgáṁ ná vrā́ mṛgáyante* in RV. 8. 2. 6 may refer to the chasing of wild beasts with 'firebrands' in hunting, reading *vrā́* (inst. sing.) instead of *vrā́ḥ* or understanding it with Pischel as elliptical for *vrābhiḥ*.

The above suggests that 'glow' either of fire or of dawn, is perhaps the true meaning of *vrā́-* and this is also supported by the I.-E. element **u̯r̥-* (or **u̯l̥-*) 'to burn', found here as well as in the following: *ulkā́-* 'firebrand' or 'meteor', *ulkuṣí-(mant-)* and *ulmuka-* 'firebrand', *ulbaṇa-* 'hot' Vj. 196, 17, *várcas-* 'splendour'; old HG. *walm* 'warm', old Bulg. *varъ* 'glow-heat', *variti* 'to cook', Lith. *isz-vora* 'soft boiled vegetable food', Lett. *wārs* 'soup', *wārīt* 'to cook'—Leskien, Alt. Bulg. Element. p. 13—old Slav. *varŭ* 'heat' *vrěti* 'to cook, to be hot', *vrutŭ* 'hot', Lith. *vìrti* 'to cook'—Kluge. Etym. Wb. d. deutsch. Sprache, s.v. *warm*—etc. Cf. also Walde, s.v. 3. *u̯er-*, p. 269.[1]

samuṣpalā́-

saṁvánanī samuṣpalā́ bábhru kályāṇi sáṁ nuda: ámūṁ ca mā́ṁ ca sáṁ nuda samānáṁ hr̥dayaṁ kr̥dhi. 6. 139. 3.

Previous Scholars: Sāyaṇa hazards a conjecture, *samuṣpalā samyak uptaphalā satī.* Whitney: "A conciliator, a love-awakener (?), do thou, O brown, beauteous one, push together; push together both yon woman and me; make [our] heart the same". He remarks, "The mss. hardly distinguish *sy* and *sp*, but ours, in general, seem as distinctly as the case admits, to read *samuṣyalā́* in a; yet SPP. has *-uṣpa-* (noting one ms. as reading *-uṣya-*), and, as he has living scholars among his authorities, the probability is that he is right. Save here and at XIV. 1. 60. (*úṣyalāni* or *úṣpa-*), the word appears to be unknown".

Samuṣpalā́- is probably identical with **samut-sparā́-* 'conquering' (: *spr̥-* 'to conquer'), entailing a loss of final unexploded *t* before *s* as in *ut-sthā-*: **uṣṭhā-*: Vern. *uṭh-*. See Turner, Bulletin of the School of Oriental studies, V, p. 130f. Compare *jáyantī* and *spáraṇī* in 5. 5. 3, *vr̥kṣáṁ vr̥kṣam ā́ rohasi vr̥ṣaṇyátī 'va kanyálā: jáyantī pratyātíṣṭhantī spáraṇī nā́ma vā́ asi,* with *saṁvánanī* 'winning over' and *samuṣpalā́* in the above verse.

Úṣpala- 'framepieces of a bedstead' in 14. 1. 60, *Bhágas tatakṣa catúraḥ pā́dān Bhágas tatakṣa catvā́ry úṣpalāni: Tváṣṭā*

---

[1] Walde, *loc. cit.*, tries to show that the meaning, in the Baltic and Slavonic languages, 'to be hot' etc. came from 'to cook' < 'to stir' < 'to mix water' < *u̯er-* 'to make wet', and suggests that Arm. *varem* 'I light', *var* 'burn' and Germ. *warm* are to be separated from them. He does not take into account the Sans. examples amongst them.

pipeśa madhyató 'nu várdhrān sā́ no astu sumaṅgalī́, seems to be altogether a different word from the above. It can, however, hardly be different from *utpala-* in Kauś. 35. 26, *dīrghotpale 'vagṛhya saṁviśati* and 36. 7, *śayanapādam utpale ca*, the former of which the commentators explain, *maṁcakeśe* (??) [prob.- *keṣe*, the (side-)poles of the bedstead] *adhaḥ kṛtā* (? *-tvā*) *tatra saṁviśati* (Dār.), and *khaṭvām adhomukhapaṭṭikāṁ gṛhītvā ......svapiti* (Keś.). Assuming *utpala-* to be the correct form, the appearance of *uṣpala-* can be explained as coming first through a Prakritic tendency to *uppala-* and then by ms. corruption becoming *uṣpala-*. Other instances of *pp* (प्प) appearing as *ṣp* (ष्प) are found elsewhere, cf. Whitney's remarks with regard to *pippalī́-* at 6. 109. 1 and *píppala-* at 9. 9. 20.

suśīma-

lā́ṅgalaṁ pavī́rávat suśī́maṁ somasátsaru : úd íd vapatu gā́m áviṁ prasthā́vad rathavā́hanaṁ pī́varīṁ ca prapharvyàm. 3. 17. 3.

Previous Scholars: Sāyaṇa: '*karṣakasya sukha-karam.*' BR. suggest emendation to *susīmam* 'having a good furrow'. For *somasátsaru* (p. *somaśat-saru*, VS., MS., KS., and Vas. Dh. *-pit-saru*, Ppp. *-pitsalam*), which Whitney considers impracticable, Weber conjectures a noun *uman* 'strap' and emends to *soma* (=*sa-uma*) *satsaru* 'with strap and handle'. For the rest and *variæ lectiones* see elaborate discussion of the verse by Whitney, who renders: "Let the plow (*lā́ṅgala*), lance-pointed, well-lying, with well-smoothed handle, turn up (*ud-vap*) cow, sheep, an ongoing chariot-frame, and a plump wench".

Suśīma- in ŚBr. 6. 44. 3, where it is used to explain *suṣad-*, evidently contains the root *śī-* 'to lie', see BR. It also appears in Kauś. 76. 23, *iṣo tvā sumaṅgali prajāvati prajāvati suśīma iti prathamam*, in the following sūtra (the same expression), and in 77. 6, *samṛchata svapatho 'navayantaḥ suśīmakāmāv ubhe virājāv ubhe suprajasāu*, etc. Bloomfield (suggested also by BR.) emends in all these cases to *susīma-*, but if *suśīla-* is substituted for *suśīma-* the meaning suits all right. *Śīma-* and *śīla-* 'habit' thus appears to be parallel formations with *śī-* 'to lie', originally meaning simply 'inclination'. In the above verse *suśíma-* probably refers to the inclination of the pole to the stump of the plough.

As most of the verses of this hymn are found also in different texts (Ppp., RV., VS., MS., TA., TS., Vas. Dh.) but nowhere in the same order or all together, it is possible that this verse is culled from a different context and *soma* may well be a vocative and *sátsaru=sát-tsaru-* 'well-handled'. With this understanding, which does not require change of accent or any other supposition, the verse may be translated: 'Let the plough, furnished with a lance (*i.e.*, the share), well-inclined, of a good handle, O Soma, turn up', etc.

In this connection may be considered RV. 10. 93. 14, *prá tád duḥśíme pṛ́thavāne vené prá rāmé vocam ásure maghávatsu: yé yuktvā́ya páñca śatā́ 'smayú pathā́ viśrā́vy eṣām*, where both *duḥśíma* and *pṛ́thavāna-* have been considered proper names. Now King Vena, who is notorious in tradition as a perpetrator of evil deeds (cf. Sörensen's Index to MBh., *s.v.* Vena, and W. Kirfel, Das Purāṇa Pañcalakṣaṇa p. 145f., 15–17; 234f. 10–33; 251, 3–10), had a son called Pṛthu. Thus, with the above meaning of *śíma-*, *duḥśíma-* 'evil-disposed' may well be his epithet, while *pṛ́thavāna-* may mean 'having Pṛthu (as a son)'—see suffix *-āna* under *párśāna-*—and thus be another epithet.[1]

[1] The above was approved by the University of London as a thesis for the degree of Doctor of Philosophy in July, 1930.

INDEX OF WORDS.

Sanskrit.

INDEX OF VEDIC PASSAGES.

AV.

CHAPTER 2

Theism in the Āyurveda

The Hindu medical works, treating of the living organism, as they do, have incidentally to say something about the basic principles of life. The moment they begin to discuss the conception and growth of the foetus in the mother's womb, or to trace each individual disease to its root-causes, or to lay down rules governing the good conduct of life-all of which are considered integral parts of the Ayurveda—some remarks on this head become inevitable. When, for instance, the Ayurveda posits that the male and the female seed, united, in their normal, healthy conditions, in the mother's womb at a time when this latter is favourable for their reception, produce the foetus, the question naturally arises whether these two are competent by themselves to start the living organism and build the body, or whether something else, totally different from either of them, has to be assumed, which starts life and sets the building properties in the seeds in motion. A second issue, necessarily connected with the first, is whether the mental, moral and physical characteristics of the person thus born are all traceable, through the seeds, to the parents inasmuch as the characteristic virtues of the effect are determined by those of the cause. If they are not, and if no other appreciable cause, since the inception of his life, can be traced for some of them, are we justified in attributing them to mere chance, or must we perforce assume that this life is only a continuation, and the causes, not apparent herein, must have had their being in a previous one ? Similarly, in the case of diseases, some cases of them are hereditary and some others are attributable to deviation from the mode of life leading to good health; but there remain still certain others which seem to be destined to baffle all enquiries after the cause. How are they to be explained ? Again, as individual philosophy determines the man, shaping his attitude towards life and therefore forcing itself, whether he is aware or not, through all his undertakings, it becomes incumbent on the Ayurveda, advising, as it does, on the good conduct of life, to affirm in the most clear and cogent terms what view a person should take of life. Are birth and death the two extreme points determining the span of our existence, or does the latter extend both ways beyond them ? If it does, is it this existence of ours with all its accompanying pleasures and pains and many other such contrasts, that will rotate *ad infinitum*, or have we a finer entity that runs through these rotations, uniting them into one whole, as a piece of thread unites the flowers in a garland, that is unaffected by these contrasts, and that can, therefore, discard them at pleasure, thereby putting a stop to further rotations ? Is it only a chance or in the mere nature of things that we are here and the world goes as it does ? Or is

* First published in *Kalyanakalpataru*, 1934

there some Principle, some force, that comprehends all existence, seizing it in a grasp from which there is no escape, and that evolves itself in a baffling contradiction of no-change in change? Much will depend on answers given to these questions, and we propose to see in this article what the *Ayurveda* has to offer us.

Four works, or rather three—*the Charakasamhita, the Susrutasamhita, and the Ashtangasamgraha*, with its abridged and versified redaction, the *Ashtangahridaya* of Vagbhata—represent the philosophical side of the *Ayurveda* in its best. Being the finest, as also the oldest, extant, contributions of some of the master minds on the subject, they have been an inexhaustible store of material for the later writers, who have seldom, if ever, ventured to differ from the views expressed in them. Of these, again, Charaka has dealt with the above questions most elaborately and systematically, offering arguments and counter-arguments, with a force that belongs only to originality and conviction; Sustuta briefly summarises the most generally accepted views, supplementing and defining them with some of his own; while Vagbhata is still more concise, mentioning only the mature conclusions incidentally and without pretension. Following the Sanskrit maxim "the needle first, the caldron next" (*Suchi-kataha-nyaya*), we shall take up Vagbhata first, Susruta next, and Charaka last of all.

Vagbhata

Vagbhata (vide *Ashtangasamgraha, Sarira, chap.* 2), discussing the inception of the embryo, remarks that when the old mense has disappeared, the new has settled, and the seat and the passage of the embryo are clean, the normal semen, in the function of the seed, impelled by the normal motor force (*Vayu*) of the body, followed by the five primary elements, assisted by the mense and immediately joined by the living entity (*Jiva*), who submits to the force of the Troubles (*Klesas*) such as attachment (*Raga*), who is impelled by his own sections, and whose motion rests with the mind (*Manas*), settles in the uterus as the embryo. As effects follow the nature of the causes, the preponderance of the semen or of the mense or their equality determines respectively the sex—male, female or neutral—of the embryo. Similar are his remarks in *Astangahridaya, Sarira*, 1. 1-4. But the import of verses 1 and 4 should be noted. Verse 1, which compares the manifestation of the spirit (*sattva*), impelled by his own actions and Troubles, in the united seminal and menstrual fluids to that of the fire in the churning stick, under the impulse of the right collocation, would imply the unity and omnipresence of the spirit like that of fire, its plurality and motion properly belonging to its object of adoption, viz. the mind (*Manas*), just as they belong to stick in the case of the fire. Verse 4 says that as effects retain the characteristics of the causes, the spirit assumes different forms like molten iron and moulds. This amounts to saying that the spirit in man is essentially the same as in the lowest living entity. The same idea is contained also in Sutra 2.23, "one should view even a worm or an ant as one's own self". In Vagbhata's opinion the mind appears to be inseparable from the individual self (*sattva, Atma, chetana*) until Freedom (*Mokhsa*); that is why he says, "the mind, the organs of sense, and birth in different species (of the embryo) are due to the self" (*Ashtangahridaya, Sarira* 3.5); cf also *Ashtangasamagraha, Sarira* 5, the passage beginning with etc. and the commentator Indu's remarks thereon, "so the mind originates in the Self, since it does not come from anywhere, being permanently attached to the Self."

Indu (vide *Ashtangasamgraha, Sarira*, chap. 5) summarises the philosophy of Vagbhata thus, "The Self is eternal, immune from change, is neither born nor dead; owing to its contact with the mind and others it receives the appellations 'born', etc.; the contact, again, is due to the nature of the *Avidya*; when the contact disappears on the exhaustion of the *Avidya*, it is in its pure essence and is termed 'free'; without a continuous agent there can be no memory of childhood and other states of life, without which there can be no undertaking of works with a motive, and such works as the body become impossible. It, again, acts of its own accord, getting, as a result of it, bondage or freedom. Bondage and freedom are the effects of his own actions, which serve as the cause. Surely, the body is not possible without the Self as the agent, to this effect is also the assertion of the holy Charaka, "he who can say that a pot can be made by earth, the stick and the wheel, without the potter, or a house by earth, grass and wood, without the house-builder, may say that the body is made by the materials combining themselves. Thus, the Self is conscious, the cause, and eternal, while the primary elements (Mahabhutas) are unconscious, transient and disrupting themselves every moment. Had the latter been permanent, growth of phenomena would have been impossible. Surely, a single thing cannot be the same and otherwise, but this is seen; so the elements are transient, acquiring the appellation of 'Person' (*Purusha*), when presided over by the Self."

In discussing whether one's span of life is fixed or has variations, Vagbhata (vide *Astangasamgraha, Sutra*. ch. 9) remarks that it is determined by one's own actions in a previous life (*daiva*) as much as this (*purushakara*) These two classes of actions may either go hand in hand or conflict with each other, in which latter case the stronger prevails. So that the treatment of the same disease, other things being equal, may be easy, much more difficult, or may even fail, according as *daiva* and *purushakara* favour each other, *daiva* is against but *purushakara* is stronger, or *daiva* overrides *purushakara*.

The author repeatedly advises us to shun atheists (Nastikas) and atheistic thought. (cf. *Ashtangasamgraha, Sutra*. III. 79. 114). He often mentions the two worlds, this one and the next, and praises one who is forgetful of neither and who fares well in both (cf. *Ashtangasamgraha, Sutra*. III. 38; *Ashtangahridaya*, 25). One is advised to worship deities for general welfare as also for getting rid of certain diseases (cf. *Ashtangasamgraha, Sutra*. III. 22). His remark at the end of the fifth chapter of the *Sarirasthana* in *Ashtangasamgraha* is interesting. This body, which has just been analysed, becomes the cause of bondage or of freedom according as it is viewed collectively or separately.

Susruta

In the first chapter of the *Sarirasthana*, Suruta first of all recounts the twenty-five basic ingradients (Tattvas) of the human body and the universe, and traces their mutual relations, following the *Samkhya* system. The cause of all beings, itself uncaused, marked by three properties (*Sattva, Ralas* and *Tamas*) and eight forms (*Avyakta, Mahat, Ahamkara* and the five Tanmatras), the source of the whole universe, is the Unmanifested (*Avyakta*). Alone, it is the resort of the innumerable souls (Kshetrajnas). From the Unmanifested evolves Intelligence (*Mahat* or *Buddhi*) and from Intelligence, Egoism (*Ahamkara*), both retaining the three characteristic properties of the Unmanifested. The latter is of three kinds, *Sattvika, Rajasa* and *Tamasa*, according to these three properties. From the Sattvika Egoism, helped by the Rajasa, evolve the eleven organs, five of sense, five of action and mind (Manas), which shares the characteristics of both. From the Tamasa Egoism, assisted by the Rajasa, evolve the five sense-essences (Tanmatras), the sound, the touch, the vision, the taste and the smell, each in its purest essence. Their developments are the sound, the touch, the vision. the taste and tne smell, from which evolve the five elements (Bhutas)—Ether (Vyaman), Wind (Anila), Fire (Anala), Water (Jala) and Earth (Urvi). These are twenty-four First Principles (Tattvas), all of which are unconscious ( ). The twenty-fifth is the Person (Purusha), which, connected with both the cause and the effect, is responsible for their consciousness ( ). Although the source (Prakriti, Pradhana or Avyakta) is unconscious, it is said to work for the freedom of the Person (Purusha). Now for the similarities and dissimilarities between the Source and the Person. Both are without beginning, without end and without tangible characteristics; both are eternal, supreme is one, unconscious and possessed of three properties, contains the germs of everything, when unmoved, and bears them forth, when moved by contact with the Person, and is not indifferent, the Persons are many, conscious, devoid of any of the three properties, neither containing germs, nor bearing them forth, and indifferent. Then, as effects are similar to the causes, all these developments are full of sattva, rajas and tamas. Being manifested in them and full of them, the Persons retain their properties. This, he says, is the view of some.

Next, he says that in Vaidyaka the wise consider Nature, God, Time, Chance, Destiny and Evolution as the Source. The elements must be viewed as full of them and possessed of their properties, since they produced the whole mass of elements, marked by their characteristics. Its importance is ever asserted for medicine, since in medicine there is no thought beyond that of the elements. For it has been said that the collection of materials necessary for the being of the Person originates in the elements, and the organs and the objects of the organs are described in the Ayurveda as elemental. And here is the dictum, "It is maintained that man perceives a sense-object by the corresponding sense-organ and not by a different one, undoubtedly because they have the same origin." Again, in the Ayurveda the souls (Kshetrajnas) are not described as all-pervasive and eternal. Reasons are adduced for establishing the eternity of the Souls that are not all-pervasive. In the Ayurveda the souls, that are not all-pervasive but eternal, are said to wander about in the bodies of the lower animals, men and gods, owing to good and evil actions. They are inferential, extremely minute, conscious, eternal, manifesting themselves in the union of the male and female needs. For this reason it has been said that the Person is an assemblage of the five primary elements and the soul. This Person of action is the subject of medicine. In brief, the eightfold source, the sixteen evolutes, and the souls are recognised in this as in any other science.

In the third chapter of the same book, while discussing the formation of foetus, he applies certain epithets to the soul that should remove all misapprehension about its character. It is the Field-knower (Kshetrajna), the Knower (Jna), the subject of the sensations of touch, smell, sight, hearing and taste, the Person, the Creator, the Goer, the Witness, the Ordainer, the Speaker, it is indestructible, inexhaustible and unthinkable. Again, at the end of the fifth chapter, after having analysed the different parts of the body, internal as well as external, he remarks : "The all-powerful (i.e. the Soul) who is extremely minute, cannot be seen in the body with this eye, but he is seen by those who have the sight of knowledge or of austerities." His remarks at the end of the second chapter are also interesting : "Those who have, in their previous births, charged their minds with the thoughts of the scriptures, become ever devoted to them, share an abundance of the Sattva-guna, and remember their previous births. The actions which impel a person follow him also in his rebirth, and he shares the very same virtues that he practised in a previous body."

That the author is a strong theist will appear from his remarks, to quote only a few, at Sarira. II. 48, "the foetus may get deformed owing to the atheism of the parents, the sins committed in a previous birth, and the irritation of the humours"; at III. 33, "those that are devoted to the gods and the Brahmans and habituated to purity and good conduct, and are congenial, bear highly meritorious offspring, while those that are of an opposite description have worthless children"; and at IV, 80, "purity, theism, study of the Vedas, respect for the superiors, hospitality, and worship are the marks of the Brahman body (the best body characterised by an abundance of the Sattva-guna, according to him).

Charaka

The views of Charaka may be summarised thus : Mind, soul and body are like three rods; the animate world lives in their union, on which rests everything.

The Ayurvedic Person

This union is called the Person (Purusha), who is conscious and who forms the subject-matter of the Ayurveda (Sutra. I. 45-46). The body and the mind are the home of diseases; but the Supreme Soul is incapable of being affected, eternal, and responsible for consciousness with the help of the mind, the properties of the five elements, and the organs of sense (ibid. 54-55). This Person, endowed with a proper share of the powers of body and mind, should have three pursuits (Eshanas), the pursuit of life, the pursuit of wealth, and the pursuit of the other world. As loss of life means loss of everything, the pursuit of life should be one's foremost consideration. Its preservation, in brief, consists in observance of the laws of health by the healthy and alertness on the removal of the ailments by the diseased. Next to life, one should be mindful of wealth, there being no greater sin than having a long life without means. For its acquisition one should resort to agriculture, animal-rearing, trade, State service, or any other profession that is sanctioned by honest people, and that brings in livelihood and prosperity (Sutra. XI. 3-5) Third in order comes the pursuit of the next world.

CHAPTER 3

The Uṇādisūtras: A Review

1. The Uṇādisūtras with the Vṛtti of Śvetavanavāsin. Edited by T. R. Chintamani, M. A. Madras University Sanskrit Series No. 7, Pt. 1. Madras, 1933. 10″ × 6½″. Pp. xiv, 236, 46. Price Rs. 3/.

2. The Uṇādisūtras with the Prakriyāsarvasva of Nārāyaṇa. Edited by the same. M. U. S. Series No. 7, pt. 2. Madras, 1933. 10″ × 6½″. Pp. xii, 149, 63. Price Rs. 2/8/0.

3. The Uṇādisūtras of Bhoja with the Vṛtti of Daṇḍanātha Nārāyaṇa and The Uṇādisūtras of the Kātantra School with the Vṛtti of Durgasiṁha. Edited by the same. M. U. S. Series No. 7, pt. 6. Madras, 1934. 10″ × 6¼″. Pp. xiv, 107, 51, 72, 24. Price Rs. 3/.

The Madras University and the editor may be congratulated for having undertaken the publication of the Uṇādisūtras in various recensions and already published the above three nicely got up volumes, each furnished with indexes of Sūtras and words and the first two also with those of authorities and quotations. The importance of the Uṇādisūtras as an authoritative guide to the position of the accent and the right sequence of sounds in a large number of nominal stems cannot be exaggerated; one cannot, however, say as much of their etymological contribution, which not infrequently consists in an arbitrary analysis into a verbal root and a suffix, all other phonetic require-

* First published in the *Journal of the Bihar and Orissa Research Society*, vol. XXII, 1936, pp. 122-42.

ments being supplied by *nipātana*[1]. All this has been recognised by the commentators[2]. There appears to be a general agreement, also in holding the Uṇādi-derivatives as nouns (*saṁjñā-śabda*), which, coupled with a view implicitly held by some that all of them are current in non-Vedic Sanskrit, has misled many commentators into attributing mostly fanciful meanings to purely Vedic words. That this view cannot be altogether correct is, however, clear from II. 82[3], *dhṛser dhiṣ cha saṁjñāyām*, whereupon Ujjvaladatta remarks, *saṁjñādhikāre punaḥ saṁjñāgrahaṇaṁ prāyeṇoṇādīnāṁ yaugikatvasūchanārtham*, and from the large number of Vedic derivatives which are very often found to be *yaugika* in sense.

Almost every school of Sanskrit grammar has its own Uṇādisūtras[4], but the most important are those of the Pāṇinīyan school, since the others are mostly based on these and almost universally ignore the accent. The authorship and the date of composition of these Sūtras, the earliest that we possess, are obscure. We know that they are very old, since they have been frequently quoted in the Kāśikā and

[1] Cf. Pāṇ. 3.3.1, उणादयो बहुलम् and the Vārttika on it, बाहुलकं प्रकृतेस्तनुदृष्टेः प्रायसमुच्चयनादपि तेषाम्। कार्यसशेषविधेश्च तदुक्तं नैगमरूढिभवं हि सुसाधु ॥

[2] Cf. Śveta. I. 1, उणादिप्रत्ययान्ताः संज्ञाशब्दाः। तेन तेषामत्र स्वरूपसंवेदनस्वरवर्णानुपूर्वीमात्रफलमन्वाख्यानम्, and Nārā. I. 1.vs. 1-4, 3. vs. 1-2.

[3] The references in this article are to Ujjvala's text, except when some other commentary is being considered.

[4] Besides those that are being reviewed here, there are Uṇādisūtras attached to the Saṁkṣiptasāra, the Supadma and to the grammars of Chandra, Śākaṭāyana, Vāmana (cf. Winternitz, III, 403, fn.4) and Hemachandra.

were presumably known even to Kātyāyana and Patañjali,[1] and we also know that they are later than Pāṇini's grammar, since not only have they quietly adopted throughout the *pratyāhāras*, the *saṁjñās*, the *paribhāṣās*, and the *anubandhas* of the latter, but there are a few of them which appear to have been necessitated to record exceptions to the corresponding Sūtras in that grammar[2]. More than this we do not know. That some have fathered them upon Śākaṭāyana[3] and others upon Vararuchi[4], *alias* Kātyāyana, appear to be nothing more than guesses, the former based on the statement of Yāska, Nir, I. 12[5], and on a Kārikā[6] to Pāṇ. 3.3.1 that it was Śākaṭāyana, amongst the grammarians, who held that all nouns are derived from verbs, and the latter on the assertion of Durgasiṁha that it was Kātyāyana who composed the Kṛt-sūtras, Śarvavarman having held that the derivatives were *rūḍha* like the word *vṛkṣa*[7]. Much more plausible is Goldstücker's conclusion that the Uṇādi list[8] '*must be of*

[1] See Goldstücker, Pāṇini: His place in Sanskrit literature, p. 131ff; especially the footnotes to pp. 132-135.

[2] *E.g.* II. 65, च्विरव्ययम् : Pā. 1.1.39, कृन्मेजन्त: and IV. 226, गतिकारकयो: पूर्वपदप्रकृतिस्वरत्वम् : Pā 6.2.139, गतिकारकोपपदात् कृत्.

[3] *E.g.* Nāgeśa.

[4] *E.g.* Vimala Sarasvatī.

[5] तत्र नामान्याख्यातजानीति शाकटायनो नैरुक्तसमयश्च। न सर्वाणीति गार्ग्यो वैयाकरणानाञ्चैके।

[6] नाम च धातुजमाह निरुक्ते व्याकरणे शकटस्य च तोकम्। यन्न पदार्थविशेषसमुत्थं प्रत्ययत: प्रकृतेश्च तदूह्यम्॥

[7] वृक्षादिवदमी रूढा: कृतिना न कृता: कृत:। कात्यायनेन ते सृष्टा विबुद्धिप्रतिबुद्धये॥—Durgasiṁha at the beginning of the Kṛdvṛtti.

[8] *Op. cit.*, p. 139. By the *Uṇādi list* he could have only

Pāṇini's own authorship'; but, even as it is, it does not carry conviction. His main argument in favour of this view is that without such an assumption Kātyāyana's 'strictures' upon some of Pāṇini's rules[1]—esp. those upon the so-called inconsistencies of his *anubandhas*—become no better than a madman's raving. Evidently, he did not notice that Kātyāyana, Patañjali or Kaiyaṭa did not consider *pha*, *ḍha*, *kha*, *chha*, *gha* in sū. 7. 1. 2., *ṭha* in 7. 3. 50, or *la* in 3.4.77 as *anubandhas* or *its*[2], but *sthānins* and that, this being the case and there being no qualifying words in the Sūtras, Kātyāyana was merely testing if, within a grammatical context, they were universally applicable. Had this not been the case we should have hardly found such expressions in the Vārttika and the Mahābhāṣya as *ṭhādeśe varṇagrahaṇaṁ ched dhātvantasya pratiṣedho vaktavyaḥ : paṭhati, paṭhitum* on 7.3.50 (*ṭhasyekaḥ*),

meant the essentials of the present Uṇādisūtras, for a mere list of suffixes without reference to the respective roots and the various phonetic operations has hardly any meaning. A modification of this view is that of Pathak (Annals of the Bhandarkar Oriental Research Institute vols. IV, pp. 111-136 and XI, pp. 90-93) who holds that Pāṇini is the author of the present treatise. Mangala Deva Shastri (Proceedings and Transactions of the Fourth Oriental Conference vol. II, p. 466ff.) would have it that it is earlier than Pāṇini. The same remarks would apply to these two views as well.

[1] Most of these rules, with Kātyāyana's and Patañjali's remarks, have been quoted by Goldstücker, *op. cit.*, pp. 132-33.

[2] Cf. Pā. 1.3.3,7,8 and Patañjali on 1.3.3, एतच्चात्र युक्तं यदित्कार्यभावादित्संज्ञा न स्यात्। यत्रेतकार्यं भविष्यति तत्रेत्संज्ञा and on 3.4.77, with reference to ल, इत्कार्याभावादत्रेत्संज्ञा न भविष्यति, upon which Kaiyaṭa has तस्यां च सत्यां लोपे च कृते स्थान्यभावादल्विधित्वाच्च स्थानिवद्भावाभावादादेशो न भविष्यतीत्यर्थः। Kaiyaṭa also has on 7.1.2, ये त्वनुणादयः खल्घञादयस्तेषु खघयोरित्संज्ञया भाव्यम्। 'खित्यनव्ययस्य' 'चजोः कु घिण्ण्यतो' रिति लिंगात्.

or *lādeśe sarvaprasaṅgo'viśeṣāt.............. asyāpi prāpnoti : lunāti, labhate* on 3.4.77 (*lasya*). Besides, we should not also forget that Kātyāyana himself has said, *prātipadikavijñānāch cha pāṇineḥ siddham*, on 7.1.2, which Goldstücker has quoted in footnote 209, but evidently overlooked in course of discussion. There is, however, no doubt that an analysis into roots and suffixes, essentially the same as that in the present treatise, had already been done for most of the words before Pāṇini's time and that Pāṇini was so far conversant with it as to feel the necessity to frame a few rules especially covering such cases[1]. Thus we may not be far from the truth, if we hold that the present Uṇādisūtras are an adaptation of this analysis to Pāṇini's system by some grammarian who came after Pāṇini but before Kātyāyana and Patañjali, if the *auṇādika* derivations mentioned in the Mahābhāṣya are considered sufficient, as they do appear to be, to indicate his priority[2].

[1] Cf., besides उणादयो बहुलम् 3.3.1 and ताभ्यामन्यत्रोणादयः 3.4.75, थाथघञ्क्ताजबित्रकाणाम् 6.2.144, न्यङ्क्वादीनाञ्च 7.3.53 and ति-तु-त्र-त-थ-सि-सु-सर-क-सेषु च 7.2.9 along with the Kāśikāvṛtti.

[2] Cf.

Mahābhāṣya	Uṇādisūtra
Pratyāhārasūtra 7, 8. अक्षर =अश् + सरन्.	III. 70, अशेः सरन्.
1.1.4 जीर- in जीरदानु- (which appears also in 6.1.66 as an instance of व् disappearing before र्) =√ ज्या+रक् or √जीव्+रक्, but the remarks are directed against √जीव्+रदानु according to Kaiyyaṭa and Nāgeśa.	Our present Uṇ. has no such rule, but cf. Bhoja 81, जीवेरदानुक्.

These Uṇādisūtras appear in two different recensions, the Daśapādī and the Pañchapādī. The former has been commented on by Māṇikyadeva and followed by Viṭṭhala in his commentary on the Prakriyā-

1.1.26 लोत-, गर्त derived with -त (तन् acc. to Kaiyaṭa).	III. 86, हसिमृग्रिण्वामिदमिल्पूधूर्विभ्यस्तन्.
1.1.61 कंस = √कम् + स, along with 6.1.162 हंस-, वत्स-derived with स and 8.3.59 वर्स-, तर्स- (स supported by Bhaṭṭoji in Prandh) also with the same suffix.	III. 62 वृतृवदिहनिकमिकषिभ्यः सः.
परान् शृणातीति परशुः	I. 34 आङ्परयोः खनिशृभ्यां डिच्च (कुः).
1.4.3 स्त्रियामाख्यायेते स्त्र्याख्यौ। यदि कर्मसाधनः। कृत्स्त्रिया धातुस्त्रियाश्च न सिध्यति। तन्त्र्यै लक्ष्म्यै श्रियै भ्रुवै etc., upon which Kaiyyaṭa remarks, न हि तयोरीकारोकारौ स्त्रियां विहितौ.	The words are derived in III. 158, III. 160, II. 57 and II. 68 respectively, none of which are *stryadhikāravihita*.
3.4.77 शाला-, माला-, मल्ल– derived with-ल.	Kaiyaṭa has शाला (मा ?) मलिभ्य औणादिको लन्प्रत्ययः and Śveta. 177 remarks शोममालीभ्यो (शोमामलिभ्यो ?) लः इति कैयटाचार्यः पठति स्म उणादिसूत्रम्, But this Sū. is not found in the present Uṇ.
4.1.3 स्त्री- = √स्त्यै + ड्रट्.	IV. 165, स्त्यायते ड्रट्.
सूतेः सप् प्रसवे पुमान्, upon which Kaiyaṭa has, सू इत्येतस्य धातोः सप्प्रत्ययो (?) भवति सकारस्य पकारो भवतीत्यर्थः। औणादिको मसुन्प्रत्ययः ह्रस्वश्च बाहुलकात्।	IV. 177, पाते र्डुम्सुन्, on which Bhaṭṭoji in Prauḍh. and Jñānendra in Tattvabodhinī, after referring to Mbh. and the readings of Nyāsa and Rakṣita, 'पुनाते र्मक्सुन् ह्रस्वश्च', and others, 'पूञो डुमसुन्', remark, 'उपेयप्रतिपत्त्यर्था उपाया अव्यवस्थिता इति तत्वम्'.

kaumudī, and the latter by Ujjvaladatta and his numerous predecessors and successors. It is remarkable that, while Bhaṭṭoji Dīkṣita in his Prauḍhamanoramā often refers to the Daśapādī, Ujjvala seems to be unaware of its existence. The two recensions differ not only in the order and division of the Sūtras, but sometimes even in the wording of the Text. Bhaṭṭoji, *op. cit.*, has recorded most of these differences.

Amongst the extant Uṇādi-vṛttis on the Pañchapādī the oldest and, in many respects, the best is that of Ujjvaladatta. The peculiar charm of Ujjvala's commentary and its superiority over others mostly consist in the attempt at noticing every peculiarity of a word formed with an Uṇādi-suffix—not only in its own use, but even in that of its secondary derivatives, and in the large number of apt quotations from diverse sources[1] in support of his statements. In this respect

6.1.67 दर्वि-, जागृवि-with-वि.	IV. 53, वृदृभ्यां विन् and IV. 54, जृशृस्तृजागृभ्यः क्विन्, respectively.
6.1.123 गो- =√ गम् + डो.	II. 67, गमे र्डो.
7.1.2 शङ्ख-, षण्ढ-with-ख and -ढ respectively.	I. 104 and IV. 104 (acc. to the reading of Bhaṭṭoji; Ujj. has शण्ढ-) respectively.
7.3.50 पाण्ठ-, शण्ठ-, षण्ठ-, with -ठ.	I. 105, कणेष्ठः, II. 104 (acc. to Kaiyaṭa, शमे र्जानदाच्युस्थिति ठः), and II. 105 (acc. to Kaiyaṭa, पणोऽन्येभ्योऽपि दृश्यते इति ठः).
7.3.59 अर्क- =√ अर्च् + क 7.4.13 राका-, धाका-, with -क	III. 40, कृदाधारार्चिकलिभ्यः कः .
8.3.59 कूसर-, धूसर- with -सरक्.	III. 73, कृधूमदिभ्यः कित् (सरन्).

[1] The number of the authorities quoted by him is more than 150 and they range over almost all the branches of Sanskrit literature.

it bears comparison with the great Mādhvīya-dhātuvṛtti of Sāyaṇa. Of the many commentaries[1] previous to his, he names six, *viz.* the Prāchinavṛtti, the Satī-vṛtti, and the Vṛttis of Govardhana, Puruṣottama-deva or Deva, Kṣapaṇaka, and Nagna, of which the last two, as suggested by the meanings of the words, may be identical. His only weak point appears to have been his obviously imperfect acquaintance with the Vedic language, and herein he has been excelled by Bhaṭṭoji Dīkṣita, whose Prauḍhamanoramā on the Uṇādi portion of the Siddhāntakaumudī is a masterpiece of critical interpretation of the Sūtras. Bhaṭṭoji is largely indebted to Ujjvala for the non-Vedic materials of his commentary, but his strongest point is his uncommon mastery of the Vedic language, along with that of the Pāṇiniyan literature as a whole, with the help of which he not only criticises and corrects his predecessors, but also restores in many cases the correct text of the Sūtras,—a feature rarely met with in the other Vṛttis, two of which we shall examine here.

The Uṇādi Sūtras and Vṛttis of the other schools are mostly concerned with the derivations and meanings of the words, and are often insipid and of a doubtful authority, for want of support with literary quotations. Two of these, *viz.* those attached respectively to the schools of Bhoja and Śarvavarman, we shall review here.

With these remarks on the Uṇādi literature in

[1] Cf. उणादिवृत्तयोऽनेका भूरिभिः सूरिभिः कृताः। तास्त्विदानीं विपर्यस्ताः सूत्रशब्दार्थधातवः ॥ ता एवाथ समालोच्य ग्रन्थानन्यांश्च विस्तरात्। सर्वतः सारमाकृष्य मया वृत्ति विरच्यते ॥ Intro. vs. 4-5.

general, let us now proceed to examine the above publications.

Śvetavanavāsin's Uṇādivṛtti

The editor states in his Introduction, p. ix, that, according to Śvetavanavāsin, Śākaṭāyana is the author of the Pāṇiniyan Uṇādi-sūtras[1], which is hardly correct, since there is such a word as *ādi* after Śākaṭāyana in the text, *yeyaṁ śākaṭāyanādibhiḥ pañchapādī virachitā* etc., quoted by him. Śvetavanavāsin's Vṛtti is far less elaborate and appears to be far less reliable (at least the present edition) than Ujjvala's work. His knowledge of the Vedic language must have been poor: sū. 362 he reads (in common with Ujjvala) *dadhiṣāyyaḥ*[2] (= *dadhi* + √ *so* + *āyya*), which is only a mistake for Ved. *didhiṣāyya*-and 364 as *stuvaḥ kṣeyyaś chhandasi*, giving as example, *staukṣeyya-*, which is non-existent and a mistake for Ved. *stuṣéyya*; cf. Sk. and Prauḍh.[3] for both the cases; in 301-302 he reads *-knu*, instead of*-ktnu*, as the suffix and derives *kṛṇu-*, *ḥanu-* and *jiganu*[4], which are really mistakes for Ved. *kṛtnú*, *hatnú-*, and *jigatnu-*, cf. Sk. and the remarks in Prauḍh. directed against the Daśapādīvṛtti; in 345 he reads *-kāku* for *-kāru* as the suffix, which leads to the absurd example *pṛdāru-* = *vṛśchika-* or *sarpa-* in 347, the real Ved. word being *pṛdaku-*, found in the other

[1] This inaccurate statement has already been repeated by Pathak and Chitrao (Word-Index to Pāṇini Sūtrapāṭha and Pariśiṣṭas, Introduction, p. V): श्वेतवनवासिना च स्वकृतटीकायां तथैव (*i.e.* शाकटायनप्रणीतानीति) निरदेशि !

[2] Saṁkṣiptasāra, Kṛchchheṣoṇādipāda 671, has *didhi*+√ *so* +*āyya*. The references are to the edition of Śyāmācharaṇa Kaviratna, Calcutta, San. 1308.

[3] Sk.=Siddhāntakaumudī and Prauḍh.=Prauḍhamanoramā.

[4] Bhoja, too, has *kṛṇu* and *jiganu-* in 2.1.74 and 2.1.76.

Vṛttis; in 348 he reads *-agnuch* for *-aknuch* and gives, as example, *vajagnu-* for *vachaknu-*, cf. Prauḍh. and the name *Gārgī Vāchaknavī* in Bṛ. Ār. Up.; sū. 630, showing the formation of Ved. *réknas-* is also faulty and should read, *richer dhane ghich cha*, as in Sk., cf. Bhaṭṭoji's remarks in Prauḍh., this reading being suggested also by *kittvāt kutvam* (undoubtedly for *ghittvāt kutvam*) in the Vṛtti, which appears to have escaped the notice of the editor.

Even in the meanings of the later Sanskrit words Svetavanavāsin is often not very accurate : cf., for instance, (sū. 14) *kanduḥ* = *pākasthānam* (also Nārāyaṇa and Saṁkṣiptasāra, Kṛchcheśoṇādipāda 543); (36) *gaḍuḥ* = *vadanaikadeśaḥ*; (127) *yakṣmaḥ* = *mukharogaḥ*; (146) *plīhā* = *vyādhiviśeṣaḥ*; (153) *nirṛthaḥ* = *paśūnāṁ saṅghātaḥ*; (264) *dhanuḥ* = *śaraḥ*; (277) *vasnam* = *dravyam*; (343) *tasaraḥ* = *tantuvāyaḥ*; (345) *bhayānakaḥ* = *bhīruḥ* (cf. Saṁkṣiptasāra, *l.c.* 600, *bhīruko bhayānakaḥ kātaraś cha*); (723) *ūrṇā* = *chhāgaloma*, etc. Certain words, too, in his own sentences appear with wrong genders, but for this probably the editor is, at least partly, responsible : cf., for instance, (150) *artha-* n., (152) *auṣadha-* m., (158) *pṛṣṭha-* m., (274) *phena-* n., (353) *anta-* n., (389) *ādeśa-* n., etc.

Moreover, in some instances the editor's preference of certain texts over others found in his own mss. is highly questionable. In sū. 87 he reads-*ḍuk* and *tarḍūḥ*, while his own ms. B has *-duk* and *tardūḥ* in agreement with all the other known Uṇādi-vṛttis. He reads sū. 93 *garmuṭ cha* against A. *gro much cha* and B. *gro muṭ* and gives the example, *garmuṭ*, against A. *garmut*. Now, this is not only against all the Uṇādi-vṛttis and the Vedic records of the word *garmut-* >*gārmutá-* it is also against the text of the Vṛtti adopted by himself which has *muḍāgamaḥ*, not *muḍādeśaḥ*. In 110 he adopts the example *chāṇḍāla-* against *chaṇḍāla-* of A. and C., but cf. Bhaṭṭoji's remarks in Prauḍh. against the possibility of such a form here. In 159 he prefers *sedhra-* to *sidhra-* of B., which is not only read by Ujjvala and others, but required by the *anubanadha k* of the suffix. He reads *vīyu-* in 344 against *pīyu-* of B., which agrees with all the other Vṛttis, and gives, as example, *viyālaḥ vṛkṣaviśeṣaḥ* (cf. Bhoja 2.3. 101, *viyālaḥ chāraḥ*), for which every other Vṛtti reads *piyāla-*, the well-known tree. In 357 he has the absurd *dūtaḥ preṣakaḥ* (!) against *preṣakaraḥ* of B.

Besides those mentioned by the editor, two other printing mistakes may be noted—sū. 536, *prājāpatiḥ* for *pra-* and p. 193 below, *uraḥ vṛkṣaḥ* for *vakṣaḥ*.

Nārāyaṇa's Uṇādivṛtti

The Uṇādivṛtti of Nārāyaṇa is brief and precise. He tries to justify the etymologies and the rules as far as possible, but that he finds the former unsatisfactory is clear from his remarks[1] under sū. 3. Interesting also are his remarks under sū. 130 about the pronunciation of *padma-* as *patma*[2], presumably in his own province, inasmuch as this tendency of de-voicing

[1] अस्माद्धातोरियं संज्ञा साध्येति मुनिशासने। किं कुर्मोऽर्थान्वयः कश्चिल्लब्धश्चेत् कृतिनो वयम् ॥ etc.

[2] पद्मं हि पद्यतेरुक्तं न पते र्माधवादिभिः। स्पष्टो दकारश्चोदीचां तकारोक्तिरतो भ्रमः ॥

is characteristic of south Indian mss. and publications in general. He seems to have been much more conversant with the Vedic language than either Ujjvala or Śvetavanavāsin and has accurately interpreted *āyavaḥ*=*martāḥ* (sū. 2), *mahā*=*mahatvam* (150), *darśataḥ* = *darśanīyaḥ* (382), *vidathaḥ* = *yajñaḥ* (388), *jāgṛviḥ* = *vinidraḥ* (489), *ūrdaraḥ* = *kusūlaḥ* (727), etc., but has apparently been misled by his predecessors in the meanings of *apvā* = *devayūtham* and *amīvā* = *jalam* (143) and *niṣaṅgathiḥ* = *dhanurdharaḥ* (526), and in the retention of sū. 370 *dadhiṣāyyaḥ* without any remark.

Nārāyaṇa does not appear to have seen Ujjvala's Vṛtti, but must have been highly influenced by Śvetavanavāsin. All the references to *vṛtti* or *kāchid uṇādivṛtti* are traceable to the latter, with whom he has also shared in the defective texts and interpretations in a few instances. Sū. 684 he reads, with Śveta., *pāter ḍatiḥ* (Ujjvala and Bhaṭṭoji : *pāter atiḥ*) and remarks, *idaṁ prāgukter heyam*, and gives, as example to the next rule (*vāter nit*), *vatir vāyuḥ*, which appears to be non-existent[1]. Ujjvala and Bhaṭṭoji have *vātir vāyuḥ* and quote Rabhasa in support. With Śveta., too, he explains the word *mithuna-* in Sū. 663 as standing for masculine and feminine, although he is not satisfied in his mind.[2] While in Sū. 598 he explains the same word *mithune* as *maithune dyotye* and gives the apparently absurd meaning *maithunechchhāvatī strī* to the word *suśarman-*, which he thinks is the aim of the rule. Ujjvala, Viṭṭhala and Bhaṭṭoji all

[1] But cf. Saṁkṣiptasāra, *l. c.*, 712 वापात्योर्डतिः।

[2] एवं व्याख्या क्वचिद्वृत्तौ यश आद्याश्च पुंस्त्रियोः। न दृष्टा इति भीतिर्नः को वा शब्दान्तमीक्षते॥

explain *mithuna-* in these two rules as a coupling of *upsarga* and *dhātu*[1].

The text appears to be carefully edited, but a few anomalies are still noticeable. In sū. 362 the editor adopts *mūrtaḥ* against *muhūrtaḥ* of ms. G, although the text clearly supports the latter and Bhoja, whose view is represented here, also has it. The sū. *lūṣ-śiṅghi-dhāñbhyaś cha* is incorporated in the Vṛtti to sū. 357 for no apparent reason, while Ujjvala, Bhaṭṭoji, Śvetavanavāsin, etc. read it as a separate rule. Sū. 241, *śviter daś cha* (not found also in Śveta.), does not appear to have been intended as a separate Sūtra by the author, but to have been mentioned only as a text found in the Ṭīkāsarvasva, although not found in his own mss., and this view is supported also by ms. A which omits the Sūtra. *Vatsara-* and *vatsala-* (for *patsara-* and *patsala-*) in 347, *mithin-* (for *mathin-*) in 444, and *mṛdvīketī* (for *mṛdviketi*) in 453, appear to be printing mistakes, as they go against the sense of text and are not supported by any editorial remarks, while *bhojaktaḥ* in 516 and *kvichid* in 607 have clearly to be corrected to *bhojoktaḥ* and *kvachid* respectively. The word *karmaṇāṁ* in the quotation, *karmaṇāṁ chinute śubham*, in 590 appears to be a corruption of *karmāṇaṁ*, cf. Ujjvala under the same rule, *karmāṇaṁ kurute śubham* etc. Unfortunately, the Trivandrum edition of the Ṭīkāsarvasva presents the same text.

[1] But cf. Saṁkṣiptasāra, *l. c.* 739 सोमर्विृशृभ्यो मिथुने and its Vṛtti, सुपूर्वं मा सुमामानौ स्त्रीपुरुषौ, एवं सुपूर्ववृञ् सुवर्माणौ, तथा शृ हिसायां सुशर्माणौ.

The Uṇādisūtras of Bhoja with the Vṛtti of Daṇḍanātha Nārāyaṇa

The Uṇādisūtras of Bhoja, indicating, as they do, the position of the accent as well with the same *anubandhas* as in the Aṣṭādhyāyī, form a very important treatise indeed, while Daṇḍanātha's commentary is the prototype of Nārāyanabhaṭṭa's Uṇādi-vṛtti in respect of brevity and aptness. Daṇḍanātha appears to have taken a great care for the precision of meanings and is generally far more accurate than most of the other commentators on the Uṇādi, cf., for instance, *grahaṇiḥ agnyādhāraḥ* (sū. 212), *plīhā śarīrāntaravayavaḥ* (278), while others are satisfied with the meaning *vyādhi-viśeṣaḥ* in both the cases; *jīrviḥ vṛddhaḥ, jāgṛviḥ jāgarūkaḥ* (235), while some have been pleased to treat them as substantives; and so on. Several interesting and rare words also appear in his commentary, e.g., *kalmalīkaṁ jvālaḥ* (369), cf. *kalmalīkin-* in RV. II. 33.8; *pavīraṁ vījāvapanam* (652), cf. AV. III. 17.3, *lāṅgalaṁ pavīrávat*; *khaḍūraḥ khuralīsthānam* (661), Cf. J.B.O.R.S., vol. XVII, pt. I, p. 66, where this meaning was guessed for the word in AV. XI. 9(11). 16 from its inferred connection with *khalūrikā-* ; *magguśaḥ nakulaḥ* (753), cf. Eng. *mongoose*; *avasam pātheyam* (777), cf. Yāska I. 17, *padvadavasaṁ gāvaḥ pathyadanam*. It is unfortunate that the text of such a valuable work could not be presented in a better form, and the pity is that there should appear a considerable number of such textual errors as could be easily detected with the help of a little critical study. We subjoin a list of those that we have come across and that have not been noticed by the editor.

[Sū. 12] *rāhuḥ saiḥmikeyaḥ* : for ... *saiṁhi-*. [36] *vaniṣṭhuḥ ūrvaikadeśaḥ* : for ... *udaraikadeśaḥ*? [48] *nīlaṅguḥ timiḥ* : for ... *kṛmiḥ*? [63] *pājyartibhyo ḍit* : for ... *ṅit*[1]. [77] *taner ḍuḥ* : for ... *ḍaūḥ*[1], cf. Pāṇ. Uṇ. *taner daū sanvach cha*. [81] *jīvaradānuḥ* : for *jīradānuḥ*, according to the sense of the Sūtra and the Vṛtti, which must have been misunderstood, and to Vedic usage, cf. also Nārāyaṇa, p. 143, l. 6. [97] *śigruḥ saubhājanakaḥ* : for ... *saubhāñjanakaḥ*. [113] Sū. *dūśca*, Vṛ. *drūś chābhyāgamaḥ*, while Nārāyaṇa on I.86 remarks, *bhojamate tro duk cha*. Thus *duk* appears to be the correct reading, inasmuch as *ū* at the end of the *āgama* is superfluous, the suffix itself being *-ū*. Thus the examples *tadrūḥ*, *dadrūḥ*, appear to be corruptions of *tardūḥ*, *dardūḥ*, it being noted that there is nothing in Sū. or Vṛ. to indicate the disappearance of *r* from the roots[2]. [131] The Vṛtti appears to be a corruption for *tiṣṭhateḥ savya upapade ṛnpratyayo bhavati ḍich cha*. [133] *yāteḥ* : for *yateḥ*, otherwise *vṛddhi* is meaningless. Pāṇ. Uṇ. also has this latter reading. [239] Correct the examples to *varṇasiḥ*, *parṇasiḥ* and *sānasiḥ*. The *āgama* is *n*, not *nu*, cf. *nuṭ* and *thuṭ* in Sūtras 335 and 336 respectively. [265] A similar mistake is noticed in the example *garmuṭ*, which should be *garmut* (= √*gṝ*+(*m*)*ut*). [292] *umapade*: for *upa-*. [301] *praryanuju-jyate* : for *parya-*. [324] *uṣtaṁ* : for *uṣaḥ*. [337] *pāṭ baliḥ* : for *pājaḥ balam*. [358] Where is the example

[1] Cf. sū. 127 for the effect of the indicative *ḍ*.

[2] Cf. the remarks of Ujjvala on I. 92, repeated in Prauḍha., भोजदेवशब्दानुशासने तु दरिद्रातेर्यालोपश्चेति तिपा निर्देशात् रिश्च आ चेति संहितापाठे र्याशब्दलोपे दद्रूरित्यपि साधितम्। तथा रश्च इश्च आश्चेत्यन्तसदेशद्वितीयरेफलोपेन दर्दूरित्यपि साधितम्।

for the alternative *numāgama* (*viz.*, *kaṇṭaka-*)? [364] The syllable *ṭaḥ* appears to have been dropped after *viṣakī-*. [368] *śalākā* and *dūṣikā* are out of place amongst regular derivatives with *-kīkan* and should, if their inclusion is right, be *śalīkā* and *dūṣīkā* respectively. [370] *saṁkusukaḥ* : for *saṁkasukaḥ*. [381] *kalaviṅkaḥ gṛhavāṭakaḥ* : for ... *gṛhachaṭakaḥ*? [395] *iṣeḥ* in Sū. : for *uṣeḥ*, as in Vṛ. [427] *ḍichach* : for *ḍī-*, if the example is right. [449] *sṛṅgāṭaḥ jalaviśeṣaḥ* : for ... *jalajaviśeṣeḥ*? and *ālikam* : for *alikam*. [470] *ḍapratyayaḥ* in Vṛ. : for *ḍha-*. [518] °*kukundau* in Vṛ : for °*kakundau*. [543] *pāmam* : for *pāpam*. [557] *parivapanam* : for *paripava-* and *nichayam* : for °*yaḥ*. [569] *ambaḥ* : for *āmbaḥ*, see Nārāyaṇa on IV. 103. [578] *valabhiḥ* : for *valabhī* in Vṛ. [588] *kusumbhaḥ mahārajatam* : for ... *mahārajanam*. [598] *adharmaḥ* : for *adhamaḥ*. [608] *vaserādivatvaṁ nuṭ cha* : for ... *tuṭ cha*, as required by the example, *vastyam*. See also Nārāyaṇa on IV. 121. [637] *vindhraṁ* : for *vīdhraṁ*. [645] *kiñji* in Sū. : for *kañji*, cp. example and Narā. on III. 138. [654] *kimmīraḥ* : for *kirmīraḥ*? [660] *kavūraḥ ṣaḍī* : for *karchūraḥ śaṭī*. [675] Sū. *iḍāvatsaraḥ*, Vṛ. *idvatsaraḥ* : both wrong for *idāvatsaraḥ*. [700] *bhṛṣṭa-* (*bhraṣṭa*, acc. to the corr. of the editor)*tilāsatīchūrṇam*: for *bhṛṣṭatilātasīchūrṇam*? [722] *śṛṇoteḥ* : for *śṛṇāteḥ*. [771] *āṭarūṣaḥ pāśaḥ* : for ... *vāsā*, cf. *vāsā āṭarūṣakaḥ* in 772. [793] ex. *dastyūhaḥ* : for *dātyūhaḥ* (= $\sqrt{}$*dā* + *tyūha*). Similarly in Nārā., p. 149, l.1, *datyahaḥ* has to be corrected to *dātyūhaḥ*.

The Uṇādisūtras of the Kātantra School with Durgasiṁha's Vṛtti

These Sūtras and the Vṛtti (based on a single

ms.) are so very badly edited that it would have been much appreciated, had the editor waited for other mss. The disadvantages of having to depend upon a single ms. are, no doubt, many, but still there are many instances of textual errors whose continuance can only be attributed to the editor's insufficient acquaintance with the Kātantra School and failure to exercise his critical judgment sufficiently, as will be clear from the appended notes. The Catalogus Catalogorum records two other mss. of the Sūtras, one of which contains also the Vṛtti of Durgasiṁha, and it is very likely that more mss. would be available in Bengal, where this school of grammar is still assiduously studied and where most of the best works of this school have been produced. Nor is this the first publication of the Sūtras. Gurunātha Vidyānīdhi of Calcutta, in his edition (in Bengali character) of the Kalāpa with many commentaries, published them as an appendix, some thirty years ago. The text of the Sūtras published by him differs slightly from that in the present edition, while the Vṛtti, the authorship of which is not mentioned there, appears to be a shorter recension of Durga's Vṛtti. The Sūtras are divided into five Pādas, but end with sū. 260 (IV. 66) of the present edition and, indeed, the fresh *maṅgalācaraṇa* at the beginning of the fifth Pāda of the latter would probably indicate a later addition of the rest by a different hand. We shall refer to the Bengali edition with the letter B in the following notes, which may help to improve the text in a later edition.

The editor has invariably spelt the name Durgasiṁha as Durgasimha (°सिम्ह) in Roman and Durga-sihma (°सिह्म) in Devanāgar. It is curious how this anomaly could have escaped his notice, considering how many times the name is repeated. [Sū. 17] *dakārānto guṇaś cha* : unintelligible and not found in B; a corruption for *akārānto'guṇaś cha* (which certainly the *pratyaya* is)? [18] *maṅkura-* in Vṛtti : *makura-* in Sū., *mukura-* in B. [19] B has *śāvaśe-* in Sū. and *tālavyādirayam* in Vṛ., which agrees with Pān. Uṇ., Mahābhāṣya, and use. [20] *naṭādyarthaḥ* and *naṭāditvāt* in Vṛ. : for *nadā°* as in B, since the *gaṇa* that takes the feminine suffix *ī* is called *nadādi* in Kātantra, cf. sū. 106, below. [34] *kaserūḥ tṛṇaviśesaḥ mūlam* : for ... *tṛṇaviśeṣamūlam*, as in B. [46] *palala-* in Vṛ.: for *palvala-*, as in Sū. and B. [51]*dhṛñ* in Sū. and *dhṛñ ādhāre* in Vṛ : for *dṛṅ* and *dṛṅ ādare* respectively, as in B; since there is nothing in Sū. or Vṛ. to indicate a change of *dh* to *d*. [53] *patantaḥ* : for *patataḥ*. [55] *śyāmā* : for *śyāmaḥ*. [65] *varṇuḥ nādaviśeṣaḥ* : for ... *nada°*. [68] *pātha-*, read also in B. : for *pītha-*, cf. Kātantra, Ākhyāta -Vr. 152 and Nārāyaṇa and Ujjvala, II. 7. [70] *udapūrvaḥ* : for *utpūrvaḥ*. [71] *prothaḥ aśvaghoṣāntaram* : for ... *aśvaghoṇā°*; B has *aśvanāsā*. [72] *rodatīti* : for *rodi°*. *undraḥ* : for *udraḥ*, as in B. [104] (*januḥ*) *jarjāriḥ* : unintelligible, B has *januḥ jananam* instead. [114] *prathiḥ*: for *prabhiḥ*, cf. 203. [123] *iṣikā viruṇīśalākā* : for ... *vīraṇa°*, cf. Ujjvala IV, 21, *iṣīkā śaraśalākāvīraṇakāṣṭhikā cha*. B has *iseḥ kīkaḥ* as the Sū. and *iṣīkā* as the example. [124] *tintiḍīkā tilavṛkṣaviśeṣaḥ* : should be simply ... *vṛkṣaviśeṣaḥ*, as in B, which reads *tintīḍīkādayaścha*, *-kīka* being considered the suffix. [137] *naṭāditvādiḥ* : for *nadāditvādīḥ*. [138] for *phanasaḥ*, B has the usual form *panasaḥ*. [139] *valabhiḥ. naṭāditvādiḥ*:

for *valabhī. nadāditvādīḥ.* B omits *śali* and *vali* from the Sūtra. [141] *yathāsaṁkhyaṁ* is out of place. B has *yathāvidhānam* instead. [142] Sū. *grnāmnyupadhāt kviḥ* should be *gṝnāmyupadhāt kiḥ.* B has *gṝ nāmyupadhāch-cha kiḥ. Nāmin-* is a technical term, *svaro'varṇavarjo nāmī,* Kāt. Sandhi. 7. Similarly in Vṛ. *nāmnyupadhāch-cha dhātoḥ kviḥ* should be *nāmyupadhāchcha dhātoḥ kiḥ, nāmni upadhā yasya* should be *nāmī* etc. and *gṛ nigaraṇe* should be *gṝ nigaraṇe.* [146] B has another Sūtra, *sṛṅgāra-bhṛṅgāra-kuñjarāḥ,* after this. The explanation of these forms in the Vṛtti without any remark seems to indicate that the Sūtra has been dropped here. *Nvātvāgamo* is unintelligible (corruption for *nvāgamo*?). [149] *striyāmādā* is Kāt., Chatuṣṭaya-Vṛ. 255, and there should be no query mark after it. [151] The Sūtra should be *iṣyaśibhyāṁ takaḥ* as in B. [161] *aviḥ* and *tariḥ* : for *avīḥ* and *tarīḥ,* respectively, since the suffix is *ī.* [164] B reads *kṝgṝ°* and gives *kṝviḥ, gṝviḥ* as examples, which should be *kīrviḥ* and *gīrviḥ* respectively, according to Ākhyātavṛtti 418. *Kurviḥ* and *girviḥ,* found here, are also impossible. Pān. Uṇ. has *kṛviḥ* < √ *kṛ* and *jīrviḥ* < √ *jṝ,* but cf. Mugdhabodha 1132, *kṝgṝjāguḥ kiḥ* (according to the reading of Durgādāsa; Rāmatarkavāgīśa has *jṝśṝ°.*). [168] (*aratniḥ*) *kaniṣṭhi kāṅguliḥ* should be *vistṛtakaniṣṭhikāṅgulir hastaḥ* as in B. [170] *kaṇīchiḥ kalāviśeṣaḥ* should be ... *latāviśeṣaḥ* as in B. Nārāyaṇa, IV. 72, also has *latā.* [172] *duṣe kālite*: for *duṣeḥ kārite,* Kāt. Ākhyāta 187. [174] *ṛjīṣaṁ paśuvachanam* seems to be a mistake for...*piṣṭapachanam* found in B and Amara. [182] *hateḥ* in Sū. : for *hanteḥ,* as in B and the Vṛ. [186] *vahatram* : for *vahitram.* [191] Probably before ... *tīti kuṇḍaḥ* we have to supply '*kuṇa śabde*' (found in B) *kuṇa*°. [193] *śo nūkaraṇe* : for *śo tanūkaraṇe*. [199] *śarīramadhmam* : for °*madhyam*. [204] *dhṛñ* in Sū. should be *dṛñ* or *dṛ* as in B. Compare the Vṛtti and the example. [206] *ṛk* in Sū. and Vṛ of this as well as the following two Sūtras is a mistake for *vuk* and *ṛḥ* in 209 for *vuḥ*, found in B. *Vu* = *aka*, according to Kāt. Kṛt. 484, which has been wrongly quoted in 208 as *yuṛjhāmanākāntāḥ* for *yuvu*°. [216] With this Sū. ends the fourth Pāda in B. [227] √*vāsi* in the Sū. seems to be out of place, since *vāsara*- cannot be regularly formed with the suffix -*sara*. B has neither the root nor the derivative. [230] *ḍa* : for *ḍraṭ*, and *ḍakāro nadādyarthaḥ* : for *ṭakaro* etc. [252] *gṛ nigaraṇe* : for *gṝ* etc. [260] Here ends the fifth Pāda in B and along with it the whole work, the total number of Sūtras being 267. [292] *sihma*- : for *siṁha*-. [297] *sṛṇāteḥ* in Sū. and Vṛ. and *sṛ* in Vṛ. appear to be mistakes for *śṛṇāteḥ* and *śṝ* and therefore also *sūrpaḥ* for *śūrpaḥ*. [308] *tavaṣa uvargāditi utvam* : for *tavargasya ṣaṭavargād* (Kāt. Ākhyāta. 409) *iti ṭatvam*. [310] *muhūrtaṁ dinapañchadaśo'ntaḥ* : for ... *dinapañcha-daśāṁśaḥ*. [316] *athavā* ... = *athavā vikalpenantāś churādayaḥ* and there should be no query mark. [332] *samūhamaṇḍalaṁ* : for *samūhaḥ maṇḍalam*. [339] *dṛ* : for *dṝ*. Read '*ṛdantasyer*' '*nāminorvor*' *iti dīrghaḥ* for *kṛdantasya* "*āraminorvi*" *iti dirghaḥ*, for Kāt. Ākhyāta. 258 and 418 are being quoted here. [345] Correct *kṛdantasyo* ... etc. to '*ṛdantasyer*' (Ākhyātā. 258) '*svarā-dāvivarṇovarṇāntasy*' (Ākhyāta. 178) *etyādinā uv*. [361] *nayanti* should be *na yanti*. '*Nasya tatpuruṣe lopyaḥ*' is a complete Sūtra (Chatuṣṭaya. 280). *Māmātyavivakṣā-yām* appears to be a corruption for *sāmānyavivakṣāyām*, which should go with the next sentence, not the previous one. [388] *asi* in Sū. : for *aśi*. "*Kaṣa saṁyoge*" *kṣaḥ* : for "*kaṣa saṁyoge*" *kakṣaḥ*?

CHAPTER 4

The Vedas

§1. THE SOURCES

THE *Veda* consists of *Mantras* and *Brāhmaṇas*. *Mantras* are of four varieties—three mainly concerned with the sacrifice (*yajña*), viz. (i) verses for recital (*Ṛc*), (ii) verses for chanting (*Sāman*), and (iii) prose formulae (*Yajus*), and the last (iv) *Atharvāṅgirasaḥ*, formally indistinguishable from either (i) or (iii), with magical and sacramental rites. A settled collection of each of these presenting normal euphonic features is a *Saṁhitā*, to wit, *Ṛg-Veda-Saṁhitā*, *Sāma-Veda-Saṁhitā*, *Yajur-Veda-Saṁhitā* (called "Black" or "White," according as *Brāhmaṇa* portions are included or not), and *Atharva-Veda-Saṁhitā*. The *Brāhmaṇas*, dependent on these, are prose treatises elaborating and eulogizing sacrifices. They are attached to one or the other of the *Saṁhitās* and are considered to include the mystic and philosophical *Āraṇyakas* and *Upaniṣads*, treated in the next chapter. Each of the *Saṁhitās*, and some *Brāhmaṇas*, developed different canonical recensions in course of time.[1]

Indian tradition lost all count of the age and authorship of the *Vedas*, persistently crediting them, as it does, with eternity and impersonality. The accredited seers (*ṛṣis*) are no more than media of revelation at the beginning of each aeon. Max Müller's was the first attempt to fix the period of composition, on purely arbitary grounds,[2] as between 1200–600 B.C. Curiously enough this view has found favour with most scholars who have since spared no pains to offer corroborative arguments and fought tooth and nail, if anybody had the temerity to challenge its authenticity. From astronomical references in the texts Tilak in his *Orion* (Bombay, 1893), and Jacobi in a paper in *Festgruss an Rudolf von Roth* (Stuttgart, 1893), "simultaneously and independently of each other," arrived at 4500–2500 B.C. (the former pleading, further, for the maximum limit of 6000 B.C. for some of the earliest hymns). Patient scrutiny discloses the essential soundness of their conclusion which has been further confirmed through various other articles by Jacobi.[3]

For the sake of convenience the varied philosophical conceptions of the *Vedas* will be presented here under the captions (i) Religion, (ii) Theology, (iii) Monotheism, Pantheism and Monism, (iv) Ethics, (v) Cosmology and Cosmogony, (vi) Eschatology, (vii) Psychology, and (viii) Logic.

* First published in S. Radhakrishnan (ed.), *History of Philosophy: Eastern and Western*, vol. 1, London: George Allen & Unwin, 1952, pp. 40-52.

§2. RELIGION

Consideration of the deities worshipped by the *Vedic* people will occupy us in the next section. Their worship consisted mainly of offering of hymns, obeisances and oblations. Although, later, these appear only as parts of the *yajña*, there is evidence to indicate the independent value attached to the first two acts, separately or conjointly. At the *yajña*, before one or more fires were ceremonially kindled, favourite articles of food—milk, honey, melted butter, grains, and their preparations, flesh, and the stimulating juice of the plant *soma*—were offered with the utterance of *Yajuses*, recital of *Ṛcs*, and chanting of *Sāmans* according to set rules and conventions. Great sacrifices called *śrauta-yajñas* required the specific services of several priests, but the sacramental domestic rites (*gṛhya-karman*) could be performed by the householder and his wife with or without the assistance of any officiating priests. The fire-god Agni is asked to carry the oblations, committed to his care, to the gods, or to fetch the latter to receive them. The *yajña*, originally conceived to secure the goodwill of the gods granting mundane happiness and a delectable heavenly life after death, developed endless varieties and was clothed with ever-increasing mysticism with the march of time. *TS*. 2. 5. 5. 6 calls it a "razor-edge," which may as easily bring about blessings as death, and inculcates right conduct in the initiate. It became an independent means of achieving any object and usurped to itself reverential faith (*śraddhā*) at the cost of the gods,[4] who had been its primary recipients (cf. *RV*. 2. 26. 3; 10. 151; *TS*. 1. 6. 8. 1; *VS*. 19. 77; *TB*. 3. 12. 3. 2; *KB*. 2. 8). Accordingly, the gods themselves and even Prajāpati, the Creator, appear frequently in the *Brāhmaṇas* as sacrificers. The *yajña* became mystically equated with Prajāpati, Viṣṇu, the year, or death.

The *Mantras*, too, are invested with similar mystic powers even in the earliest hymns and hence called Brahman, like the mysterious power of the gods. A purely devotional tone, however, shorn of any consciousness of compelling power, runs through innumerable hymns. Terms of endearment, fondly addressed to the gods, also bear this out (§3). Meditation on the nature and glory of the gods is emphasized in *RV*. 1. 24. 1; 3. 62. 10; 5. 1. 4, etc. Powers and efficacy of austerity (*tapas*) are celebrated in *RV*. 10. 154. 2, 4, 5; *TS*. 5. 3. 5. 4; *KB*. 2. 8; *TB*. 3. 12. 3. 1. *TS*. 5. 2. 1. 7 mentions the nomadic ascetic (*yāyāvara*) who "pursues that which yields peace and tranquillity, clenches his fist, controls speech," and *RV*. 10. 136 dilates upon the mystic and superhuman character of the hairy anchorite (*muni*), who naked or clad in brown dirt (cf. *AB*. 7. 13), "moving in the haunts of the *gandharvas*, the *apsarases* and the deer," enjoys communion with the gods. Ethics which will occupy us later (§5) permeated all these religious activities. It is noteworthy that no reference to images or temples occurs unless *deva-māna*, "a building of a god," in *RV*. 10. 107. 10, be the solitary instance. *RV*. 4. 24. 10 (and perhaps also 8. 1. 5) seems to refer to some sort of fetishistic image of Indra, which could be sold or hired. Totemism and animism as such do not occur, but animism prompted by the sense of the immanence of God is abundantly in evidence (§3).

Beside this picture, is to be set that of the widespread popular belief in the potency of charms, spells and magic. Although stray references are scattered throughout *Vedic* literature, it is the special province of the *Atharva-Veda* and its ritual work, the *Kauśika-sūtra*, which thus anticipate the *Tantras*. The charms are directed mostly against demons and sorcerors, diseases and accidents, as also towards securing welfare, peace and harmony, but a few are certainly designed to secure advantage over rivals or even to injure enemies. Here, too, the gods are the friends and the demons the enemies of the *Vedic* people, and black magic is condemned as strongly in the *AV*. itself as in the other *Vedas*.

§3. THEOLOGY

Superhuman might and wisdom, luminosity, immortality, benevolence and intolerance of sin characterize *Vedic* gods and their appurtenances.[5] Bases for their conception are principally of three different kinds: (1) The grander aspects of nature. The degree of nearness to these leads to a further classification[6] into (i) transparent, e.g. heaven (*dyaus*), earth (*pṛthivī*), sun (*sūrya*), dawn (*uṣas*), wind (*vāta* or *vāyu*), fire (*agni*), waters (*āpaḥ*), along with the various river-deities and the beverage-deity *Soma*; (ii) translucent, e.g. Pūṣan, Viṣṇu, Indra, Rudra, Apāṁ-Napāt, etc.; and (iii) opaque, e.g. Aditi, Varuṇa, Mātariśvan, the *Ṛbhus*, etc. (2) Certain functions, e.g. artificer (*Tvaṣṭṛ*), stimulator (*Savitṛ*), Lord of prayer (*Bṛhaspati* or *Brahmaṇaspati*), etc. And (3) abstract notions, e.g. faith (*śraddhā*), wrath (*manyu*), disease or dissolution (*nirṛti*), etc., which are often mere apostrophes and play but a secondary role. Animals, plants, and inanimate objects, including man-made articles, are sometimes similarly apostrophized to grant peace and prosperity.

The conception is on the whole anthropomorphic. But anthropomorphism here is often indefinite in outline—fairly distinct about translucent, opaque and function-gods, but shadowy about the rest. This attitude underlies occasional attribution of differences in age, stature and mutual relationship (*RV*. 1. 27. 13; *AV*. 1. 30. 2), parentage, and acquisition of immortality through drinking *soma* (*RV*. 9. 106. 8), performing austerity or certain rites (*RV*. 10. 167. 1; *AV*. 4. 11. 6; *ŚB*. 11. 1. 2. 12), or favour of certain deities (*RV*. 6. 7. 4; 4. 54. 2). Again, all this is denied, they being "equally great" (*RV*. 8. 30. 1) and "sons of immortality" (*RV*. 6. 52. 9; 10. 13. 1). They live in heaven, but are classed (*RV*. 1. 139. 11; *AV*. 1. 30. 3) also as inhabiting heaven, atmosphere and earth—Sūrya, Vāta and Agni respectively representing them symbolically (*RV*. 10. 158. 1; *TS*. 7. 3. 12). Individual gods like Indra, Varuṇa, or Savitṛ often appear as the highest. Max Müller explains this as *henotheism* or *kathenotheism*, which makes each god in turn the highest and independent of the rest.[7] The better explanation may, however, lie in the natural tendency of the devotee to extol the deity engaging his attention for the time being, or more probably in the widespread belief in their equality and even in their unity (cf. *RV*. 1. 164. 46; 8. 58. 2; 10. 114. 5; and §4).[8]

Great cosmic activities (such as creating and stabilizing heaven and earth, planting the sun on high, digging the courses of the rivers and ordaining their constant downward flow, etc.) are attributed to some of the gods and they are busy fighting the disturbers of the cosmic order, the great demons of drought, darkness, etc., whom they ultimately overpower. The cosmic order, conceived as immutable and inviolable, is called *ṛta*, literally "the course (of things)". *Ṛta* must have immediately covered also the religious and moral orders, these, too, being regarded as equally immutable and inviolable. The gods, especially the Ādityas and their leader Varuṇa, are zealous guardians of this extended *ṛta*. But not only that: they are also born in or out of it (*ṛta-jāta*), abide by it (*ṛtāvat*), and flourish in it (*ṛtāvṛdh*). Men supplicate them also to remove or annihilate the smaller spirits causing trouble or disease, to help overpower enemies, and to eliminate the "tortuous" course of sin or forgive slips. They are affectionately called "father," "mother," "brother," "friend," "comrade," or "relative"—terms indicative of the cordial relation and implicit faith subsisting between the worshipper and the worshipped. But there are sceptics, too, flatly denying the existence of Indra (or, for that matter, of any divinities), for "who has seen him?" (*RV*. 2. 12. 5; 8. 100. 3; *AV*. 11. 2. 28, etc.), and the *ṛṣis* are at pains trying to refute them.

The battles of the gods and the demons, both offspring of Prajāpati, form a frequent topic in the *Brāhmaṇas*, but *ŚB*. 11. 1. 6. 9. 10 appears to lift the veil when it authoritatively denies any such occurrences. The *Brāhmaṇa* cited is a variation of *RV*. 10. 54. 2, which stigmatizes Indra's battles as an "illusion" (*māyā*). *RV*. 3. 53. 8 and 6. 47. 18 also ascribe Indra's assumption of forms to his *māyās*. This fact, read in the light of §4 and of epithets[9] like "sons of (the) great might," "of the reality," "of immortality," "of consciousness" (Dakṣa)[8], "of infinity (Aditi)"[8] (*RV*. 8. 25. 5A; 8. 69. 4C; 10. 13. 1C; 6. 50. 2A and 8. 25. 5B; 7. 60. 5D), and "born of the mind, allied with the mind" (*TS*. 1. 2. 3. 1), clearly indicates that the *ṛṣis* were conscious that the gods and their myths were but different aspects of the self-same immanent *principle*. Their attitude (recognized in the *Bhāgavata-Purāṇa* 10. 87. 15) is the one recommended in the *Bhagavad-Gītā* 10. 41, viz. whatever entity exhibits magnificence, beauty or might has its being in an aspect of the spirit of God.

§4. MONOTHEISM, PANTHEISM AND MONISM

The reference to *RV*. 3. 55, "the mighty divinity of the gods in one," makes explicit the idea of oneness underlying the paradox of mutual generation[10] and alternative supremacy of the gods. It is further clarified in *RV*. 1. 164. 64, which avers that sages describe diversely that which is One, and in 10. 114. 5, where the wise sages with their words are said to turn into many the eagle (*suparṇa*) which is really one. The conception of the supreme *being* as an eagle might have been suggested by the sun—a great creative, controlling and vivifying force in the *Vedas*,[11] which is often so fancied and which appears to have led to another important conception, that of the golden embryo (*hiraṇya-garbha*).[12] This one *being* finds mention in the *RV*. under various unqualified appellations such as "unborn" (*aja*) (1. 67. 3; 1. 164. 6; 8. 41. 10, etc.), "spirit" (*asura*) (5. 63. 3. 7; 10. 177. 1), "father" (*pitṛ*) (1. 160. 2; 164. 22; cf. 1. 160. 4; 4. 56. 3), or "one" (*eka*) (1. 164. 46; 8. 56. 2; 10. 129. 2). But two hymns on "the All-doer" (*Viśva-karman*) (10. 81–2) and one on *Hiraṇyagarbha* (10. 121) set forth vividly its character as the all-embracing creator, controller and supporter of the universe. In 1. 164. 31 He appears in the role of the guardian (*gopā*), who, never resting, moves hitherwards and away and, "robing Himself in centripetal as well as centrifugal elements, rolls recurrently amongst the entities." The *AV*. presents Him besides as the "heavenly *gandharva*" (2. 1. 2; 2. 1), the "supporter" (*skambha*, 10. 7–8), the "ruddy one" (*rohita*, 13. 1–4), the "vital principle" (*prāṇa*, 11. 4), and the "time" (*kāla*, 19. 53–4). This monotheism is often tinged with pantheism. Thus *RV*. 5. 3. 1C speaks of all the gods being in Agni, 3. 54. 17B in Indra and 1. 35. 6C round Savitṛ "as round the axle-point," while the burden of 10. 100, addressed to the All-gods (*Viśve-devas*, refers to Aditi as "all" (*sarvatāti*). Similar is the trend of 10. 82. 6 and 10. 121. 7, 8. But when *RV*. 1. 89. 10 equates Aditi with everything conceivable, including "what has been, or will be, born," pantheism passes into monism.

Monism is indicated also in *RV*. 8. 58. 2, where, on the analogy of there being only one fire, one sun and one dawn that function everywhere, it is concluded that "*one* became diversified into all this." Similarly, in 2. 35. 2, 8 it is said of the god Apāṁ-Napāt, "Son of the Waters," that all the other entities, which he himself has created, are "but his branches." *VS*. 31. 19AB says: "Prajāpati moves inside the embryo—unborn, He produces Himself in various manners"; to which *AV*. 10. 8. 13CD adds: "He produced the whole universe with one half—where is that light which is His (other) half?" Immanence and transcendence implied in this last passage appear also in the *Puruṣa-sūkta* (*RV*. 10. 90. 3CD): "All the beings (together) constitute one-quarter of Him—His three-quarters are immortality in heaven" (cf. also *AV*. 10. 7. 8, 9). Monism is highly elaborated in the two *skambha-sūktas* of the *AV*. (10. 7–8).

A corollary of monism is the identification of the individual with the universal soul, which appears to be postulated in *RV*. 4. 26, where Vāmadeva identifies himself with various mythic personages and gods, and in 10. 61. 19, where another sage declares, "I am all." *VS*. 8. 9 emphasizes the vastness and secrecy of the self (*aham*, "I"), while *AV*. 10. 7. 17AB proclaims that "those who recognize the Brahman (i.e. the universal soul) in man (*puruṣa*) know Him who is stationed at the summit (*parameṣṭhin*)" (cf. also *TB*. 3. 10. 8). Reference to the two souls (or, to the body and the soul?)[13] as two birds resting on the same tree—one eating sweet fruit, but the other lustrous without eating—is to be seen in *RV*. 1. 164. 20. Soul must be the theme also of verses 21, 22, 30, 31 and, most probably, of 37 in this mystic hymn. The two *skambha-sūktas* (*AV*. 10. 7–8; so *ŚB*. 10. 5. 4. 15, 16; 10. 6. 3; 11. 2. 13 among others) have anticipated most of the ideas of the *Upaniṣads*.[14]. Even the principle of illusion (*māyā*)[15] of the Advaita Vedāntin appears forestalled in 10. 8. 34: "Where gods and men rest like spokes in the nave—I ask you of the Flower (i.e. the quintessence) of the Waters,[16] (of the place) where it is deposited with *māyā*." The whole position regarding the soul and its liberation is summed up in 10. 8. 44: "(It is) free from desire, wise, immortal self-born, satiate with sap (*rasa*), not deficient in any respect; knowing only it one fears not death—(it) the self (*ātman*), (that is), wise, un-aging, young." Similar is the trend also of *VS*. 31. 18–19.

§5. ETHICS

The concept of *ṛta* (§3) invested the moral order with sublimity and inviolability and its working with inevitability and justice, anticipating thus the doctrine of *karman*. "Divine ordinance (*vrata*), was similarly extended to include "vows" or "conduct." The gods (§3) assess merits of thoughts, speeches or deeds from the inside (*RV*. 2. 27. 3; 8. 18. 15), dispensing rewards or punishments accordingly. "Agreeing or agreement with reality" (*satya*), and "negation of *ṛta*" (*anṛta*), later restricted to truth and falsity of speech respectively, appear in moral contexts to represent virtue and vice generally (cf. *RV*. 7. 49. 3; *TB*. 3. 7. 12. 3). Malign intention, swearing, falsehood, imprecation, calumniation, back-biting, dishonesty, sorcery, gambling, debt, egoistic enjoyment, wantonness or adultery, theft and any injury to life are sins (*RV*. 1. 23. 22; 4. 5. 5; 7. 104. 1–25; *AV*. 6. 112. 3D; *VS*. 30. 5, 13; *MS*. 4. 14. 17; *TB*. 3. 7. 12), while honesty, rectitude, fellow-feeling, charity, non-violence, truthfulness, salutary and agreeable speech, continence and control of senses (*brahmacarya*), reverential faith, and austerity are virtues highly extolled (cf., further, *RV*. 10. 117. 154; *AV*. 11. 5; *GB*. 1. 2. 1–4; *VS*. 19. 77; 26. 2; *KB*. 2. 8). Only compunction for slaughtering the victim could have prompted the remark that it did not die, but went to heaven (*RV*. 1. 162. 21; *AB*. 2. 6). Three performances of sacrifices, improper eating, and inordinate acceptance are further sources of trouble (*TS*. 1. 1. 13. 3; *PB*. 19. 4. 10–11). Even association with sinners might contaminate (*AV*. 7. 65. 3). Incapacity to understand (*RV*. 7. 86. 6; *ŚB*. 4. 4. 5. 23), or confession (*ŚB*. 2. 5. 2. 20) might lessen the heinousness; condonation, nevertheless, is solicited for unconscious, accidental or unavoidable sins (*TB*. 3. 7. 12. 1–4).

Mutual love, respect and agreement, obedience to parents, community of pursuits, agreeable and salutary address, and conjugal love and obligation are enjoined amongst the members of a family (*AV*. 3. 30; *RV*. 1. 73. 3D; 10. 34. 2). The wife enjoys a high, affectionate status (*RV*. 3. 53. 4A; 10. 85. 46; *TS*. 6. 1. 8. 5; *ŚB*. 5. 2. 1. 10). A woman might occasionally choose her husband (*RV*. 10. 27. 12; cf. *TB*. 2. 4. 2. 7) and remarry (*AV*. 9. 5. 27–8), but polygamy, not polyandry, is approved (*TS*. 6. 5. 1. 4; *ŚB*. 9. 4. 1. 6; *GB*. 2. 3. 20).[17]

Socially, a man is born with debts to seers, gods, manes, men and animals, repayable respectively with *Vedic* study, sacrifice, procreation, hospitality and offering, called the five "great sacrifices" (*TS*. 6. 3. 10. 5; *ŚB*. 1. 7. 2. 1–5; 11. 5. 6. 1). Society, consisting apparently from the earliest times of the priestly (*brahman, brāhmaṇa*), ruling (*rājanya, kṣatriya*) and professional (*viś, vaiśya*) classes, is strengthened by admitting a servitor class (*śūdra*), the erstwhile *dāsas* (cf. *AV*. 4. 20. 4–8; 5. 22. 7; *TS*. 3. 2. 6. 2). Ārya, however, continues to designate only the first three. But evidence of rigidity of the caste-system is as yet lacking. An Ārya's life comes to be divided, first during this period, into four successive stages (as student, householder, forest anchorite and mendicant), called "hermitages" (*āśramas*), where one could toil for spiritual progress,[18] *AB*. 7. 15 expressly denying any prosperity for one who has not toiled.

Politically, the king, chosen and liked by the people (*RV*. 10. 124. 8C; 173. 1; *AV*. 4. 8. 4), is their guardian (*RV*. 3. 43. 5), having devoted friends (*RV*. 1. 73. 3B = 3. 55. 21B) and feeding on the rich (*RV*. 1. 65. 7B). Solicitude for courteous speech (*VS*. 26. 2), concord and harmony (*RV*. 10. 191), and the optimum condition of prosperity (*VS*. 22. 22; cf. *RV*. 1. 91. 20) in the state reveals a high sense of civic responsibilities.

The goal of right conduct is variously held out as prosperity (*RV*. 1. 189. 1; 8. 97. 13), heaven (10. 154. 4; *AV*. 11. 4. 11), or immortality (*AV*. 11. 5. 19). But in *RV*. 10. 31. 2 right conduct according with one's conscience and understanding seems to be stressed as an independent value.

§6. COSMOLOGY AND COSMOGONY

To the *Vedic* Indian the universe consisted of three regions—earth, atmosphere, and heaven which lay beyond the vault of the sky. The immutability or regularity in the position, succession or behaviour of the phenomena of nature was attributed, as already noted, to an all-pervasive order, termed *ṛta*. The self-sustenance of the sun, the manifestation of dawn or storms, etc., are sometimes referred to an innate power, termed *svadhā* (*RV*. 1. 64. 4; 4. 13. 5; 7. 78. 4). The mythic fixation of heaven and earth with pillars is only figurative, there being distinct statements to the contrary (cf. *RV*. 2. 15. 2; 4. 56. 3; 10. 149. 1). The question of the origin or creation of the universe, which evoked considerable interest (cf. *RV*. 1. 164. 4; 10. 31. 7; 81. 2, etc.), has been mythologically treated in various hymns, *Brāhmaṇas* and *Brāhmaṇa* portions of the Black *Yajur-Veda*. As there is little of philosophical import in them, we shall be concerned here mainly with *RV*. 10. 72 and 129—and a number of relevant texts found elsewhere—for a true estimate of the higher thoughts on the subject.

According to *RV*. 10, 129 there was, at the primeval stage, neither "non-being" (*a-sat*) not "being" (*sat*); no trace of air or heaven; of any covering,[19] refuge, water, or deep abyss; of death or immortality, night or day; "there breathed that *one* windless through *its* innate power (*svadhā*)," besides which there was nothing else. Gloom being then enveloped in gloom, all this was indistinguishable "fluid" (*salila*).[20] Then that one "which was to come into being"[21] (*ābhú*) and had been concealed with "void" (*tucchya*) became manifest through the majesty of *tapas* (i.e. inherent determined urge). Upon this appeared desire which was the first seed of the mind. The wise investigating in their hearts with contemplation (*manīṣā́*) found the bond (i.e. cause) of being in non-being. Their rope of assessment spread across, gauging above and below, found that there were "impregnators" (*retodhā́ḥ*) (and) "great powers" (*mahimā́naḥ*)—"innate urge" (*svadhā*) below, "arduousness" (*práyati*) above. (Verses 1–5.)

This hymn posits that before the emergence of the sensible world there was something which cannot be described in terms of being or non-being[22]—that is, cannot be referred to time, inasmuch as not only were there no events to lead to its conception, but even the mind and the senses along with the whole phenomenal world were as yet inchoate. "*Tapas*" appears frequently in cosmogonic contexts (cf. *RV*. 10. 190. 1; *AV*. 10. 7. 1; 11. 8. 2, etc.), and the *Brāhmaṇas* positively attribute to Prajāpati its assumption, prior to creation. It is very significant, however, that *AV*. 11. 8. 6 has: "*tapas* was there, and *karman*—then they adored the *highest*." It is probable that here we have the germ of the theory of collective

karman that leads to the emergence of the universe, and that ***tapas*** merely stands for its potentiality like ***apūrva*** or ***adṛṣṭa*** in later conceptions. ***Arṇava*** in this passage and ***salila*** above, both meaning "the heaving ocean," and ***ap*** "water" (*AV*. 10. 2. 7; 8. 34–40, etc.) in such contexts can have reference only to the formless, limitless, inchoate energy that is the perennial spring of the universe, and doubtless represent the "cosmogonic water" (***kāraṇa-vāri***) of later literature. The "desire" was simply the urge for creation,[23] and this evoked the collective or cosmic "mind." The "impregnators" would correspond to the individual souls (***jīvātman*** or ***puruṣa***) and "great-powers" to properties constituting matter (***prakṛti***) in later philosophy. The "innate urge" and the "arduousness" would refer to these two in the reverse order.[24] To use the language of later philosophy, matter is credited here with blind tendencies and individual souls, endowed with persistent mental impressions (*vāsanā*, ***saṁskāra*** = *tapas* here), with positive effort.

RV. 10. 72 makes some further contribution to the cosmogonic idea: "In the primeval age of the gods being came out of non-being. The quarters (i.e. space) followed it (i.e. being) in their emergence; it (viz. being) issued out of (i.e. became manifest in) the world. Dakṣa was born of Aditi, and Aditi of Dakṣa. For (when) Aditi who is thy daughter was born, O Dakṣa, in succession to her were born the gods (that are) beneficent (and) cognate with immortality." (Verses 2–5). Here "being" stands for the primeval world that can be referred to time and space, while "non-being" for that which precedes it in the sequence of evolution and which cannot be so referred to. "Lying outstretched" (*uttāna-pad*), (cf. *AV*. 3. 21. 10, where "waters" (*āpaḥ*), are called *uttānaśī vārīḥ*, "lying outstretched"), can have reference only to the limitless, indistinguishable mass called *salila* or ***ap*** above. The first half of v. 4 simply explains v. 3, while its second half brings out another important feature. Aditi, literally "boundlessness" or "infinity," can stand here only for what has just now been described as ***uttāna-pad*** and ***a-sat***, and Dakṣa, literally "understanding" or "consciousness," the principle of subjectivity. Thus Dakṣa issuing out of Aditi accords well with the Sāṁkhya view as recorded in *Caraka-Saṁhitā* (IV. 1. 61. 63), in which the unmanifest (***a-vyakta***) represents the state previous to the distinction of *prakṛti* and ***puruṣa***. Whereas Aditi issuing out of Dakṣa would indicate the view-point according to which the first principle is all consciousness (***cinmātra***) and matter is only its aspect or characteristic.

Reference to creation having taken place only once is found sometimes (cf. *RV*. 6. 48. 22; 10. 74. 4 = *VS*. 33. 28), but in *RV*. 10. 190. 3 the Creator (***dhātṛ***) is said to have fashioned the various cosmic objects "as previously" (*yathā-pūrvám*) and in *AV*. 10. 7. 26 *Skambha*, while creating, is said to have "rolled out what was old." On the other hand, creation and dissolution are frequently represented as events, constantly taking place in the ultimate reality (cf. *AV*. 10. 8. 29, 39–42; *RV*. 10. 90. 2, etc.), and immortality and death as both ensconced in it (*RV*. 10. 121. 2; *AV*. 10. 7. 15).

§7. ESCHATOLOGY

That the *Vedic* Indian was fondly attached to this world, as against the next, is clear not only from the constant prayers for long life and its blessings, but also from its description as the "dearest" (*AV*. 5. 30. 17) or the "world of immortality" (*AV*. 8. 1. 1)—immortality for the mortal consisting in "being better here" (*KS*. 8. 1), or "attaining full life (i.e. of a hundred years) and being better" (*PB*. 22. 12. 2), and continuing himself through progeny (*TB*. 1. 5. 5. 6; cf. *RV*. 5. 4. 10)—and from occasional distrust of the other world (*KS*. 8. 8; *TS*. 6. 1. 1). Rebirth is even offered as a reward (*ŚB*. 1. 5. 3. 14). It is no wonder, therefore, that thoughts on the future life are mostly evoked by death, the inevitable. Here, again, myths grew round cremation, although there is occasional reference to other modes of disposal (*AV*. 18. 2. 34; *RV*. 10. 18. 10–13). Agni is said to carry and join the departed to the manes in the highest heaven, where he is to meet Yama, their pathfinder and king, and Varuṇa (*RV*. 10. 14. 1, 7, 8). The process is called *asu-nīti* or *asu-nīta*, "leading the spirit," or rather "leading to the spirit state" (cf. *RV*. 10. 15. 1c). Agni consumes only the body, and the departed soul, the "unborn part"[25] of *RV*. 10. 16. 4, issues forth as from the father or the mother (*ŚB*. 2. 2. 4. 8), furnished with a body, all lustrous (*RV*. 10. 56. 1) and free from imperfections (*AV*. 6. 120. 3). References to enjoyment by the departed of offerings made here and the delights in heaven indicate that this body—which could scarcely be gross—was conceived as endowed with the senses, similar to the "subtile" body (*sūkṣma-śarīra*) of later conception.[26]

The heavenly delights are described in *RV*. 9. 113. 7–11: "There are eternal light and swift waters; there movement is unrestrained; there is spirit food and satiety; there are joy, glee, gladness, and the fulfilment of all desires."[27] A few more heartening touches are added by other texts (*RV*. 10. 135. 7; *AV*. 3. 29. 3; 4. 34; *ŚB*. 14. 7. 1. 32–3, etc.). Agni is supplicated to carry the newly departed to this place, which is assured (*RV*. 10. 154. 2–5) for those who have undergone rigorous penance (*tapas*), or died heroically in battles, or made liberal sacrificial gifts, or adored the law of righteousness (*ṛta*). In contrast, hell where, by rights, the sinners should go is only vaguely referred to as the "deep place," "endless abyss," "intangible darkness" (*RV*. 4. 5. 5; 7. 104. 3, 17), and "lowest, black, or blind darkness" (*AV*. 8. 2. 24; 5. 30. 11; 9. 2. 10). *VS*. 30. 5 and *AV*. 12. 4. 36 are the first to call it *nāraka* or *nāraka loka*. Torments of hell are touched in *AV*. 5. 19 and described with greater detail in *ŚB*. 11. 6. 1 and *JB*. 1. 42–4.

Merits of sacrificial and charitable acts accrue to the departed in heaven (*RV*. 10. 14. 8; *VS*. 18. 64). It has been noted already (§6) that the term *karman* appears very significantly in the *AV*. (cf. also 11. 7. 17). According to the *ŚB*."a man is born to the world he has made" (6. 2. 2. 27), and one is placed in a balance in the other world for an estimate of one's good and evil deeds (11. 2. 7. 33). Thus the idea of proportionate recompense appears to be gaining ground progressively. *ŚB*. 10. 6. 3. 1, going still further, declares that as a man is constituted by his desires (*kratumáya*), he is born in the other world with reference to these.

Macdonell[26] sees a probable germ of metempsychosis in *RV*. 10. 16. 3, where the departed spirit is asked to go, among other places, to the plants and "stay there with bodies." Growing belief in rebirth becomes evident in the *Brāhmaṇas* (cf. *ŚB*, 1. 5. 3. 14; 10. 4. 3. 10) and words like *punar-mṛtyu*, "re-death," *punar-asu*, "coming to life again" (*ŚB*., *TB*.) and *punar-āyāti*, "rebirth" (*GB*.), are coined to denote it. Some scholars[28] explain *punar-mṛtyu* as "repeated death" in the other world, having no reference to rebirth, but "repeated death" of one already dead makes scarcely any sense. The reason why "re-death" instead of "rebirth" struck the *Vedic* people first seems to lie in the fact that they dreaded death, not birth[29] as in later times. Interpreted by this outlook of theirs, rebirth seems to be suggested even in *RV*. 10. 14. 8c, where the departed is asked to "come home once again,[30] and in 10. 16. 5, where Agni is supplicated to see that he may "assume life (*ā́yus*) and obtain progeny."

Adoration of the self through meditation in the right manner, as fetching more valuable rewards than worship of the gods, is preached in *ŚB*. 11. 2. 6. 13–14 and 10. 6. 3. 1–2. The view of final release from fear of death or rebirth through right knowledge of the self, along with a more philosophical outlook on the events of the world, has already found notice (§§4, 6).

§8. PSYCHOLOGY

The principal word for the entity which is responsible for all mental activities is *manas*. It often stands for the combined thinking and vivifying principle (*RV*. 1. 164. 18; 10. 57. 4–6; 59. 5, etc.), which is referred to as the "light" implanted in the heart (*RV*. 6. 9. 6; 7. 33. 8) and forms the theme of *VS*. 34. 1–6. Frequently, however, the vivifying principle alone is so termed and separated from the other (*RV*. 3. 26. 8; *AV*. 10. 2. 31–2; 8. 28, 43). The heart, generally conceived as seat of the mind, is occasionally separated from the latter, either as the physical organ with mind as its function (*RV*. 3. 26. 8; 5. 56. 2; 10. 71. 8, etc.) or as having some separate function altogether (*AV*. 3. 20. 9; 5. 21. 2; *RV*. 10. 191. 4). Rarely, however, the head is conceived as the seat of certain mental attributes (*RV*. 2. 16. 2; 8. 96. 3; 5. 57. 6). "The nine-doored lotus, enveloped with three *guṇas*" (*AV*. 10. 8. 43), where the soul resides, is evidently the heart identified with the mind. The passage is suggestive of the *Sāṁkhya* constituents of the mind (cf. also *AV*. 8. 2. 1, where *rájas* and *támas* appear together). Desire has already figured (§6) as the first seed of the mind.

Three states of the mind, viz. waking (*jāgrat*), dreaming (*svapna*) and sleeping (*supti* or *nidrā*) are indicated (*RV*. 10. 164; *AV*. 19. 56, 57), and dream is said to be "neither alive nor dead" (*AV*. 6. 46. 1) and "born of the heated mind" (*AV*. 19. 56. 5). The vital principle (*prāṇa*) is said to keep erect and awake, while others lie asleep (*AV*. 11. 4. 25). Mahīdhara equates the words *cit*, *manas* and *dhī* in *VS*. 4. 19 with the later *citta*, *manas* and *buddhi*, faculties respectively of indeterminate cognition, deliberation and determination. Agility and restlessness of the mind (as well as its range covering all distances and times) are often alluded to (*VS*. 34. 1, 4; *AV*. 10. 7. 37, etc.). The five senses (*indriya*) with the mind as the sixth appear in *AV*. 19. 9. 5. In the *RV*. *indriya* still means "relating to Indra" or "power or energy belonging to, or similar to that of, Indra." The words *indriya-saṁyama*, "control of the senses," *ekārāmatā*, "concentration of the mind," and *yukta-manas*, "concentrated in mind," appearing in *ŚB*. 11. 5. 7. 1 point to leanings towards *yoga*.

§9. LOGIC

In the *RV*. the incidence of human ignorance (1. 164. 5, 6; 10. 88. 18, etc.) and of the elusiveness of truth (5. 85. 8; 10. 139. 5; cf. 8. 100. 3) is frankly admitted. The means of attaining truth appeared to be (i) direct perception with the senses or the mind (1. 184. 2; 8. 25. 9; 10. 67. 2 and 130. 6), (ii) statement of one who knows (1. 164. 4; 10. 129. 6), and (iii) investigation with the mind, i.e. reasoning (10. 81. 4; 129. 4, 5). Asceticism (*tapas*) as a source of special insight finds mention not only in the *Brāhmaṇas* and the other *Vedas*, but even in the *RV*. itself (*TS*. 5. 3. 5. 4; *RV*. 8. 59. 6). Infallibility and independence of the *Vedas* as a source of knowledge is already insisted on in the *Brāhmaṇas* (cf. *ŚB*. 10. 4. 2. 21, 22; *TB*. 3. 12. 9. 1). Immediate or perceptual (*pratyakṣa*) and mediate or non-perceptual (*parokṣa*) knowledge are frequently distinguished in the *Brāhmaṇas*.

Enquiry about material and efficient causes is common (*RV*. 10. 81. 2, 4; 168. 3), and the development of meanings of *nidāna*, "bond" > "root-cause" (*RV*. 10. 114. 2; 130. 3), *bandhu*, "connection" > "cause" (*RV*. 10. 129. 4; *AV*. 4. 1. 3), *nābhi*, "navel" > fountain-head" (*VS*. 23. 59), and *ārambhaṇa*, "grasping," "tackling" > "achievement" (*RV*. 10. 81. 2 = *VS*. 17. 18), point to the same direction. Similar development or coining of a few more technical terms may be noted here with their sources in parentheses: thus *kāraṇa*, "cause" (*GB*.), *kṣetra*, "field" >

"sphere" or "scope" and ***kṣetra-vid***, "knowing the subject" (*RV*.), ***nānātva***, "difference" (*Br*.), ***pakṣas***, "wing" > "side" or "party" (*RV*.), ***prakṛti***, "source," "original form" (*GB*.), ***prākṛta***, "original" (*ŚB*.), ***vikṛti***, "change" or "modification" (*ŚB*.), ***bhūta*** and ***bhuvana***, "entity" (*RV*.), and ***majmana***, ***mahiman*** or ***mahman***, "greatness" or "power" > "quality" (*RV*.; cf. *AV*. 10. 2. 12).

Statements supported by reasons indicated with the particles ***khalu***, ***vai***, ***hi***, etc., are frequent. An instance of an analogical reasoning (*RV*. 8. 58. 2) has already been cited (§4). A type of deductive reasoning, styled *mīmāṁsā* and consisting of (i) *vicikitsā*, "doubt," (ii) *mīmāṁsā*, "deep deliberation," and (iii) *sthiti*, "final position" is frequent in the *Brāhmaṇas*.[31] Such terms as *prāś*, "query" or problem," *pratiprāś*, "opponent in debate" (*AV*. 2. 27), *praśnin*, "questioner," *abhipraśnin*, "counter-questioner," *praśna-vivāka*, "arbiter" or "umpire," and *maryādā*, "limitation," i.e. "conventional rules" (*VS*. 30. 10) indicate the popularity of debate. Habit of presenting thought in pairs, distinct or dichotomic, such as (i) *iṣ* (refreshment), *ūrj* (strength), *iṣṭa* (sacrifice), *pūrta* (charity), *nāman* (essential nature), *rūpa* (external form), etc., or (ii) *vidyā* (knowledge), *avidyā* (ignorance), *sat* (being), *a-sat* (non-being), etc., becomes more and more common. In the *Brāhmaṇical* portions indulgence in long lists of associated concepts, set off against one another, in describing different collateral subjects or situations is frequent (cf. *AV*. 12. 5; 13. 4; 15. 2–7). Attempts at definition through etymologies or otherwise are not infrequent (cf. *AV*. 3. 13. 1–14; 11. 8. 34; *KB*. 2. 8; *ŚB*. 4. 1. 4. 1).

The intimate connection of thought and speech is often emphasized (*RV*. 6. 9. 6D; 10. 71. 2; 177. 2). According to *KB*. 2. 7 all sensations have to be converted into speech before they find expression, while in 9. 3 mind and speech are said to contain everything. In *RV*. 1. 164. 45 and 8. 100, 10, 11 *vāc*, "voice," "speech," appears in the role of an all-inclusive sonority and is called *rāṣṭrī*, "sovereign ruler," in the latter place and in *RV*. 10. 125, where its mystic divine character, guiding and controlling the activities of gods, men and all other entities, is especially stressed. *RV*. 10. 71 lays particular emphasis on the care and accuracy with which the agreeable and salutary contents of speech are to be presented and understood, while *AV*. 10. 8, 33 declares that speeches are impelled by the "unprecedented one" (*a-pūrva*); and speaking rightly, they go to the great *Divinity* (*Brāhmaṇam*).

§10. CONCLUSION

The above survey brings out in bold relief the emergence of certain characteristic features of later Indian religious and philosophic thought.

The various *bhakti* cults are anticipated in respect of their emphasis on the character of the favourite deity as an aspect of the Absolute (§3). and on the tenderness of devotion and strictly ethical conduct of the devotee (§§2, 5). Asceticism of various types and even *Tāntric* practices are forestalled (§2). Monism of the Vedānta with a hint at *māyā* and liberation through knowledge (§4); omnipotence of the sacrifice as in the Mīmāṁsā (§2); the three *guṇas* (§8) and blind tendencies in matter (§6) of the Sāṁkhya; control of the senses and concentration of the mind (§8) of the Yoga; and right mental perspective and right speech leading to the Absolute (§9) of the Nyāya-Vaiśeṣika are also foreshadowed, besides consideration of the common problems of *ātman* (§4), *manas* (§§7, 8), the Absolute Reality (§4), the emergence of the universe (§6), *karman* (§§5, 6, 7), rebirth (§7) and liberation (§4). No wonder later thought should regard the *Vedas* as the fountain-head of all religion and philosophy.

ABBREVIATIONS

(a) *Texts*

AB.	*Aitareya-Brāhmaṇa.*
AV.	*Atharva-Veda.*
Br.	*Brāhmaṇas.*
GB.	*Gopatha-Brāhmaṇa.*
JB.	*Jaiminīya-Brāhmaṇa.*
KB.	*Kauṣītaki-Brāhmaṇa.*
KS.	*Kāṭhaka-Saṁhitā.*
MS.	*Maitrāyaṇīya-Saṁhitā.*
PB.	*Pañcaviṁśa-Brāhmaṇa.*
RS.	*Ṛg-Veda-Sarvānukramaṇī.*
RV.	*Ṛg-Veda.*
ŚB.	*Śatapatha-Brāhmaṇa.*
TB.	*Taittirīya-Brāhmaṇa.*
TS.	*Taittirīya-Saṁhitā.*
VS.	*Vājasaneyi-Saṁhitā.*

(b) *Treatises*

ASL.	Max Müller, *History of Ancient Sanskrit Literature.*
BRV.	Bloomfield's *Religion of the Veda.*
GRASS.	Grassmann, *Wörterbuch zum Rig-veda.*
GRR.	Griswold, *The Religion of the Rigveda.*
GVB.	Geldner, *Vedismus und Brahmanismus.*
HIL.	Winternitz, *History of Indian Literature* (Eng. Trans.), Vol. I.
IP.	Radhakrishnan, *Indian Philosophy*, Vol. I.
MVG.	Macdonell, *Vedic Grammar.*
MVM.	Macdonell, *Vedic Mythology.*
MVR.	Macdonell, *A Vedic Reader.*
MW.	Monier-Williams, *A Sanskrit English Dictionary.*
OST.	Muir, *Original Sanskrit Texts*, Vols. I–V.
RPVU.	Keith, *Religion and Philosophy of the Veda and the Upanishads.*

NOTES

1. For these and other details, see *HIL*, pp. 55–225.
2. *HIL*, pp. 292 ff.
3. Noted in *HIL*, p. 295 n.
4. *RPVU*., pp. 456, 462.
5. cf. *RV*. 10. 63. 4, and Yāska's *Nirukta*, VII, 4–13.
6. First made in *BRV*. p. 96, pp. 150 ff., with minor differences.
7. *ASL*., pp. 526, 532, 546.
8. *MVM*., pp. 26 f.
9. cf. *OST*., V, pp. 51 f.
10. cf. Heaven and Earth: gods; Aditi: Dakṣa; Savitṛ, an Āditya: gods; Puruṣa: Virāj, etc.; *MVM*., 12; *OST*., V, p. 50.
11. cf. *RV*. 1. 115. 1; 3. 62. 10; 4. 53. 6.
12. *MVM*., 13. cf. *RS*. Intro., 2. 14–15.
13. Differently, *GVB*., p. 96 n.
14. *GVB*., p. 105 n.
15. cf. also *RV*. 3. 53. 8; 6. 47. 18; 10. 54. 2; *ŚB*. 11. 1. 6. 10 discussed above, §3.
16. See §6.
17. *OST*., V. pp. 457 ff.
18. *IP*., p. 132 n.[1] cf. Keith, *RPVU*., p. 470 n.[2]
19. *Kim ā varīvaḥ*, "what covered" (: √ *vṛ*), *OST*. IV. 4; "what did it contain?" *MVR*., p. 207 and *MVG*.; "what rolled forwards and backwards? (: √ *vṛt*), i.e., was there the wind?" *GVB*., p. 88, with Grass. and *MW*.
20. "Chaos, lit. flood," *GVB*., *loc. cit*.
21. cf. *MVR*., *loc. cit*.; "the germ of life," *GVB*., *loc. cit*.; against, "void," Grass., *MW*. and others.
22. *GVB*., *loc. cit*.; *IP*, p. 101.
23. *GVB*., *loc. cit*.
24. cf. *ibid*., p. 89.
25. cf. *OST*., V. p. 217.
26. *MVM*., p. 166.
27. *ibid*., p. 168.
28. Keith, *RPVU*., p. 464.
29. See para. 1 of this section.
30. This "home-coming" is referred to heaven, *MVM*., p. 166; *GRR*., p. 316.
31. cf. *OST*., III. p. 21.
32. *RPVU*., p. 483.

OTHER REFERENCE BOOKS (SELECT)

Bergaigne, *La Religion Védique*: Bloomfield, *The Atharvaveda and the Gopatha-Brāhmana*; Deussen, *Philosophie des Veda*: Hillebrandt, *Vedische Mythologie*: Hiriyanna, *Outlines of Indian Philosophy*: Hopkins, *Ethics of India*: Macdonell and Keith, *Vedic Index of Names and Subjects*: Oldenberg, *Die Religion des Veda*: Ragozin, *Vedic India*: Rapson, *Cambridge History of India*, Vol. I: Zimmer, *Altindisches Leben*.

CHAPTER 5

The Rāmāyaṇa

1. INTRODUCTORY REMARKS

THE *Rāmāyaṇa*, a national epic like the *Mahābhārata*, in the truest sense of the term, has exerted profound influence on the thoughts and feelings and conduct of the Indian people ever since it saw the light of day. It has set up ideals of manhood and womanhood which have been cherished and imitated by people of all classes and denominations and have thus helped to ennoble them and succour them in their tribulations. It has served as an inexhaustible source of inspiration to the great Indian poets, using Sanskrit, Prākṛta or the vernacular as the vehicle, who have drawn upon it not only for their themes but even for poetical conception and imagery.

But in spite of its unsurpassed popularity, and mostly because of it, it has not come down to us in the original form in which its author, Vālmīki, conceived it, but as considerably overlaid and disfigured with interpolations of all sorts. Moreover, it appears today in at least three important recensions, the West Indian, the Bengal and the Bombay, which differ from each other to such an extent that about one-third of the verses in each is found in neither of the other two.[1] Jacobi, who in his *Das Rāmāyaṇa* (Bonn, 1893) has made by far the greatest contribution to the critical study of the text of the *Rāmāyaṇa*, holds that of the seven books constituting the present-day *Rāmāyaṇa* the whole of the seventh and parts of the first are comparatively later additions. Even if he is right, they must have been made very early, as all the recensions have them and all later tradition includes them. Discussing the age[2] of the *Rāmāyaṇa*, he comes to the conclusion that it must have originated before the fifth or probably in the sixth or the eighth pre-Christian century. The present gleanings of philosophical views are made from the Bombay recension which, according to the experts, contains mostly the oldest version and is the one most widely used. It is hoped that they represent the spirit of the *Rāmāyaṇa* fairly correctly and will not lack corroboration from the other recensions. The references in the present article are to the second Nirṇayasāgara Press edition (Bombay, 1902).

* First published in S. Radhakrishnan (ed.), *History of Philosophy: Eastern and Western*, vol. 1, London: George Allen & Unwin, 1952, pp. 75-84.

2. THE SOCIAL AND INTELLECTUAL BACKGROUND

The *Rāmāyaṇa* envisages a society in which the order of the four castes (*varṇas*) and that of the four stages of life (*āśramas*) are firmly established, and the various occupations and professions are suitably attended to; firm faith in the *Vedas* and the sayings of the seers (*ṛṣis*) is ingrained; sanctity of the cow and the *brāhmaṇa* is repeatedly emphasized; and a sense of the overriding importance of religious and moral duties (*dharma*) amounts to an obsession. *Vedic* studies and rites are attributed even to those that are designated *vānaras* (apes), and *rākṣasas* (ogres). The cities (and presumably also the villages) abound in places of worship, with or without images and called *āyatanas* and *caityas*. Ascetics of various types, who usually live in hills and forests, roam about the country and are highly respected. On the other hand, there are also the unbelieving sceptics (*nāstikas*) who are a constant source of worry to the pious. The king, who rules with the consent of the people and on the advice of wise ministers and is called the protector of the *varṇas* and the *āśramas* and defender of *dharma*, has to be very careful in his private life, lest he should set a bad example to the people.[3]

On the intellectual side, great emphasis is laid on education (*vinaya*) as bringing out and adding to the innate virtues, and the following subjects, besides others, appear, from express or tacit references, to be cultivated: *Vedas*, *Upaniṣads* and the six auxiliaries to their study (viz. phonetics, rituals, etymology, grammar, metrics and astronomy), codes on law and duty (*dharma-śāstra*), legendary and mythic lore (*Purāṇa*), politics (*artha-śāstra* and *rāja-nīti*), military science (*dhanur-Veda*), logic (*ānvīkṣikī*), astrology and palmistry (*jyotiṣa*), fine arts (*vaihārika-śilpa*), medicine, and agriculture, cattle-breeding and commerce (*vārttā*). The terms *śruti* (direct revelation), and *smṛti* (sacred tradition), so common in later literature, have already gained currency. Practical effects of a sound mastery of grammar, phonetics, logic and the Scriptures mark the conversation of the cultured and are highly appreciated, while theories of politics are at the tip of the tongue of anybody, man or woman, talking about the king or the State. In addition to this, a general belief in omens and portents, the fantastic and the miraculous, and the powers of magic, sacred formulae and austerities may be inferred.

3. PHILOSOPHICAL UNDERCURRENTS AND GENERAL OUTLOOK

Darśana[4] in the sense of "view," "attitude towards life," or "philosophy," and *pradarśana*,[5] interpreted by commentators as "knowledge of subtle, non-perceptual matters by means of authority and inference," are terms of common occurrence. In spite of the repeated indulgence in description of miraculous facts or situations, immutability of the laws of nature and of the order of things appears to be recognized in such statements as: "Just as old age, death, time or divine decree is never impeded amongst all beings..."[6] "Three couples (*dvandva*) operate indiscriminately among animals; you should not be (affected) like this about them that are inevitable";[7] "earth, wind, ether, water and light abide by their own nature, following the eternal course";[8] "Nobody touching the burning flame of fire escapes being scorched";[9] "No animal in this world can be absolutely immortal."[10] Frequent use of the terms *maryādā* (bounds) and *sthiti* (settled state of existence), with reference to natural as well as religious or moral affairs also points to the same conclusion. A good number of technical terms[11] scattered throughout the work indicate strong undercurrents of philosophical speculation, and although testimony of the supersensitive sages as revealed in the Scriptures is, as a rule, held in high esteem and preferred to the depositions of perception and inference in subtler matters,[12] nothing appears to be too sacred to be immune from the searching logical criticism (*ānvīkṣikī*) of the Lokāyatikas[13] who are fairly in evidence.

The general outlook seems to be characterized by a sensible optimism, grounded, as it apparently is, on a dispassionate view of the inevitable concomitants of life. Unlike later literature and the teachings of the *Upaniṣads* notwithstanding, life is nowhere looked upon as a bondage and final release (*mokṣa*) from the concatenation of births and deaths does not appear to be openly preached as a desideratum. "No living being," it is said, "is immune from calamities,"[14] and "uninterrupted happiness is not easy to secure,"[15] but "joy comes to a person, if he holds on to life, even after a hundred years."[16] "A heartless evil-doer causing anxiety to created beings does not survive even though he be the lord of the three worlds."[17] "All piles end in decay, elevations in fall, connections in separation, and life in death."[18] "Just as two pieces of wood may come together in the ocean and, after a while, separate, so wives, sons, relatives and wealth come upon a man and slip off, their separation being inevitable. No living entity can escape the course of nature, so one is powerless, lamenting over the dead."[19] Considering that "life is constantly and irrevocably gliding off like the stream, one should direct one's self towards happiness, for all created beings are held to deserve happiness"[20] and one of the five congenital debts is that to one's own self, repayable with pleasurable experience.[21] But true happiness cannot be had by pursuing it per se, but is derivable only from *dharma*.[22]

4. THE DOMINANT IDEAS

The ends of human existence.—The ends which motivate human activities and which every normal human being should strive to attain (*puruṣārtha*) are, according to the *Rāmāyaṇa*, three in number and hence collectively called *tri-varga*. They are *dharma* (spiritual merit), *artha* (wealth or material advantage), and *kāma* [(gratification of) desire or pleasure]. Of these *dharma* is the supreme and the other two should be subordinated to it. One who is actuated only by *artha* comes to be hated in this world, while excessive seeking of pleasure cannot be commended, as it leads one promptly to grief.[23] One should judiciously and harmoniously pursue each of the three at its right moment,[24] but one who pursues only pleasure to the neglect of the other two wakes up after a fall like one asleep at the tree-top.[25]

Dharma is ubiquitous in the *Rāmāyaṇa* and has been used almost indiscriminately for the end as well as the means, viz. any or all of the religious, social and moral duties, enjoined by the Scriptures or recognized by the wise as such. The conception of *dharma* has been of profound significance in Indian thought of all times and its etymology is a pointer to its connotation. In *Vedic* times *dharma* in its variant form *dhárman* (:√*dhṛ* "to hold," "to support") meant "prop" or "support" and "law" or "ordinance"; later it naturally developed the senses "innate property of a thing," "customary law," "religious injunction" and "duty." All these meanings it has ever continued to have, so that *dharma* has been understood and interpreted as that which supports the universe as well as the society. "*Dharma* is supreme in this world" and "the most potent refuge."[26] "Material advantage or pleasure issues out of *dharma*; one gets everything through *dharma*; *dharma* is the sustaining power (or quintessence) of this universe."[27] *Dharma* guards one who guards it,[28] and "those who are devoted to truth and *dharma* have no fear of death."[29] But the fruit of *dharma* alone does not accrue to one who has earned it, but who is bound up (also) with the fruit of *a-dharma*, its opposite, nor does *dharma* destroy *a-dharma*: one gets the fruit of the one as surely as that of the other.[30]

But the course of *dharma* is subtle and extremely difficult of apprehension even by the wise.[31] The inscrutable ways of events in this world often raise doubts as to its pretensions.[32] Owing to frequent apparent anomalies in recompense in the shape of prosperity or adversity in this world, the potency and even the existence of *dharma* and *a-dharma* are sometimes challenged and the absoluteness of might, wealth or expediency advocated,[33] while those who deny themselves enjoyment and undergo austerities for the sake of *dharma* are ridiculed.[34]

Theology and Religion.—By the time of the *Rāmāyaṇa* the *Vedic* deities have become completely anthropomorphized and a host of new deities has been introduced. Their immortality is not absolute, being only an exaggeration of the ordinary human span, and their positions are now considered attainable by human beings through virtuous actions. But three super-deities Brahmā, Viṣṇu and Śiva, credited respectively with the cyclic evolution, maintenance and merger (*sṛṣṭi*, *sthiti* and *laya*) of the universe and deemed as three functional, personal aspects of the Absolute (Brahman), appear on the scene. They form the Trinity and are given, jointly as well as individually, all the epithets of the Absolute such as "unborn," "eternal," "immutable," "all-pervasive," "infinite," "the source and container of all," etc.[35] The impersonal Absolute as the source of Brahmā is termed *a-vyakta*[36] (unmanifest), or *ākāśa*[37] (the All-pervasive one), and as *ātman* or *paramātman*[38] (the soul of all beings), the individual soul receiving the characteristic designation *bhūtātman*[39] ("the spirit apparent in the senses and sensations"), or *liṅgin*[40] ("endowed with indicators"). The inscrutable power in the Absolute that is responsible for the evolution, duration and merger of the universe and for its assumption of personal forms is termed *māyā*.[41]

In religion the *Vedic* mode of worship is supplemented by the worship of images in temples. The articles of offering also are augmented by flowers, scents, sweets and all the best varieties of food, and, in fact, it has become a truism that "the deities of a person have the same food as he himself."[42] "Sitting in right posture" (*āsana*),[43] "control of the breath" (*prāṇāyāma*),[44] "meditation" (*dhyāna*),[45] and "absolute concentration of the mind" (*yoga* and *samādhi*), and vows of all sorts are frequently mentioned in this connection. Austerity, study of the prescribed portion of the *Veda*, liberality to the *brāhmaṇas* and the needy, hospitality, and adoration of the manes as well as the *brāhmaṇas* form other items of pious work. Great liberalism in the matter of worship seems to prevail and bigoted sectarianism of the later times is clearly out of the question.

Asceticism is in the air and, besides confirmed ascetics of various orders,[46] every pious man or woman exhibits ascetic traits in his or her habits. There seem to be two classes of hermits, *tāpasas* and *śramaṇas* (both including women),[47] the subtle distinction between them, if any, is not apparent from the text. *Bhikṣu* and *bhikṣiṇī* for the male and the female hermit respectively are also met with.[48] Although regular asceticism is often resorted to for attaining objects, ordinarily wellnigh impossible of attainment, there seems to be a much higher motive for the best of the ascetics who are presented as striving after absolute placidity of the mind through control of the senses and passions, freedom from desires and compassionate kindliness towards all living beings.[49] It has been stated above that "final release" (*mokṣa*), is not openly preached, but there are occasional hints that this is what they are striving after, their goal being indicated by the ambiguous term *brahma-loka* (the word of Brahman or of Brahmā).[50] The last stage of asceticism seems to be characterized by absolute disregard for the creature comforts and constant meditation on the self.[51]

Ethics.—Ethical virtues, as an integral part of *dharma*, have found so much emphasis in the *Rāmāyaṇa* that it is virtually "ethics turned poetry," and its success in this difficult task may be gauged by the immense popularity and veneration it has enjoyed among millions of Hindus throughout the ages. Kindly regard for all animal existence, truthfulness, self-control, forbearance, tolerance for the shortcomings of others, hospitality and succour even to an enemy who seeks it, and purity in mind, speech and act are some of the virtues highly extolled.[52] Devotional regard for the parents, the teacher, the elder brother, the husband and the master and the corresponding affectionate regard in them for the others are emphasized again and again. Monogamy and chastity form one of the highest virtues for both the sexes.[53] Women, who are normally dependent on the father, the husband or the son, are entitled to tender courtesy under all circumstances, and no females must be killed.[54] The wife, who is the inalienable self of the husband and his comrade in the pursuit of *dharma*, enjoys solicitous care and supreme authority in domestic life.[55] Her character is her best armour,[56] and the respect and even veneration that a chaste and devoted wife, reputed for her character, enjoys is unparalleled, and is hardly less than that enjoyed by any great ascetic. The king, who owes his position to the loving consent of the people, is to be looked upon as a god in disguise, since it is he who is the guarantor of the *dharma*, welfare and life of the people.[57] But he commits a heinous crime, if he, while enjoying the privileges, neglects his duty.[58] The judge and the criminal who is justly punished, both go to heaven.[59] It is not a sin to kill one who has struck first, for one has to save one's life as best one can.[60] But even in war one must not kill an enemy who is not fighting, has taken to hiding or sought refuge with folded hands, is running away or drunken.[61] Killing of a king, a woman, a child or an old man, or desertion of a dependent is considered a great sin.[62]

The absoluteness of moral conduct is emphasized more than once.[63] But its disparagement is sometimes met with in the speech of one engaged in immoral action or as an outburst of passion, roused by occasional non-appreciation of moral virtue in this world. Thus in the speech of Indrajit killing the magic Sītā: "That a woman should not be killed, as you say, O monkey, anything that causes suffering to the enemy has to be done";[64] or in the speech of Rāma offended with the behaviour of the ocean: "The world honours a boastful, evil-hearted, shameless fellow who rushes about and chastises everybody,"[65] and "Chastisement is the supreme expedient for a man in this world, I should think, fie upon forgiveness, sweet words or presents to the ungrateful."[66]

The criteria of moral judgment appear to consist in (1) consideration for the other world, (2) regard of the élite, (3) effect on other people's morals, and (4) one's own conscience and self-respect.[67]

Fatalism.—Fatalism is frequently exploited in the *Rāmāyaṇa* as a refuge in irremediable adverse circumstances. "That which surpasses logic is fate (*daiva*) and its course is unimpeded amongst all entities."[68]

Fate matures in time and the two are so inseparably connected that often time (*kāla*) is held responsible for all that happens.[69] Sometimes fate is looked upon as predestination (*niyati*) ruling absolutely over all that is, as in the address of Rāma to Tārā:[70] "*Niyati* is the author in this world; *niyati* is instrumental in achievements; *niyati* is responsible for the undertakings of all entities in this world. Nobody does anything; one is not one's master even in respect of one's undertaking; the world rolls on its inherent state, and time is its supreme resort. Time does not transgress itself; time is not to be avoided; and having attained its inherent state, nothing transgresses. For time there is no relationship, no logic, no powers; connection with friends and relations is no consideration; it is beyond one's own control. But one, who sees rightly should observe the evolution of time: *dharma*, *artha* and *kāma* are achieved in the course of time." Often, however, fate is regarded as the maturation of the deferred potentialities of one's actions (*karman*) in this or a previous life, thus entailing a belief in transmigration.[71] The two concepts are evidently due to two angles of vision: the one looking upon the individual as a tiny particle buried in the immensity of the universe, and the other regarding him as distinct from other individuals and hence responsible for whatever he comes by, injustice or chance being ruled out.

Despite this homage to *daiva*, the importance of human effort (*puruṣakāra* or *pauruṣa*) is nowhere disparaged. In fact, success is considered to be dependent on both.[72] The second of the above conceptions also implies the importance of *puruṣakāra*, for *daiva* here is the fruition of some previous *puruṣakāra*.[73] Some protagonists of *puruṣakāra* would even pity *daiva* as powerless before human effort, while not to be submissive to time (i.e. *daiva*) is considered a great virtue.[74]

Materialism.—The views of the materialists, who are vehemently condemned as *Nāstikas* (nihilists), time and again, appear summed up in the speech of Jābāli to Rāma:—

"A creature is born and annihilated alone; it has no relations or comrades. Therefore, a man who is affected by the consideration that it is his mother or father should be looked upon as a lunatic. For men 'father,' 'brother,' home,' 'wealth' are all like a halting stage for a traveller, and no sane persons become attached to them. The father is just the initiator, but it is really the seminal and menstrual fluids combined in the mother's womb that leads to a man's birth. At death one meets the inevitable end: this is the way of things and one need not be aggrieved. Those that give precedence to wealth and spiritual merit are really to be pitied—not the others, since it is they who suffer misery here and annihilation at death. People busy themselves with funeral rites and offerings to the manes: just look at the extravagant waste of food, for what can a dead man eat? If food eaten by one is transferred to the body of another, similar offerings should be made in favour of those that are living abroad instead of supplying them with provender. 'Sacrifice,' 'give,' 'receive initiation,' 'practise penance,' 'renounce'—such texts inducing liberality have been composed by clever people. Therefore, an intelligent person should make up his mind that there is nothing else, and entertain that which is directly apprehended by the senses and reject the rest."[75]

These materialist ideas of Jābāli look like an exact replica of the views of Cārvāka who, however, is nowhere mentioned by name.

5. CONCLUSION

It will appear from the foregoing survey that the *Rāmāyaṇa* presents a practical philosophy, underlining ethics and religion, in the shape of a poem of engrossing human interest. The higher philosophical truths and the views of the heretics are touched only incidentally in presenting a verisimilitude of the cultural atmosphere. No philosophical Schools, except *ānvīkṣikī* favoured by the Lokāyatikas, are mentioned by name, nor views that are peculiar to any particular School, although the general trends and the numerous technical terms show that philosophical speculations along various lines must be rife. Sectarianism is not in evidence, although pious devotion to various deities is frequently alluded to. On the whole, the philosophy of the *Rāmāyaṇa*, free from dogmatism and sectarian prejudice as it is, deserves to have a universal human appeal for all times to come.

NOTES

1. Macdonell, *History of Sanskrit Literature*, p. 308.
2. *op. cit.*, pp. 100–111.
3. II. 109. 9; VII. 43. 19.
4. II. 21. 64; 109. 3; III. 66. 14; IV. 18. 59; 28. 65; VI. 22. 32; 64. 2; VII. 50. 16, etc.
5. VI. 50. 40.
6. III. 64. 75.
7. II. 77. 23. The couples are variously interpreted by the commentators as "hunger and thirst, grief and stupor, old age and death," or "birth and death, pleasure and pain, gain and loss," or "existence, birth, increase, decay, change, disintegration."
8. VI. 22. 23.
9. IV. 30. 18; VI. 118. 17.
10. VII. 30. 9; also 10. 17.
11. cf. *anupapanna* (illogical), VI. 64. 11; *anumāna* (inference), IV. 6. 9; 10. 34; VI. 18. 37; "inferential knowledge," 52. 13; *avyakta* (unmanifest), I. 70. 19; *ākāśa* (free space), > (the Absolute as the all-pervasive one), I. 34. 4; II. 110. 5; VII. 110. 10; *indriya* (organ of sense), V. 9. 29; *indriyārtha* (object of sense), V. 9. 29; VI. 93. 22; *upapatti* (reasoning), V. 9. 39; *upapanna* (logical), II. 118. 15; *tattva* (the ultimate reality), in *tattva-jña* (knower of the ultimate reality), II. 77. 24; *tamas* (one of the *guṇas*), II. 109. 17; *tarka* (logical analysis), IV. 32. 9; VI. 2. 7; *tri-varga* [group of three (viz. spiritual merit, wealth and pleasure)], IV. 38. 23; *niḥśreyasa* (the highest good), VI. 64. 8; *nisarga*

(nature), IV. 58. 30, 31; *nyāya* (reasoning or syllogism) III. 50. 22; VII. 22. 24. 30; *pañcatva* (merger in the five elements), IV. 11. 46; V. 13. 23; *pañca-varga* [group of the five (senses)], II. 109. 27; *puruṣārtha* (object of human pursuit), IV. 64. 10; V. 13. 18; *brahma-bhūta* (become Brahman), I. 33. 16; *bhāva* (entity), II. 94. 18; *bhūta* (being), III. 64. 75; VII. 34. 39; (animate being), II. 77. 23; (primary elements) > (the senses including mind), VII. 96. 21; *bhūtātman* (the individual soul), VI. 93. 22; *maryādā* (bounds, settled order, propriety), II. 35. 11; III. 64. 64, etc.; *māyā* (the inscrutable divine power), V. 54. 37; VII. 104. 2. 4. 5; 110. 11; *māyā-yoga* (obviously = *yoga-māyā*), "*māyā*" as *yoga* (*q.v.*). I. 29. 9; *moha* (delusion), II. 54. 30, and *sammoha* (delusive), VII. 84. 9; *yoga* (self-concentration), II. 20. 48; III. 6. 6; *rāga* (passion), II. 2. 44; V. 55. 16; *rājasa* (due to *rajas*, a constituent of *prakṛti*), V. 55. 16; *rūpa* (being), VI. 116. 30; *lakṣaṇa* (definition or accurate description), VI. 64. 6; *vāda* (debate), I. 14. 19; VI. 17. 52; *vipāka* (fruition of *karman*), V. 68. 4; *vyāviddha*, III. 9. 27, and *vyāhata* II. 106. 18 (self-contradictory): *saṅga* (attachment), II. 37. 2; *sattva* (one of the *guṇas*), VII. 58. 6; (mind), II. 39. 32; (spirit), II. 21. 39; *samādhi* (self-concentration), IV. 30. 16. 17; VII. 49. 8; *svabhāva* (innate nature), VI. 22. 23; 64. 6.

12. III. 50. 22.
13. II. 100. 38–39.
14. III. 66. 6.
15. II. 18. 13.
16. V. 34. 6; VI. 126. 2.
17. III. 29. 3.
18. II. 105. 16 = VII. 52. 11.
19. II. 105. 26–28.
20. II. 105. 31, cf. also vv., 19–21.
21. II. 4. 13–14. The other four are to the gods, the sages, the manes, and the *brāhmaṇas*, repayable respectively with sacrifice, study, begetting a son, and gifts. Compare these with the Five Great Sacrifices
22. III. 9. 30–31.
23. II. 21. 57–58.
24. II. 100. 62–63.
25. IV. 38. 20–22, cf. II. 53. 13.
26. II. 21. 41; VII. 3. 10.
27. III. 9. 30.
28. II. 25. 3.
29. VI. 46. 32.
30. V. 51. 28–29.
31. IV. 18. 15.
32. II. 39. 11; 52. 17; III. 52. 39; 64. 52; V. 28. 12–13.
33. VI. 64. 6–9; 83. 14–42; 13. 2–5.
34. II. 109. 13; VI. 13. 2.
35. II. 110. 3, 5; VI. 117. 13–26; VII. 6. 2.
36. I. 70. 19.
37. II. 110. 5; VII. 110. 10.
38. IV. 10. 15, VI. 113. 34; 111. 11; VII. 41. 7.
39. VI. 59. 55; 93. 22.
40. V. 13. 40.
41. I. 16. 15; 29. 9; V. 54. 37; VII. 104. 2, 4, 5; 110. 11.
42. II. 103. 30; 104. 15.
43. II. 99. 15.
44. II. 4. 33; VII. 7. 6.
45. II. 6. 3.
46. III. 6. 2–6.
47. I. 14. 12; IV. 18. 33; II. 29. 13; II. 38. 4; III. 74. 7. 10; IV. 50. 38–39.
48. II. 29. 13; IV. 3. 2, 23.
49. II. 99. 13–16; III. 1. 15, 21; V. 26. 45–6.

50. I. 33. 16; 34. 4; II. 19. 33; 21. 53; 94. 19; III. 5. 28, 31. 41; 74. 13, 35.
51. II. 67. 23.
52. II. 33. 12; 109. 31; VI. 113. 43; 18. 27–28; II. 109. 21.
53. II. 64. 43; 29. 16; 117. 23–9.
54. I. 32. 21 f.; II. 61. 24; IV. 33. 36, 39, 61; II. 78. 21.
55. II. 37. 24; III. 10. 21; IV. 24. 37–8; 65. 23–4.
56. VI. 114. 27.
57. II. 102. 4; III. I. 18–20; IV. 18. 41–3.
58. III. 6. 11.
59. IV. 18. 61.
60. II. 96. 24; VI. 9. 14.
61. VI. 80. 39; IV. 11. 36.
62. II. 75. 37.
63. II. 109. 4; VI. 113. 42–4.
64. VI. 81. 28.
65. VI. 21. 15–16.
66. VI. 22. 45.
67. II. 109. 3–9, 16–19. 24–5.
68. II. 22. 20.
69. II. 24. 33; 88. 11; III. 68. 21; 72. 16; VI. 32. 13; 95. 48.
70. IV. 25. 4–8.
71. II. 39. 4; 53. 19; 109. 28; III. 49. 27; VI. 111. 25–6; 113. 37–8.
72. I. 18. 47; V. 36. 19; VI. 73. 6.
73. II. 23. 7, 16–20.
74. II. 1. 31.
75. II. 108. 3–17.

BIBLIOGRAPHY

Editions of the text:

(Bengal recension): Ed. by G. Gorresio. 5 Vols. Paris, 1850.

(N.W. recension): Ed. by Viśvabandhu Śāstrin and Bhagavad Datta. Vols. I–VII. Lahore.

(Bombay recension): Ed. with the Tilaka commentary by V. L. Pansikar. 4th revised ed. Nirṇaya-sāgara Press, Bombay, 1930. Ed. with the commentaries, *Tilaka*, *Śiromaṇi* and *Bhūṣaṇa* by S. K. Mudholkar. 7 Vols. Bombay, 1913–20.

Translations:

(into English Verse) by R. T. H. Griffith. Banaras, 1895. New ed. by M. N. Venkataswami. Bombay, 1915.

(into English Prose) by Manmathnath Dutt. Calcutta, 1892–94.

Studies:

JACOBI, H.: *Das Rāmāyana*. Bonn, 1893.

VAIDYA, C. V.: *The Riddle of the Rāmāyaṇa*. Bombay and London, 1906.

RUBEN, W.: *Studien zur Textgeschichte des Rāmāyaṇa*. Stuttgart, 1936.

MACDONELL, A. A.: *History of Sanskrit Literature* (London, 1913), pp. 302–17.

WINTERNITZ, M.: *History of Indian Literature*, Vol. I (English translation by Mrs. S. Ketkar. Calcutta, 1927), pp. 475–517.

CHAPTER 6

Some Phonetic Peculiarities of the Bengali Dialect of Manbhum

§ 1. General Remarks

This dialect is spoken not only in the modern district of Manbhum but also in the portions of Ranchi, Bankura, Birbhum, Burdwan, and the Santhal Parganas, contiguous to it. It may roughly be considered to have two varieties, a western (W) one, spoken in and about, and to the west of, Purulia, and an eastern (E) one, elsewhere. Except where something in particular has been noted, the sounds, as a rule, are to be considered identical in their articulation and behaviour with those of the standard colloquial Bengali (SB.) as recorded by Dr. S. K. Chatterji in his *Origin and Development of the Bengali Language* (ODBL.), *Bhāṣāprakāś Bāṅgālā Vyākaraṇ*, and other works.

The most remarkable phonetic peculiarities of this dialect, which, conjointly, are also distinctive of it, are:—

(1) A very short [i] as well as [u] between a vowel and a consonant which is distinctly felt but produces a momentary, almost consonantal impression, *e.g.*, [la^{i}th < lathi] 'kick', [ʃa^{i}r < ʃari] 'row', [ã^{u}ṭh < ãṭhu], 'knee', [kha^{u}k < khauk] 'let him eat', [ṭha^{u}kra^{i}n < ṭhakurani] 'goddess', etc. This phenomenon will be referred to hereafter as 'squeezed' [i] or [u].

(2) A very light, almost vocalic [j] as well as [w] after consonants, followed by vowels, in syllables other than the first, *e.g.*, [ɦɔ̀r^{j}a < ɦɔ̀ria], 'negligent form of the personal name [ɦɔ̀ri]', [khel^{j}e < khelia] 'having played', [meʃ^{w}a < maʃua] 'mother's sister's husband', [rɔ̀gɦ^{w}a < rɔ̀gɦua], 'negligent form of the personal name [rɔ̀gɦu]' etc. In effect, the previous vowel is not made to feel the strain as normally before a conjunct.

(3) A pure nasal consonant, probably identical with the original Sanskrit Anusvāra, before [g, gɦ, ɟ, ɟɦ, d, dɦ, and b] in certain native words, *e.g.*, [ko^{m}ga] 'a particular plant', [ʃa^{m}gɦa] 'wooden beam in thatched houses', [a^{m}ɟir] 'guava', [ba^{m}ɟɦa] 'barren,' [ba^{m}dɔr] 'monkey', [ka^{m}dɦ] 'shoulder', [ta^{m}b^{u}] 'tent', [tu^{m}ba] 'gourd', etc. Together with the previous pure vowel, it corresponds, as a rule, to a nasal vowel in SB., *e.g.*, [ca^{m}d: ʧãd] 'moon', [bi^{m}dɦ: bĩdɦ] 'hole', [rɛ^{m}da: rɛ̃da] 'plane', [ʃa^{m}ɟɦ: ʃãʒɦ], etc. Before [g, gɦ], however, and in combination with them it corresponds to SB. [ŋ] or [ŋg], *e.g.*, [ra^{m}ga: raŋa, raŋga] 'red', [co^{m}ga :

---

* First published in *The Journal of the Asiatic Society*, vol. XVII, no. 2, 1951, pp. 65-72.

[1] Accepted for the Indian Linguistics Section of the 15th Oriental Conference, held in Bombay, November, 1949.

ʤoŋa] 'pipe' or funnel', [ʃa^{m}gɦa: ʃaŋa, ʃaŋga] 'wooden beam in thatched houses', etc. It also develops often before the same consonants, after a vowel immediately preceded by [n] or [m], presumably because such a vowel tends to be nasal, *e.g.*, [nɛ^{m}ɟ: lɛʤ] 'tail', [ni^{m}d: nid] 'sleep', [mɛ^{m}ɟmɛ^{m}ɟ: mɛʤmɛʤ] 'onomatopoetic suggesting fatigue', [ma^{m}ɟa: maʤa] 'to cleanse by rubbing', etc. Sometimes it replaces nasal consonants in colloquializing Sanskritic forms still in use, *e.g.*, [mɔ^{m}dɔ] for *manda*, [rɛ^{m}ga] and [nɔ^{m}da] 'negligent forms respectively of the proper names *raṅga* and *nanda*', etc.

This 'pure nasal consonant' is undoubtedly the same as the reduced nasal described in ODBL., pp. 360ff., but only a step advanced towards decolourization. To the ears of the present writer the colouring due to the following stop is imperceptible.

(4) A fondness for aspiration, which, if inherited, is seldom lost even when it is in the final sound and never when it is followed by a vowel. In this it is sharply distinguished from SB. which has a remarkable tendency to deaspirate all medial and final aspirate sounds, cf. inherited words, [maɟɦ: maʤ] 'middle', [kɔtha: kɔta] 'talk', [piṭhali: piṭuli] 'paste of powdered rice', etc. along with the native or borrowed, [ugɦa: uga] 'file', [ulkhi: ulki] 'tattoo', [gɔ^{m}dɦɔl: gɔ̃dɔl] 'infants' feeding spoon', [√cã̃cha: √ʤãʤa] 'to scrape', [ḍɔbɦa: ḍoba] 'pool', [√libɦ: √nib] 'to be extinguished', [laṭhim: laṭim] 'top', [bɔ^{m}dɦɛɟ: bondeʤ] 'orderliness', etc. Original aspiration is often transferred, when a sound or a syllable has been lost: [pagɦa] < S. *pragrāha* 'tether', [tothe < tohate] 'in thee', [naikhɔ < naɦikɔ] 'is not', [kakhɛ < kaɦakɛ] 'to whom', etc. The eastern dialect, especially as spoken by the upper classes, shows the tendency of SB. to a limited extent, but the western one never misses an aspirate sound and possesses even aspirate forms of [n], [m], [r] and [l], thus [√pɔɽɦ] < S. *√paṭh* 'to read', [muɦɛ̃] 'in the face' < S. *mukha*, [kumɦir] < S. *kumbhīra* 'crocodile', [kumɦar] < S. *kumbhakāra* 'potter', [√panɦa] < S. *pra-√snu*, 'to ooze through teats', [unɦan] 'oven', [pɔrɦa] 'to wear', [culɦa] 'oven', etc. The lower classes often introduce aspiration in sounds which originally do not appear to have had any, *e.g.*, [ɟabhɛ] 'you will go', [cĩɽɦa] < S. *cipiṭaka* 'flattened rice', [ʃɛ̃kha] 'to bake', etc.

(5) A preponderance of nasal sounds. The contributory factors are mainly: (i) Retention of all inherited and developed nasal sounds (excepting a few cases of change of initial [n] to [l]) in common with SB. (ii) Formation of the gerund with [-ʝɛ̃] or [-ĩ] of verbal roots ending in vowels, which happen to include all causative and denominative roots, *e.g.*, [khaʝɛ̃] 'having eaten' [: √kha], [dhuʝɛ̃] 'having washed' [: √dhu], [mɔraĩ] 'killing,' causative of [√mɔr] 'to die,' [cɔɽaĩ] 'slapping,' denominative from [cɔɽ] 'slap', [keṭh^{w}aĩ] 'being chilled,' denominative from [kaṭh] 'wood,' etc.,—the western variety, especially as spoken by the lower classes, extending it even to the rest, *e.g.*, [pɔ̃ɽɦ^{j}ɛ̃: E. pɔ̃ɽ^{j}ɛ] 'having read' [: √pɔɽɦ], [kaṭ^{j}ɛ̃: E. kaṭ^{j}ɛ] 'having cut' [: √kaṭ], etc. As gerunds, besides their own proper uses, enter into three tense-formations, the effect is enormous: thus for instance, [khaʝɛ̃] 'having eaten' enters into [khaʝɛ̃cɦɛ] he has eaten,' [khaʝɛ̃chilɔ] 'he ate,' and [khaʝɛ̃ tha^{i}kbɛk] 'he shall have eaten'. And (iii) tendency to nasalize a syllable immediately preceding or following a nasal one *e.g.*, [khãʝɛ̃: khaʝɛ̃], [cɔɽãĩ: cɔɽaĩ], [bhũĩ] < S. *bhūmi*, 'earth', [ṭhãĩ] < S. *sthāna* 'place', [mũʝɛ̃], locative of [mu] 'mouth', [dhũã] < S. *dhūma* 'smoke,' [rũã] < S. *roman* 'hair,' etc., besides all vowels after [n] or [m] generally.

With these remarks we proceed to record certain individual peculiarities of the sounds.

§ 2. Individual Sounds

1. Vowels

[ɔ]

This vowel is modified into a variety [ɔ̇] approaching [o] (but by no means identical with it), when it is followed immediately or in the next syllable by either of the close vowels [i] and [u], original or epenthetic, full or squeezed, or by a 'light' [j] or [w]: *e.g.*, [ɦɔ̇ri, ɟɔ̇du, dɔ̇i, bɔ̇u, ɦɔ̇ⁱlɔ, ɦɔ̇ᵘk, rɔ̇ⁱkkha (= S. *rakṣā*), ɔ̇ⁱddɔ (= S. *adya*), pɔ̇ⁱṛlɔ < pɔ̇ṛilɔ, ɦɔ̇rʲa < ɦɔ̇ria, rɔ̇gɦʷa < rɔ̇gɦua, mɔ̇ᵘd-dada < mɔ̇dhu-dada]. But it remains unaffected, if the conditioning element belongs to a compounded word or a suffix whose separate existence is meant to be felt: thus [pɔt-bɦula, gɦɔr-i, gɦɔr-ṭi, lɔt-ṭuku], but [pɔ̇ṛi, pɔ̇ṛuk < √paṛ], [gɦɔ̇ṭi < gɦɔṭ], [ʃɔ̇tu, dɦɔ̇nu] 'endearing nicknames respectively of [ʃɔ̇tiʃ] and [dɦɔnɔɲɟɔj]', etc. In pronouncing [ɔ̇] the upper lip remains inert, while the lower one is rounded, whereas in pronouncing [o] both are equally active; thus the difference between the first vowels in [bɦɔ̇ri] and [bɦor] or [ʃɔ̇ruk] and [ʃora] can be distinctly felt. But [ɔ̇] in SB. seems to be somewhat more rounded. Under any other conditions [ɔ] remains unaffected, thus differing from its behaviour in SB.: cf. [bɦalɔ, kalɔ, bɔṛɔ, tɔtɔ, ɦɔ̇ⁱlɔ, ɔnɔbɔrɔtɔ, mɔn, pitɔl] with SB. [bɦalo, kalo, boṛo, toto, ɦolo, onoboroto, mon, pitol], respectively.

[ɔ] tends to replace [o], when [a] follows in the next syllable, intervened by a consonant, cf. [goch: gɔcha] 'bunch', [bɦok(h)] 'hunger': [bɦɔkha] 'hungry', [rog] 'disease',: [rɔga] 'diseased', [ḍor] 'cord': [ḍɔra] 'stripe', [goṛ] 'leg': [√gɔṛar] 'to kick', [goɟ] 'peg': [gɔɟal] 'nail', etc. If, on the other hand, [a] follows immediately, [o] tends to change to [u] cf. [lua < loha] 'iron', [rũã] < S. *roman* 'hair', [buaⁱl: SB. boal, H. boari] 'a kind of fish', [puati: SB. poati] 'pregnant', etc. Often, however, there is no following [a], *e.g.*, [mɔṭ]: H., SB. [moṭ] 'baggage', [gɔ̃ṛ]: SB. [gõṛ] < S. *gonḍa* 'fleshy navel', [kɔ̃th: SB. kõt] < S. √*kunth* 'exertion to evacuate', etc. This tendency is to be contrasted with the opposite one in SB. of frequently changing [ɔ] into [o].

[ɔ] sometimes corresponds to [a] in SB.: cf. [√bɔna: √bana] 'to make', 'to cut', etc., [sɔɟa: saɟɦa] 'to arrange or make', [bɛɦɔja: bɛɦaja] 'shameless', [bɦɔta: √bɦata] 'to fill up (a pit)', the definitive suffix [-ṭɔ: -ṭa], the verbal suffixes [-thɔm:-tam, *e.g.*, bɔ̇ⁱlthɔm: bɔ̇ltam] and [-lɔm: -lam, *e.g.*, gɛlɔm: gɛlam], etc.

The change, in words of three or more syllables of [ɔ] or [a], when followed by [i] or [i:] in the next syllable, to [u]—so common in SB.—is almost totally absent here, cf. [ɛkhɔni: ekhuni] 'just now', [kuṛaⁱr: kuṛul] < S. *kuṭharī* 'axe', [tɛ̃tɔ̃ⁱl : tɛ̃tul < OB. tentɔli] 'tamarind', [ṭhaᵘkraⁱn :ṭhakrun < ṭhakurani:] 'goddess,' [piṭhali: piṭuli] 'paste of powdered rice', [madɔ̇li: maduli] 'amulet', etc. An exception appears, however, to be made in the eastern dialect in favour of the ending [-ɔni:] and its extension [-ɔnʲa], cf. [nɔ̇ruⁱn (< S. *nakhaharaṇī*), chɛ̃ckaᵐduni f. & -dunʲa m., lacunʲa, raᵐdɦuni, ḍɦakuni, ʃiɲtuluni, ciruni, kuruni], etc.

[a]

The change of [a] to [e] or [o] through the influence of a preceding [i] or [u] respectively, so common in SB., is altogether unknown here, cf. [cĩṛa: cĩṛe, piṭha: piṭhe, muṭha: muṭho, ɟuta: ɟ͡ʒuto]. Final [a] of gerunds changes universally to [e], but the one in the previous syllable is, as a rule, not affected, cf. [ra^{i}kh^{j}e: rekhe, khãɟe: khee], etc. Unlike SB. any other [a] following [i] or [j] remains unaffected, although the one in a previous syllable may, in the eastern dialect, change to [e]: [ɦɔ̀r^{j}a: ɦɔ̀re; ɦɔ̀^{i}lda: ɦɔ̀lde; ɟel^{j}a, W. ɟal^{j}a: ɟ͡ʒele: ɦẽ^{i}ṛ^{j}a, W. ɦãṛ^{j}a: ɦẽṛe; ɦe^{i}tar, W. ɦath^{j}ar: ɦeter]. Likewise [a] after [u] or [w] is not changed to [o], although the one in the previous syllable may, in the eastern dialect, change to [e]: [ɦãṛi-khek^{w}a, W.-khauka:-kheko; bɦeṛ^{w}a: bɦeṛo, H. bɦʌṛua; ɟed^{w}a < ɟɔ̀du, ɟadɔb; rɔ̀gɦ^{wa} < rɔ̀gɦu].

In a few sporadic instances [a] corresponds to SB. [ɛ]: [ḍɦa^{m}ga: dɦɛŋa; naŋṭɔ, naŋṭa: nɛŋṭa; lakar: nɛkar; kha^{m}da, f.-di: khɛ̃da, f. khɛ̃di:].

[i]

The phenomenon of squeezed [i], already mentioned, originates in either (1) an anticipatory (*i.e.*, metathetic or epenthetic) or (2) an original [i], squeezed between a vowel and a consonant or consonants, *e.g.*, (1) [ra^{i}t < rati, pa^{i}kh < pakhi, ra^{i}kh^{j}e < rakhia, de^{i}kh^{j}e < dekhia] and (2) [ɦɔ̀^{i}lɔ < ɦɔ̀ilɔ, kha^{i}lɔm < khailɔm, ã^{i}ṭhɔ < ãiṭhɔ (< S. *āmṛṣṭa*)]. It is universal in originally polysyllabic words, but selective in di-syllabic ones: *e.g.*, [bɔ̀^{i}ʃbɛk < bɔ̀ʃibɛk, pɔ̀^{i}ṛlɔ < pɔ̀ṛilɔ], but [ɦati, cabi, baṭi] etc., as against [ra^{i}ʃ < raʃi, ba^{i}ṛ < baṛi (< S. *vṛddhi*)]. An epenthetic squeezed [i] appears before the Sanskrit conjuncts *kṣ* and *jñ* (followed by *a* or *ā*), which are (in perfect agreement with medieval Bengali) pronounced as [kkh (j)] and [gg (j)~] respectively, the [j] element being already evanescent: *e.g.*, [bhɔ̀^{i}kkh(j)ɔn] = S. *bhakṣaṇa*, [a^{i}gg(j)ã] = S. *ājñā*. Squeezed [i] never appears after [i], thus [miṭbɛk < miṭibɛk, miṭlɔ < miṭilɔ].

Unlike SB., [i] is retained here and not changed to [e], even when followed by [a], [e] or [ɔ] in the next syllable: thus [gila, gile, gilɔ] < [√gil] 'to swallow,' or [piṭa, piṭe, piṭɔ] < [√piṭ] 'to strike.'

[u]

The same remarks apply to squeezed [u]. Examples are: (1) [a^{u}kh cf. EB. aukh] 'sugar-cane' < S. *akṣu*, *vide JBORS.*, XVII, p. 27, [ã^{u}ṭh < ãṭhu] 'knee', [ṭha^{u}kra^{i}n < ṭhakurani:] 'goddess', (2) [kha^{u}k < khauk] 'let him eat', [de^{u}k < deuk] 'let him give', etc. Epenthetic squeezed [u] can be felt before medial consonants followed by light [w], *e.g.*, [ghe^{u}ṭ^{w}a, bhe^{u}ṛ^{w}a], etc. It does not appear after [u] and tends to become rarer in the present generation.

[u] often corresponds to [o] in SB., *e.g.*, [tumar, tumadɛr: tomar, tomader] 'your' (sing. and pl.), [chua^{i}c: chõac] 'contagion', [lua: loha, noa] < S. *lauha* 'iron', [ku:n: kon] < S. *koṇa* 'angle', [rũã: rõa] < S. *roman* 'hair', [kua: koa, kuo] < S. *kūpa* 'well', [kutha : kotha] 'where' etc. The examples indicate that the [u] here is in some cases inherited and in others a substitute for [o] for which see above under [o].

As in the case of [i], [u] also does not change to [o], even when followed by [a], [e] or [ɔ], *e.g.*, [ʃuna, ʃunɛ, ʃunɔ] < [ʃun] 'to hear', or [dɦua, dɦuɛ, dɦuɔ] < [√dhu] 'to wash'.

For [u] < [ɔ, a] see under [ɔ] and for [u] < [o] under [o].

[e, ɛ]

[ɛ] is a development of original [e] and corresponds to SB. [æ], which is unusual here. The same stem presents [e] if followed by [i] or [u], and [ɛ], if by [a], [ɛ] or [ɔ]: cf. [lekhi, lekchi, lekhuk] < [√lekh] 'to write', but [lɛkha, lɛkhɛ, lɛkhɔ]. It does not, however, appear amenable to the influence of Taddhita suffixes with a consonantal beginning; compare [ɛkṭi, ɛkṭuku] with SB. [ekṭi, ekṭu].

For cases of substitution of [a] by [e], see under [a]. Raising of [e] to [i] through the influence of a following [i], so common in SB., is very rare, cf. [deʃi: diʃi, geichi: gicʃi], but [biṭi < beṭi][1] 'daughter' and [mithi < methi:].

[o]

As already noted under [u], the final or penultimate [u] of stems is not changed to [o] as in SB. under the influence of a following [a], [e], or [o]. But, as there, [o] is changed to [u], when followed by [i] or [u], *e.g.*, [gɦɔ̃ṛa < ghoṛa : gɦũṛi; nɔṛa < noṛa : nuṛi; purohit > pur(ɦ)u^{i}t]. Cases of replacement of [o] by [ɔ] has already been mentioned under [ɔ].

2. *Consonants*

Of the consonants the palatals [c, ch, ɟ, ɟɦ] deserve notice in that they are here pure stops (as in Lahnda, see S. Varma, *JRASB.*, Vol. II, 1936, p. 75) and not affricates as in SB. [ph] and [bɦ] also are never pronounced as spirants. [ṛ] and [ṛɦ], originating in intervocalic [ḍ] and [ḍɦ] respectively or independently, are carefully distinguished, although in the eastern dialect there is a tendency to represent both by [ṛ], *e.g.*, [bɔṛ] < Pr. *vaḍa* < S. *vaṭa*, [bɦā̃ṛ] < S. *bhāṇḍa*, but W. [√pɔṛh, E. √pɔṛ] < Pr. √*paḍh* < S. √*paṭh*, W. [pīṛɦa, E. pīṛa] < S. *pīṭha*, [dɔṛhɔ] < S. *dṛḍha*, etc. Confusion of [r] and [ṛ] is very unusual, cf. [baṛi] < S. *vāṭī*, but [gɦɔr] < Pr. *ghara* < S. *gṛha*. [ṛ] seems to exert a powerful influence in cerebralizing dental sounds, cf. [ḍɦa^{i}ṛ: SB. dhaṛi] 'mother of a young beast', [ḍā̃ṛ] < S. *daṇḍa* 'fine', [ḍā̃ṛa: SB. dāṛa] 'to stand', [ṭaṛɔʃ: SB. taṛɔʃ] 'influence of an inflammation or boil', [ṭũṛ] < S. *tuṇḍa* 'mouth', [ḍeṛ: SB. deṛ], etc. There is a tendency to change an initial [n] to [l], *e.g.*, [lati] < S. *naptṛ*, [lai] < S. *nābhi*, [la] < S. *nau*, [lɔkhra] < Pers. *naχrā*, [liɔr] < S. *nīhāra*, [lɔɟɔr] < Pers. Ar. *nazr*, [lɔrɔm] < Pers. *narm*, etc. Exceptions are found in (1) certain familiar and borrowed words, *e.g.*, [nak] 'nose', [nɔkh] 'nail', [niṭ] < Eng. net, [nɔkɔl], [nɔkʃa], etc.; (2) the negative and interrogative particles [nɔ], [na], [nai], but contrast [lɔ̃i, lɔo, lɔj: SB. nɔ̃i, nɔo, nɔj], and [lara: SB. nara]; and (3) words having another nasal sound in them, *e.g.*, [nɔnɔd, nim, nɔ̃muna, namta, nam, ni^{m}d, ne^{in}ɟ], etc. Literacy, however, is exerting a powerful influence in checking the tendency. The reverse one of changing [l] to [n] is rare, but cf. [nɔŋka < lɔŋka]; [nu:n] < S. *lavaṇa*, against [alɔna]; [nɔmba <

---

[1] Compare, however, Sauraseni Apabhraṃśa *biṭṭi* = *beṭī* of Hindi etc.

lɔmba], [neᵐɟ: SB. lɛʒ], all of which happen to contain another nasal sound.

§ 3. SOUNDS IN COMBINATION: SANDHI

1. *Loss of vowels*

This is especially noticeable in compounds and sporadically before a few vowel suffixes. (i) Final [ɔ] or [a] in the previous member is often lost: [ɟɔto+din > ɟɔddin] 'as many days', [bɦalɔ+manuʃʲa > bɦalmanuʃʲa] 'one posing as a good man', [thana+dar > thandar] 'perambulating night constable', [maɦina+dar > maɦindar] 'servant, esp. helping in agriculture'. (ii) [i] or [u] is reduced to its anticipatory squeezed form: [ḍhẽki+ʃala > ḍɦẽⁱkʃal] 'place for the husking apparatus', [ɦãṛi+upaʃ > ɦãⁱr-upaʃ] 'starvation to the extent of not cooking', [gɦɔ̃ṭi+ṭɔ > gɦɔ̃ⁱṭṭɔ] 'the water vessel', [mɔ̃dɦu+dada > mɔ̃ᵘddada] 'elder brother or cousin named Madhu', [ũcu+kɔpali > ũckɔpali] 'woman with prominent forehead'. (iii) Final [ɛ] in [kɛnɛ] 'why' is lost before [na] 'not' and the [a] of the latter is replaced by [ɛ] in the syntactic combination [kɛnnɛ] 'why not'.

2. *Consonantal Assimilation*

(i) Final unvoiced stops, followed by voiced ones, are voiced, their aspiration, if any, disappearing simultaneously: [ḍak+gɦɔr > ḍaggɦɔr] 'post office', [thak ga > thag-ga] 'let it remain', [rakh ga > ragga] 'go, put it', [ni:c+ɟaⁱt > ni:ɟɟaⁱt] 'low caste', [ɦat dɦua > ɦaddɦua] 'washing the hands', [rɔth+dɛkha > rɔddɛkha] 'seeing the chariot', [path dɛkh > pad-dɛkh] 'see your way', [cup diʒɛ > cub-diʒɛ] 'keeping quiet,' [cup marʲe > cummarʲɛ] 'keeping mum', [bap+bɛṭa > babbɛṭa] 'father and son'.

(ii) Dental stops, followed by palatal ones, are palatalized: [raⁱt+cɔra > raⁱccɔra] 'bat', [ɦat+chaṛa > ɦacchaṛa] 'to let go', [lait+ɟamai > laⁱɟɟamai] 'husband of a grand-daughter', [bɔd+ɟat > bɔɟɟat] 'scoundrel'.

(iii) Final [ṛ] after a nasal vowel, when followed by a cerebral stop, is reduced to [ṇ], the nasalization of the previous vowel disappearing simultaneously: [bɦãṛ+ṭɔ > bɦaṇṭɔ] 'the pot', [mãṛ+ṭuku > maṇṭuku] 'the small amount of rice-scum', [mũṛ ṭhũⁱkchɛ > muṇ-ṭhũⁱkchɛ] 'he is striking his head'. But it changes to [ḍ], if the previous vowel is pure: [ḍeṛ+ṭa > ḍeḍ-ṭa] 'just one and a half', [bɔṛ+ṭɔ > bɔḍ-ṭɔ] 'the straw-rope', [bɔṛ (< bɔṛɔ) + ṭhakur > bɔḍ-ṭhakur] 'father-in-law's eldest brother'. When followed by [l], it is assimilated to the latter: [lɔṛ+lɔ̃ṛʲa > lɔllɔ̃ⁱṛʲa] 'pert', [luṛ+luṛi > lulluṛi] 'uvula'.

(iv) [r] is assimilated to a following palatal, cerebral or dental stop or [l]: [kɔr+chi > kɔ̃cchi] 'I am doing,' [du:r+ɟa > duɟɟa] 'go away', [caⁱr+ṭa > caⁱṭṭa] 'just four', [ʃir+ḍãṛa > ʃiḍḍãṛa] 'spine', [dɦɔr+to > dɦɔt-tɔ] 'just hold', [par+na (< S. *pāraṇā*) > panna] 'breaking one's fast', [mɔ̃ⁱr+lɔ (< mɔ̃rilɔ) > mɔ̃ⁱllɔ] 'he died'.

(v) [c] and [ṭh] are assimilated to a following [ʃ]: [pãc+ʃer > pãʃʃer] 'five seers', [ɟeṭh (< ɟeṭhi:)+ʃaʃ > ɟeʃʃaʃ] 'wife of father-in-law's elder brother.'

(vi) [t+ʃ] is often changed to [cch]: [ɦat+ʃan > ɦacchan, also ɦat-ʃan] 'sign made with the hand'; [li:t+ʃɔpone > licchɔpɔnɛ, also lit-ʃɔpɔnɛ] 'every day in dream'.

(vii) [n] preceding or following [l] is assimilated to it with simultaneous nasalization of the previous vowel: [ɟan+la (< Portu. *janella*) > ɟãlla] 'window', [an+lo > ãl-lo] 'bring, O girl', [kan+la^{i}ṛchɛ > kãl-la^{i}ṛchɛ] 'it is shaking its ears', [al+na > ãlla] 'clothes-horse', [bɛl+na > bɛ̃lla] 'rolling pin', [phɔl+na (H. phʌlana) > phɔ̃lla] 'so-and-so', [dɔl+na > dɔ̃lla] 'swing'. It may be more correct to say perhaps that in the sequence [l+n] there is first of all a metathesis and then assimilation.

§ 4. An illustrative passage in Manbhum dialect (E)

ʃɔkalɛ mu dɦu^{i}tɛ ɟã^{ĩ}ɟɛ̃ ba$^{m̃}$dɦɛr a^{i}ṛ^{j}ɛ mitɔn caṭhu^{i}ɟɟar chel^{j}a opur ʃɔ$^{m̃}$gɛ ɦɔṭat dɛkha. bɔ̀^{i}llɔm, "ɦɔ̀i, opu ɟe ɦe! kɔbɛ a^{i}lɛ? ɛddin kutha chilɛ?" bɔ̀^{i}llɛk, "ar, bɦai! ʃat gɦaṭɛr ɟɔl khã^{ĩ}ɟɛ̃ ka^{i}l ʃɔ̀^{i}ndɦaj gɦɔr phirɛchi. pɔ̀ṇḍitɛr chel^{j}a, ɟɔɟmanio kɔm nai: bɦa^{i}blɔm 'ikhɛnɛ tha^{i}klɛ—ɟai kɔ̀ri kɛnnɛ—mukkhu ɦɔ̀^{i}tei ɦɔbɛk. ɛkbar be^{i}r^{j}ãĩ dekhi'. bɦaṭpaṛa, nɔbɔddip, kaʃi gɦu^{i}r^{j}ɛ bɛakɔrɔn, ka^{i}bbɔ, ʃrĩti, næj tɔkkɔ pɔṛa ɦɔ̀^{i}lɔ. bedantɔo kichu pɔ̀^{i}ṛ^{j}echi. mɔnɛr mɔtɔn ɦɔ̀^{i}lɔ nai." bɔ̀^{i}llɔm, "ba, ba! bapɛr bɛṭa bɔṭɔ, ɦe! gã^{ĩ}ɟɛ̃ro nam kɔ̀^{i}rbar ɛkṭa lok ɦɔ̀^{i}lɛ. tɔ, ibarɛ gɦɔrei tha^{i}kchɔ tɔ?" u bɔ^{i}llɛk, "ɦɔ̃, bɦai. gɦɔrduar de^{i}ktɛ ɦɔbɛk tɔ! khet-khamaro kora cai. gãɟɛ̃i ɛkṭa ṭol khu^{i}lbɔ bɦabchi." ami bɔ̀^{i}llɔm, "beʃ, beʃ. tumar kɔtha ʃu^{i}n^{j}ɛ bɔṛɔ anɔndɔ ɦɔ̀^{i}lɔ, bɔ. ɛtɔdinɛ ɟã^{ĩ}ɟɛ̃ cɦel^{j}agular ɛkṭa gɔ̀ti ɦɔbɛk. amadɛr gɔ̀^{i}mda, rɔ̀^{u}gɦ^{w}a, cɔ$^{m̃}$da tɔ bɔ̃ɟɛ̃ ɟa^{i}tei bɔ̀^{i}ʃ^{j}echɛ. de^{i}kh^{j}ɔ, bɦai, uadɛr upɔr ɔlpɔ lɔɟɔr ra^{i}kh^{j}ɔ."

সকালে মু ধুইতে যাঁইয়েঁ বা'ধের আইড়্যে মিতন চাটুইজ্জার ছেল্যা ওপুর স'গে হটাৎ দেখা। বইল্লম, "হৈ, ওপু যে হে! কবে আইলে? এদ্দিন কুথা ছিলে?" বইল্লেক, "আর, ভাই! সাত ঘাটের জল খাঁইয়েঁ কাইল সইন্ধায় ঘর ফিরেছি। পণ্ডিতের ছেল্যা যজমানিও কম নাই: ভাইব্‌লম 'ইখেনে থাইক্‌লে—য'ই করি কেন্নে—মুকখু হইতেই হবেক। একবার বেইর‍্যাইঁ দেখি'। ভাটপাড়া, নবদ্দিপ, কাশি ঘুইর‍্যে বেআকরন, কাইব্ব, স্রিতি, ন্যায় তক্ক পড়া হইল। বেদান্তও কিছু প'ইড়্যেছি। মনের মতন হইল নাই।" বইল্লম, "বা, বা! বাপের বেটা বট, হে! গাঁয়েঁরও নাম ক'ইর্‌বার একটা লোক হইলে। ত, ইবারে ঘরেই থাইক্‌ছ ত?" উ বইল্লেক, "হঁ, ভাই। ঘরদুআর দেইক্‌তে হবেক ত! খেতখামারও করা চাই। গাঁয়েঁই একটা টোল খুইল্‌ব ভাব্‌ছি।" আমি বইল্লম, "বেশ, বেশ। তুমার কথা শুইন্যে বড় আনন্দ হইল, ব। এতদিনে যাঁইয়েঁ ছেল্যাগুলার একটা গতি হবেক। আমাদের গইম্‌দা, রউঘ্‌বা, চ'ন্দা ত বঁয়েঁ যাইতেই বইস্যেছে। দেইখ্যা, ভাই, উআদের উপর অল্প লজর রাইখ্যা।"

English Translation

Having gone to cleanse my mouth in the morning, I came upon Mitan[1] Chatterji's son Opu[1] on the bank of the pond. I said, "Why, it is surely Opu! When did you come? Where have you been so long?" He said, "Don't ask, brother! Having tasted water from seven landing-places[2], I returned home last evening. Son of a Pandit, with the clientele[3] not so inconsiderable, I thought: 'If I remain here, whatever I do, I am sure to become a dunce. Let me just go out and see.' Having wandered through Bhāṭpaṛa, Nabadvīp, (and) Kāśī, I studied grammar, literature, law, and, finally, logic. I have had also a smattering of the Vedānta. It didn't come up to what I had intended."[4] I said, "Bravo! A chip of the old block, indeed! The village, too, will find in you somebody worth mentioning. So then, you are going to stay home now, aren't you?" He said, "Oh yes, brother. I have to look after the homestead[5], haven't I! The field and the threshing floor, too, have to be attended to. I am thinking of opening a Sanskrit school in this very village." I said, "Oh, very good! It gives me great pleasure to listen to your words, friend. Now, after so many days there will be some sort of salvation for the children. Our Ga^{i}mdā[6], Ra^{u}gh^{v}ā[6], (and) Ca$^{\dot{m}}$dā[6], I have to admit, are nearly gone to the dogs. You will remember, brother—won't you?—to keep an eye on them."

---

1 Endearing nicknames for Mṛtyuñjay and Upendra respectively.
2 That is 'having diverse experiences in various places.'
3 *I.e.*, the lay disciples.
4 Lit., 'It did not become like (what I had in my) mind.'
5 Lit., 'home and door.'
6 Negligent nicknames respectively for Gobinda, Raghu and Candra.

CHAPTER 7

Linguistic Aberrations in Kālidāsa's Writings

I. Preliminary remarks

§ 1. Kālidāsa appears to have succeeded, as very few other great poets of the world have done, in giving vocal expression to his noblest thoughts and sublimest experience of aesthetic pleasures by means of the simplest language conceivable for such a purpose. He may be said, relatively speaking, to have employed the language just as he found it, without taking any great liberty with it that is incompatible with its idiom. Offences against language in the shape of grammatical solecisms, fanciful meanings arbitrarily planted on words otherwise known, and coinage of words foreign to the idiom of the language,—faults which are not infrequent in writers of any great length, are comparatively rare in Kālidāsa. These find in most cases an obvious explanation either in having historical precedents or parallels or in being really no more than a resourceful application of the inherent tendencies. We propose to discuss in this paper some of these aberrations, apparent or real, as a contribution towards a correct estimate of the poetical genius of this noblest poet of ancient India.

§ 2. Without entering into controversies here, we accept with the majority of scholars the following works attributed to Kālidāsa as genuine : four poems,—(1) Ṛtusaṁhāra (RS.), (2) Meghadūta (MD.), (3) Kumārasambhava I—VIII (K.), and (4) Raghuvaṁśa (R.), and three dramas,—(5) Mālavikāgnimitra (M.), (6) Vikramorvaśīya (V.), and (7) Abhijñā-

* First published in *The Journal of the Bihar Research Society*, vol. XXXVI, pts. 3-4, 1951, pp. 1-40.

naśakuntala (Ś.).[1] For convenience' sake references are made here to the Nirṇayasāgara Press editions, unless otherwise stated.

II. Phonology

§ 3. Phonetic aberrations are few in Kālidāsa. Of these mention may be first of three cases of shortening of vowels : (1) *kākali* <°*lī* in RS. 1.8, *savallakīkākaligītānisvanair vibodhyate supta ivā 'dya manmathaḥ.* MW. mentions another occurrence of the form in the Kathāsaritsāgara and Veṅkaṭāchārya in Kale's edition of RS. quotes from Abhinanda : *sādhū 'ditaṁ kākalibhiḥ kulīnaiḥ*, while ŚK. cites the authority of Bharata's commentary on AMARA. The contention of the commentator Maṇirāma that the stem is *kākalin* (i.e., *kākalī+in*) is untenable, *vide*

1. The **other abbreviations** used are: AMARA=Amarakoṣa with Kṣīrasvāmin's comm., Poona 1941.—AV.=Atharvaveda.—BHAG.=Bhāgavatapurāṇa, ed. Pañchānana Tarkaratna, Calcutta, San 1334.—BHĀRAVI=Kirātārjunīya of Bhāravi.—BHATTI=Bhaṭṭikāvya, Chhātra Pustakālaya, Calcutta 1928, and N. S. Press, Bombay 1920.—BR.=Sanskrit Wörterbuch by Böhtlingk and Roth.—DHĀTU.=Mādhavīyadhātuvṛtti, Kashi Sanskrit Series, Benares 1935.—Dv.=Durghaṭavṛtti of Śaraṇadeva, ed. T. Gaṇapatī Śāstrī, Trivandrum 1909.—GRASS.=Wörterbuch zum Rigveda by H. Grassmann, Leipzig 1873.—JBORS=Journal of the Bihar and Orissa Research Society.—KK.=Kavikalpadruma of Vopadeva, ed. J. Vidyāsāgara, Calcutta 1904.—MANU=Manusaṁhitā.—MĀGHA=Śiśupālavadha of Māgha.—MW.=A Sanskrit English Dictionary by Sir M. Monier-Williams, Oxford 1899.—P.=Pāṇini.—RĀM.=Rāmāyaṇa, N. S. Press, Bombay Śāka 1824.—RV.=Ṛgveda.—SIDDH.=Siddhāntakaumudī of Bhaṭṭoji Dīkṣita with the Tattvabodhinī commentary, N. S. Press, Bombay 1915.—ŚK.=Śabdakalpadruma of Rādhākāntadeva, ed. K. Kāvyaviśārada, Calcutta Śaka 1850.—Ss.=Saṁkṣiptasāravyākaraṇa of Kramadīśvara with Jumaranandin's Vṛtti and Goyīchandra's Tīkā, ed. Śyāmācharaṇa Kaviratna, Calcutta San 1308.—SPEYER=Vedische und Sanskrit-Syntax by J. S. Speyer, Strassburg 1896.—TATTVA.=Tattvabodhinī of Jñānendra Sarasvatī on Siddh.—VĀMANA=Kāvyālaṁkārasūtravṛtti of Vāmana, ed. J. Vidyāsāgara, Calcutta 1922.—VĀRT.=Vārtikas of Kātyāyana on Pāṇini's Grammar.—VS.=Vājasaneyisaṁhitā.—WACKERNAGEL=Altindische Grammatik by J. Wackernagel, Vol. I, (1896), II. 1 (1905), and III (1930), Göttingen.—WHITNEY=A Sanskrit Grammar by W. D. Whitney, Leipzig 1896 (1913).

P. 5.2.115—117. (2) *Dūti* <°*tī*, K. 4. 16 ; R. 18. 53 ; 19. 18, 23, 33 ; V. 4. 25. Mallinātha twice (K. 4. 16 ; R. 19. 23) offers the explanation, *ṅībantasyā 'pi dūtīśabdasya chhandobhaṅgabhayād dhrasvaḥ*, while Raṅganātha (on V. 4. 25) and ŚK. cite respectively Rūpachintāmaṇi and Śabdaratnāvalī as authorities for the variant. BR. record an instance from the Harivaṁśa and MW. gives *dūtī* or °*ti* as f. of *dūta*. The attempt of Ujjvaladatta on Uṇādisūtra 4. 179 to explain it as a distinct formation with the suffix *ti* is futile, since the word has in every instance reference to a female messenger. Cf., in this connection, *nāḍi* for *nāḍī* in BHĀG. 2. 10. 29, *āditsor annapānānām āsan kukṣyantranāḍayaḥ*, and the compounds containing it (MW.). (3) *Vaidehibandhu* (<°*hī* + *bandhu*) in R. 14. 33, *vaidehibandhor hṛdayaṁ vidadre*. Mallinātha explains this with reference to *ṅyāpoḥ saṁjñāchhandasor bahulam*, P. 6. 3. 63. The point is whether it can be treated as a *saṁjñā*. It certainly does not satisfy the criterion laid down in Kāśikā 2. 1. 44, *saṁjñā samudayopādhiḥ* / *tena nityasamāsa evā 'yaṁ, na hi vākyena saṁjñā gamyate* /, like *Kālidāsa*, *Revatiputra*, etc., since the expounded form *vaidehyāḥ bandhuḥ* would give exactly the same meaning. Evidently, Kālidāsa took the view that as the word, compounded or otherwise, applies to Rāma alone, it might be treated as his distinctive appellation.

§ 4. There is one case of *y*>*iy* after vowel Sandhi in the word *triyambakaṁ* in K.3.44, *triyambakaṁ saṁyaminaṁ dadarśa*. This is an archaism, common in the Vedas (cf. P. 6. 4. 77 VĀRT.) and quotable also from the Rāmāyaṇa (MW.). BHĀG. 11. 28. 20 also presents *triyavastha*. It may be mentioned in this connection that DV. p. 126 records a reading *mahā̂ hi yatnas tava devadārau* for R. 2. 56 **b**, which, if genuine, would present another instance of Vedicism, viz., the peculiar Sandhi between *mahān* and *hi*.

§ 5. The passage R.6.77, *ārūḍham adrīn udadhīn vitīrṇaṁ bhujaṅgamānāṁ vasatiṁ praviṣṭam* / *ūrdhvaṁ gataṁ yasya na cā 'nubandhi yaśaḥ parichchhettum iyattayā 'lam* //, where Mallinātha explains *vitīrṇam* as *avagāḍham*, raises a shrewd suspicion that probably *vitīrṇam* here is a wrong reading for *vatīrṇam*, a case of loss of the initial vowel of *ava*. For a similar loss in *vagāhya*, *vatamsa*, *vadānya*, *valepana*, *vaṣṭabhya* and *vekṣaṇa* cf. WHITNEY §1087.a and for that in *vatokā* cf. MW., *s.v.* *Vitīrṇa* in the sense given by Mallinātha is untraceable anywhere else. If, on the other hand, it is permissible here to take it in the sense of 'crossed', then the sense itself archaic, i.e., Vedic. The commentator Nārāyaṇa (Trivandrum ed.) reads *pratīrṇam* and explains *prakarṣeṇa tīrṇam*.

§ 6. There are two cases of *ḍ* being considered identical with *l* : one in *jaḍa* > *jala* in R.9.46, *anayad āsanarajjuparigrahe bhujalatāṁ jalatām abalājanaḥ*, and the other in *tāḍa* > *tāla* in the word *karṇatāla* occurring in R.7.39 ; 9.71, etc. This treatment of the two sounds, which is frequent in classical Sanskrit and which, as based on a Prakritic tendency of *ṭ*>*ḍ*>*ḷ*, is traceable even in the Vedas (*vide* JBORS, XVII, p. 37 ; WACKERNAGEL § 194), is remarkable only on account of its rarity in Kālidāsa.

III. Morphology

A. NOMINAL

Primary Suffixes (Kṛt)

§ 7. There are two instances of *ach* for *ghañ* impugned by commentators as violating P.3.3.40, *hastādāne cher asteye* : (1) *avachaya* for °*chāya* in M. 4. $\frac{6}{7}$, *kusumāvachayavyagrahastā*, and Ś.4. $\frac{0}{1}$, *tataḥ praviśataḥ kusumāvachayaṁ nāṭayantyau sakhyau*, and (2) *uchchaya* for *uchchāya* in K.3.61, *tasyāḥ sakhībhyāṁ praṇipātapūrvaṁ svahastalūnaḥ śiśirātyayasya / vyakīryata tryambakapādamūle puṣpochchayaḥ pallavabhaṅgabhinnaḥ //*. Of these, the authenticity of the first, since it appears only in prose sentences, may be questioned, while the second, owing to the presence of a separate epithet *svahastalūnaḥ*, 'culled with one's own hands', might have been used in the sense of 'collection' or 'multitude' and not of 'culling'. The Kāśikā (Kashi Sanskrit Series edition) on P.3.3.40 has the Vārtika, *uchchayasya pratiṣedho vaktavyaḥ*, which is not found in all the MSS. and of which the Siddhāntakaumudī takes no notice. Mallinātha on K. 3. 61 cites Vallabha's caustic remarks on the proverbial carelessness of poets, but MW. records only *avachaya* and *uchchaya* and not *avachāya* or *uchchāya*. Mention may be made in this connection of the Vṛddhi of the root-vowel in the word *viśrāma* in Ś.2.6, *viśrāmaṁ labhatām idaṁ cha śithilajyābandham asmaddhanuḥ*, as violating P.7.3.34, *no 'dātto-padeśasya māntasyā 'nāchameḥ*. The form, however, is well-established in use from the Mahābhārata downwards (cf. MW.) and grammarians like Kramadīśvara (1.6) have felt themselves called upon to sanction optional Vṛddhi in √*śram*, preceded by *vi*, in similar situations. Ś.5.$\frac{3}{4}$, on the other hand, has *athavā 'viśramo 'yaṁ lokatantrādhikāraḥ*.

§ 8. There are at least five instances of *kartari kta* after transitive roots : (1) *ādṛta* in K.7.30, *prasādhanaṁ mātṛbhir ādṛtābhir nyastaṁ purastāt puraśāsanasya* ; in ibid. 8.47, *brahma gūḍham abhisandhyam ādṛtāḥ śuddhaye vidhivido gṛṇanty amī* ; and in R.13.72, *ity ādṛtena kathitau raghunandanena* ; (2) *kānta* in M. 4.1, *kuryāt kāntaṁ manasijatarur māṁ rasajñaṁ phalasya* ; (3) *niśchita* in R.12.83, *niryayāv atha paulastyaḥ punar yuddhāya mandirāt / arāvaṇam arāmaṁ vā jagad adye 'ti niśchitaḥ //* ; (4) *pīta* in R. 2.1, *vanāya pītapratibaddhavatsāṁ yaśodhano dhenum ṛṣer mumocha*, and and Ś.4.8, *pātuṁ na prathamaṁ vyavasyati jalaṁ yusmāsv apīteṣu yā* ; and (5) *prajalpitā* in K. 1. 45, *svareṇa tasyām amṛtasrute 'va prajalpitāyām abhijātavāchi / apy anyapuṣṭā pratikūlaśabadā śrotur vitantrīr iva tāḍyamānā //*. Of these the last one makes much better sense, if taken as derived according to P.3.4.71, *ādikarmaṇi ktaḥ kartari cha.* The other four, with plenty of parallel and actual uses in the whole literature, must be looked upon as based on the temporary assumption of intransitiveness by the roots in accordance with the Kārikā, *dhātor arthāntare vṛtte dhātvartheno 'pasaṁgrahāt / prasiddher avivakṣātaḥ karmaṇo 'karmikā kriyā //*, and really amount to a happy exploitation of the resources of the language. This last remark applies with equal force to the case of *puraskṛtaḥ satām* in R. 3.41, where the spirit of *matibuddhipūjārthebhyaś cha*, P. 3.2.188, if not the letter, is adhered to.

§ 9. Another formation with *kta*, viz., *nitānta* in K. 3. 4, *nitāntadīrghair janitā tapobhiḥ*, [used also in *ibid.* 7.17 ; R. 3.8 ; 14.43 ; etc.] has evoked comment from Śaraṇadeva, DV. p. 103, on the assumption that it is derived from √*tan* and therefore violates P.6.4.37, *anudāttopadeśavanatitanotyādīnām anunāsikalopo jhali kṅiti.* He passes it with the remark '*tanoter ādhṛṣīvasya rūpam*', but Kṣīrasvāmin on AMARA I.1.67 and MW. are evidently right in tracing it to √*tam*. The same critic on the same page [in unison with SS.-VṚTTI 2. 282] questions the validity of the retention of *n* also in *avamanya* in K. 5. 53., *chaturdigīśān avamanya māninī*, against P. 6.4.38, *vā lyapi*, as clarified by the Kāśikā, '*vyavasthitavibhāṣā ce'yam / tena makārāntānāṁ vikalpo bhavati / anyatra nityam eva lopaḥ /*', and suggests '*man stambhe*'—not '*man jñāne*'—as the root concerned and, alternatively, *avamatya* as the correct reading. MW., however, records the form as occurring several times in the Mahābhārata.

§ 10. There are at least four cases of apparent violation of P.3.4.21, *samānakartṛkayoḥ pūrvakāle* : (1) K. 4. 17, *suratāni cha tāni te rahaḥ smara saṁsmṛtya na śāntir asti me* ; (2) R.1.77, *avajānāsi māṁ yasmād atas te na bhaviṣyati / matprasūtim anārādhya praje 'ti tvāṁ śaśāpa sā //*; (3) R.4.2, *dilīpānantaraṁ rājye taṁ niśamya pratiṣṭhitam / pūrvaṁ pradhūmito rājñāṁ hṛdaye 'gnir ivo 'tthitaḥ //* ; and (4) Ś. 2.9, *strīratnasṛṣṭir aparā pratibhāti sā me dhātur vibhutvam anuchintya vapuś cha tasyāḥ.* But instances of this kind, especially when the subject of the gerund is in the genitive case in relation to that of the finite verb, are so common in the whole history of the language [*vide* WHITNEY § 994. **c**. and **e**.] that either the rule or its interpretation has got to be modified. SS. 3. 403 actually sanctions such cases in unison with commentators in general.

§ 11. The formation of *pralobhya* in Ś. 7. 16, *pralobhyavastupraṇayaprasārito vibhāti jālagrathitāṅguliḥ karaḥ*, as also that of the more familiar *lobhanīya* in R.6.58, *pralobhitā 'py ākṛtilobhanīyā vidarbharājāvarajā tayai 'vam / tasmād apāvartata dūrakṛṣṭā nītye 'va lakṣmīḥ pratikūladaivāt //*, appears to have reference to the Sampradāna or the Adhikaraṇa [scil., *pralubhyati asmai asmin ve'ti* and *lubhyati asmai* etc.] of the original root or to the Kartṛ or the Karaṇa of its causative form in accordance with P.3.3.113, *kṛtyalyuṭo bahulam.* Aruṇagirinātha and Nārāyaṇa render *lobhanīya* in R. with *spṛhaṇīya,* but Mallinātha with *ākarṣaṇīya,* suggesting that it has a passive reference. The same word appearing in Bhaṭṭikāvya 2. 13, *digvyāpinīr lochanalobhanīyāḥ,* has been explained by Mallinātha as well as Jayamaṅgala as derived with *kartari anīya* added to *√lobhi.* Another formation with *ya,* viz., *āśāsya* in R. 4. 44; M. 5. 20, etc., a form well-established in literature, has been taken exception to by Śaraṇadeva, DV. p. 103, on the ground that it violates P. 6. 4. 34, *śāsa id aṅhaloḥ,* and should have been *āśiṣya,* and then justified with a highly artificial and unconvincing explanation. Sāyaṇa in DHĀTU. 2. 12 appears to have rightly shown that the Sūtra in question has *śāsu anuśiṣṭau* in purview and can have no reference to *āṅaḥ śāsu ichchhāyām.*

§ 12. Two uses of *śatṛ* deserve notice. (1) In K. 4. 12, *nayanāny aruṇāni ghūrṇayan vachanāni skhalayan pade pade / asati tvayi vāruṇīmadaḥ pramadānām adhunā viḍambanā //* , the derivative is made to agree with a word that has taken the first case-ending against P. 3. 2. 124, *laṭaḥ śatṛśānachāv aprathamāsamānādhikaraṇe.* Restricted use of this nature has been sanctioned by grammarians, cf. Kāśikā, l.c., *laḍ iti vartamāne punar laḍgrahaṇam adhikavidhānārtham / kvachit prathamāsamānādhikaraṇe 'pi bhavati / san brāhmaṇaḥ / asti brāhmaṇaḥ / ....kechid vibhāṣāgrahaṇam anuvartayanti, 'nanvor vibhāṣā' iti / ....tatra yathādarśanaṁ prayogā netavyāḥ.* A similar use is found also in Kirātārjunīya 1. 8, *samunnayan bhūtim anāryasaṅgamād varaṁ virodho 'pi samaṁ mahātmabhiḥ.* (2) V.1.9, *āvirbhūte śaśini tamasā richyamāne 'va rātrir naiśasyā 'rchir hutabhuja iva chchhinnabhūyiṣṭhadhūmā / mohenā 'ntar varatanur iyaṁ lakṣyate muchyamānā gaṅgā rodhaḥpatanakaluṣā gachchhatī 'va prasādam //*, presents the form *gachchhatī* without *num;* and the commentator Raṅganātha vainly tries to dismiss it as a form in Laṭ. VĀMANA 5. 2. 80, citing '*harati hi vanarājir gachchhatī śyāmabhāvam*', impugns such forms, while WHITNEY § 449.c. notes, 'exceptions to this rule are now and then met with, even from the earliest period', and cites instances in support. RĀM. 2. 32. 8 also has '*prayachchhati sakhī tubhyaṁ bhāryāyai gachchhatī vanam*'.

§ 13. In *kāmayāna*, R.19.50, *rājayakṣmaparihānir āyayau kāmayānasamavasthayā tulām*, and Ś. 3. ½, *tataḥ praviśati kāmayānāvastho rājā*, we have an instance of violation of P. 7. 2. 82, *āne muk*, which has been conditionally passed by VĀMANA 5. 2. 83, *kāmayānaśabdaḥ siddho 'nādiś chet*. MW. records its occurrence in the Mahābhārata and BHĀG. 10. 47. 17, *striyam akṛta virūpāṁ strījitaḥ kāmayānām* [cf. also RĀM. 3. 55. 2, *sa chintayāno vaidehīm*], while WHITNEY § 1043. **f**. notes : "But decidedly more common in the epics and later is one formed with *āna* : e.g. *kāmayāna*, *cintayāna*, *pālayāna*, *vedayāna*."

Secondary Suffixes (Taddhita)

§ 14. There are two cases of violation of P. 4. 3. 11, *kālāṭ ṭhañ*, impugned by VĀMANA 5. 2. 50 and 51 : (1) *śārvara* in K. 8. 58, *śārvarasya tamaso niṣiddhaye*, and (2) *śāśvata* in K. 2. 15, *tvam eva havyaṁ hotā cha bhojyaṁ bhoktā cha śāśvataḥ*, and R. 14. 14, *sā bibhratī śāśvatam aṅgarāgam*, etc., of which the second one he justifies on the ground of usage. Śaraṇadeva, DV. p. 81, justifies both by means of a *yogavibhāga*. The dictionaries, however, show that *śāśvata* is as old as the Vedas and has been in frequent use throughout the history of the language, while *śārvara* is the form that has been preferred by the best writers as against *śārvarika*, which is rare. *Ākālikī* in K. 3. 34, *tapasvinaḥ sthānuvanaukasas tām ākālikīṁ vīkṣya madhupravṛttim*, evidently presents a divergence of meaning not contemplated in P. 5. 1. 114, *ākālikaḍ ādyantavachane*, in spite of the fact that the commentators have all (deliberately ?) ignored it. There seems to be little doubt that the meaning here is 'untimely', not 'ephemeral' or 'momentary' as the commentators would have it. BR. and MW. record a similar use from the Mṛchchhaṭika, *ākālikaṁ sapadi durdinam*. There is also a third meaning of the word, viz., 'lasting until the same time on the following day', in which it has been used in the Kalpasūtras and MANU 4. 103 and 105, and MW. is right in deriving it from *ākālam* [cf. also SS. 4. 729 Vṛtti]. The word *ādyantavachane* in Pāṇini's rule might have reference to the same [cf. the second meaning given in SIDDH.], or, if his scholiasts are right, the meaning attributed may be a further development of the other. In any case Kālidāsa's *ākālikī* appears to be a totally different word, derived from *akāla*, as rightly pointed out by MW. On the other hand, *prāsthānika* in R. 2. 70, *prāsthānikaṁ svastyayanaṁ prayujya*, which also falls in the purview of P. 4. 3. 11, accords well with the remark in the Kāśikā, '*yathākathañchid guṇavṛttyā 'pi kāle vartamānāt pratyaya iṣyate*, and really amounts to a resourceful application of the latent powers of the language. [Cf. in this connection, as a further illustration of the point, also the use of *kakudmat* in R. 4. 22, *drumavat* in R. 9. 26, *sparśavat* in K. 1.55, and *hastavat* in R. 7. 45 in agreement with the Kārikā, *bhūmanindāpraśaṁsāsu nityayoge 'tiśāyane / sambandhe 'stivivakṣāyāṁ bhavanti matubādayaḥ //*].

§ 15. *Audhasya* in R. 2. 66, *audhasyam ichchhāmi tavo 'pabhoktum*, in the Nirṇayasāgara Press edition may be no more than a MS. corruption for *ūdhasya*, which Mallinātha and MW. appear to read. It is interesting, however, to note that all the MSS. of the Paryāyamuktāvalī (JBRS, Vol. XXXI) at 21. 36 read the former as a synonym for 'milk', while MW. records a form *audhasa* from the Bhāgavata-purāṇa.

§ 16. DV., SIDDH., and SS.-VṚTTI 4.222 question the use of *pāṇḍyāḥ* in R. 4. 49, *tasyām eva raghoḥ pāṇḍyāḥ pratāpaṁ na viṣehire*, as violating P. 2. 4. 62, *tadrājasya bahuṣu tenai 'vā 'striyām*, but the former two also justify it with reference to P. 4. 4. 98, *tatra sādhuḥ*. Another case in point is *kauravyāḥ paśavaḥ* in Veṇīsaṁhāra 1. 25. Similarly the Siddhāntakaumudī would prefer to read *kambojāḥ* for *kāmbojāḥ* in R. 4. 69, *kāmbojāḥ samare soḍhuṁ tasya vīryam anīśvarāḥ*, as the latter apparently goes against P. 4. 1. 175, *kambojāl luk*.

Composition (Samāsa)

§ 17. A few peculiarities of composition (or want of it, where expected) call for notice. *Mandaṁ mandam* in MD. 1. 9, *mandaṁ mandaṁ nudati pavanaś chā 'nukūlo yathā tvām*, has been the target of much criticism as violating P. 8. 1. 12, *prakāre guṇavachanasya*, and has been justified by VĀMANA 5. 2. 87 and Mallinātha with reference to *vīpsā*. Others would avoid the issue by taking one *mandaṁ* as an adverb and the other as an adjective qualifying *tvām*. It appears, however, that *ābhīkṣṇya* or frequentation of the verb *nudati* together with its adverb is intended and the adverb only is effectively repeated instead of both. *Prakāra* (=*sādṛśya*, 'approach') is certainly not intended, inasmuch as instead of improving the meaning it would rather mar the effect. On the other hand, *vīpsā* (cf. TATTVA. on 2147), rather than *ādhikya* (Vallabha) or *nityārtha* (Mallinātha), appears to be illustrated in MD. 1. 13, *khinnaḥ khinnaḥ śikhariṣu padaṁ nyasya gantāsi yatra kṣīṇaḥ kṣīṇaḥ parilaghu payaḥ srotasāṁ cho 'payujya*, 'along which you will go, setting foot on the mountains **whenever you are fatigued** and feeding on the very light water of the streams **whenever you are debilitated**'. When, however, *prakāra* is really intended, the poet does use the compound form as in MD. 1. 14, *dṛṣṭotsāhaś chakitachakitaṁ mugdhasiddhāṅganābhiḥ*, and 2. 45, *sarvāvasthāsv ahar api kathaṁ mandamandātapaṁ syāt*, or RS. 2. 22, *mṛdupavanavidhūtair mandamandaṁ chalabdhiḥ*, and 5. 14, *stanabharaparikhedān mandamandaṁ vrajantyaḥ*.

§ 18. Quite a different problem is presented by *duḥkhaduḥkha* in MD. 2. 30, *śayyotsaṅge nihitam asakṛd duḥkhduḥkhena gātram*, inasmuch as it does not appear to be covered by any rule of Pāṇini. Since *duḥkha* is not an adjective (*guṇavachana*) here, P. 8. 1. 12 can (in spite of Mallinātha) hardly apply. Is it then just analogous in form, although opposite in sense, to *priyapriya* and *sukhasukha* sanctioned in P. 8. 1. 13, *akṛchchhre priyasukhayor ānulomye* ? Or is it in accordance with the Vārtika, *ādhikye dve bhavataḥ*, cited by Śaraṇadeva in DV. p. 122, but challenged by Jñānendra Sarasvatī on SIDDH. 2147 ? Vallabha is also of this latter view and remarks on MD. 1. 13, *ādhikye cha dvitvam āmreḍitam iti mahatyā saṁjñayā jñāpitam*. At all events, we have also in BHĀG. 11. 11. 19, *vittaṁ tva 'tīrthīkṛtam aṅga vāchaṁ hīnāṁ mayā rakṣati duḥkhaduḥkhī*.

§ 19. P. 2. 1. 65 is apparently violated (so Mallināthā on MD.) in MD. 1. 23, *katipayadinasthāyihaṁsā daśārṇāḥ*, and Ś. 2. $\frac{15}{16}$ *tat katipayarātraṁ sārathidvitīyena bhavatā sanāthīkriyatām āśramaḥ*. But it would appear from the examples given under this Sūtra, viz., *dadhikatipayam* and *udaśvitkatipayam*, when considered along with P. 2. 3. 33, *karaṇe cha stokālpakatipayasyā 'sattvavachanasya*, that the word *katipaya* is probably intended to be taken in a quantitative sense, 'a little' or 'some', and not in a numerical sense, 'several' or 'a few'.

§ 20. A suffix having the sense of *matup* after a Karmadhāraya, where a Bahuvrīhi without the suffix would serve the purpose all right, is impugned by grammarians. There are at least three instances of this apparent solecism in Kālidāsa : (i) K. 5. 16, *tvaguttarāsaṅgavatīm*, (ii) MD. 1. 11, *bisakisalayachchhedapātheyavantaḥ*, and (iii) R. 4. 44, *phalavatpūgamālinā*. These have been cited and supported in DV. in accordance with the view of some grammarians, *ekīyamate tat / ye tu lāghavārthaṁ nā 'numanyante tanmatenai 'te prayogāḥ*. Mallinātha (also Vallabha, alternatively, on MD.), however, expounds the first two as cases of Tṛtīyā-samāsa with the adjectives with *matup*.

§ 21. There are several instances of Samāsa with the particle *na* as the first member without the expected changes according to P. 6. 3. 73 and 74 : *na-prabuddhāṁ na-suptām* in MD. 2. 27 ; *nātipramanāḥ* in R. 3. 67, *nātiśītoṣṇaḥ* in 4. 8, *nātyāyatakṛṣṭaśārṅgaḥ* in 5. 50, and *nākṣikampam* in 15. 67 ; *nātibhinne* in Ś. 2.$\frac{13}{14}$; etc. This particle, they say, is different from *nañ* which is in the purview of Pāṇini's rule, and, in any case, instances of a similar use that may be cited from literature are almost innumerable (see MW.).

§ 22. There are a few cases where the compounded *nañ* is virtually used in the sense of *vinā*: (i) K. 6. 12, *tām agauravabhedena munīṁś cā 'paśyad īśvaraḥ* ; (ii) ibid. 6. 41, *gṛhayantrapatākāśrīr apaurādaranirmitā* ; (iii) R. 13. 50, *apuṣpaliṅgāt phalabandhivṛkṣam* ; and (iv) ibid. 14. 5, *svargapratiṣṭhasya guror mahiṣyāv abhaktibhedena vadhūr vavande*. These are really cases of the particle being compounded when it is connected directly with the verb and the emphasis is laid on negation rather than affirmation (*prasajya-pratiṣedha*). To these two more definite cases may be added: (i) K. 6.63, *brūta yenā 'tra vo kāryam anāsthā bāhyavastuṣu*, and (ii) R. 18. 7, *mṛgair ajaryaṁ jaraso 'padiṣṭam adehabandhāya punar babandha*. Although Samāsa in *prasajyapratiṣedha* is not generally favoured by grammarians, the remarks of Goyīchandra on SS. 7. 1 and 2 are worthy of note : '*agamakatvaṁ hi samāsa-niṣedhakāraṇam, na tu kriyayā saha sambandhaḥ / atra* (i.e. in *asūryampaśyā*) *tu gamakatvāt samāso bhavaty eva*'.

§ 23. There is one case of Dvandva with a neuter singular ending , viz., *vadhūvaram* in K. 7. 78 and Ś. 5. 15, which is justifiable only on the ground, '*sarvo dvandvo vibhāṣayai 'kavad bhavati*', Jumaranandin on SS. 7. 355 and the Kāśikā on P. 2. 4. 11, *gavāśvaprabhṛtīni cha*, sanction a good many such cases (without, however, including the one in question), e.g., *dāsīmāṇavakam, putrapautram, strīkumāram*, etc. Cf. also WACKERNAGEL II. 1, pp. 162—164.

§ 24. Several instances of Vyadhikaraṇa Bahuvrīhi, which is generally viewed with disapprobation by grammarians, are noticeable : *apāṅganetrā* in V. 1. 18 ; *aśrumukha*-in K. 6.92 ; R. 8. 13 ; 15. 66 ; *āsavagandhagarbhaiḥ* in R. 7. 11 ; *gaganagatayaḥ* in MD. 1. 46 ; *guṇodayam* in R. 4. 20 ; *jyotsnāntarāṇi* in K. 1. 25 ; *bāhuvimardaniṣṭhau* in R. 7. 52 ; *magadhapratiṣṭhaḥ* in R. 6. 21 ; *lalāṭodayam* in R. 1. 83 ; *himagarbhaiḥ* in Ś. 3. 3, etc. Such cases are so common in literature that they require no comment, and VĀMANA at 5. 2. 19 has felt himself compelled to sanction some, '*avarjyo bahuvrīhir vyadhikaraṇo janmādyuttarapadaḥ*'. The same author at 5. 2. 71 takes exception to the loss of the locative ending after the first member in *apāṅganetrā* as going against P. 6. 3. 12, *amūrdhamastakāt svāṅgād akāme*. The commentator Raṅganātha avoids the issue by supposing a Madhyamapada-lopi-Bahuvrīhi. But it is possible that *netra* is used here in the sense of 'leader' [*vide* ŚK. and MW.] and there is really a Samānādhikaraṇa Bahuvrīhi.

§ 25. The violation of P. 6. 3. 34, seen in the disappearance of the feminine ending before *bhakti* in *dṛḍhabhakti* in R. 12. 19, *dṛṣṭabhakti* in MD. 1. 36, *mānyabhakti* in K. 8. 77, and *vidita-bhakti* in Ś. 1. $\frac{1}{1}\frac{2}{3}$, seems to be only apparent, not real. For, as Bhojarāja (cited by Mallinātha on R. 12. 19 and MD. 1. 36) holds, the word *bhakti* of the *priyādigaṇa* means 'an object of devotion' as in P. 4. 3. 95 and not 'devotion', in which Kālidāsa has used it in all these cases. This explanation is accepted also by WACKERNAGEL II.1, p.52, as against the other one of holding the first member *sāmānye napuṁsakam*, given by some equally eminent grammarians. *Dṛḍhabhakti* appears also in RĀM. 2. 1. 24.

§ 26. A few anomalous formations of a slightly different nature deserve mention here : (i) *Anumeyaśobhin* in K. 1. 37, *etāvatā nanv anumeyaśobhi kāñchīguṇasthānam aninditāyāḥ*, is expounded by VĀMANA 5. 2. 59 and Mallinātha as *anumeyaṁ śobhitvam asya*. They would then drop the suffix *tva* in accordance with the dictum, *uktārthānām aprayogaḥ*, as in the words *nirākulam*, *sadhīram*, etc. MW. would admit for this case a word *śobhin*= *śobhā*. It seems easier, however, to relegate it to the to the class of Karmadhāraya formations, followed by a suffix having the sense of *maṭup*, already discussed in § 20.

(ii) *Utpakṣmala* in V.2.13, *utpakṣmalaṁ mama sakhe madirekṣaṇāyās tasyāḥ samāgatam ivā 'nanam ānanena*, presents a similar difficulty. Cf. the regular *utpakṣman* used by the poet in Ś. 4. 14.

(iii) *Rātrindivam*, formed, according to the commentators of P. 5. 4. 77, with a locative sense, has been treated as an ordinary Dvandva in R.17.49, *rātrindivavibhāgeṣu yad ādiṣṭaṁ mahīkṣitām*, and K. 2. 8, *svakālaparimāṇena vyastarātrindivasya te*. Cf. AMARA I.3.14, *samarātrindive kāle viṣuvad viṣuvaṁ cha tat*.

(iv) *Yathāpurva* (=*yathābhūtaḥ pūrvaṁ*, Mallinātha on R.12.88) in 12. 48, *tais trayāṇāṁ śitair vāṇair yathāpūrvaviśuddhibhiḥ*, together with its negative *ayathāpūrva* in R. 12. 88, *bhujamūrdhorubāhulyād eko 'pi dhanadānujaḥ | dadṛśe hy ayathāpūrvo mātṛvaṁśa iva sthitaḥ ||*, is paralleled by BHĀG 1.14.23, *taṁ pādayor nipatitam ayathāpūrvam āturam*. *Yathāpūrvatva* is cited by MW. from the Kāṭhaka-Saṁhitā 27.5, *iḍai 'va pūrvo 'pahūyā yajñasya yathāpūrvatvāya*.

§ 27. *Sugandhi* in R. 4. 45, *sa sainyaparibhogeṇa gajadānasugandhinā*, and *tulyagandhi* in 4.47, *tulyagandhiṣu mattebhakaṭeṣu phalareṇavah*, apparently violate (as pointed out by Mallinātha) either '*gandhasya 'ttve tadekāntagrahaṇam*' or '*na karmadhārayān matvarthīyaḥ*'. But such formations are so common with the best of poets [see Mallinātha on R. 4. 45] that no justification seems to be called for.

§ 28. *Pīvaroru* in K.8.36, *pīvaroru pibatī 'va barhiṇaḥ*, is obviously due to the analogy of *vāmorū, saṁhitorū*, etc., P. 4. 1. 70 The Durghaṭavṛtti and the Tattvabodhinī suggest that, in accordance with the dictum '*saṁjñāpūrvako vidhir anityaḥ*', Guṇa has not occurred here, although the stem is actually *pīvaroru*. The former gives also an alternative explanation that the second member might have been already *ūrū* in accordance with P. 4. 1.66 VĀRT., *aprāṇijāteś chā 'rajjvādīnām*. A similar case is that of *varoru* in BHĀG. 10.42.2, *kā tvaṁ varorv etad u hā 'nulepanaṁ kasyā 'ṅgane vā kathayasva sādhu naḥ*.

§ 29. Splitting of compound nouns in such a way that the word itself is indicated primarily and the person or thing only secondarily (*lakṣaṇayā*) which is, as a rule, resented by poeticians and stylists, appears in MD. 1. 42, *nīchair vāsyaty upajigamiṣor devapūrvaṁ giriṁ te* ; R. 8. 29, *daśapūrvarathaṁ yam ākhyayā daśakaṇṭhārigurum vidur budhāḥ* ; and R.16.40, *tasyāḥ sa rājopapadaṁ niśāntaṁ kāmī 'va kāntāhṛdayaṁ praviśya*. But as some of the most eminent of Sanskrit poets have resorted to this mode of expression with evident relish, it seems futile and rather squeamish to grudge it. Cf. BHĀRAVI at 18. 44, *jvaladanalaparītaṁ raudram astraṁ dadhānaṁ dhanurupapadam asmai vedam abhyādideśa*, and MĀGHA at 1 . 42, *yam indraśabdārthaniṣūdanaṁ harer hiraṇyapūrvaṁ kaśipuṁ prachakṣate*, and 3.59, *kṣuṇṇaṁ yad antaḥkaraṇena vṛkṣāḥ phalanti kalpopapadās tad eva*.

New and Obscure Words

§ 30. The following words have not been traced earlier than Kālidāsa : (1) *udayam* (indeclinable), 'at sunrise,' coined after *astam*, 'at sunset', in K. 8. 52, *se 'yam astam udayaṁ cha sevyate* ; (2) *upakārī*, 'tent', in the Prakrit form *uvaāriaṁ* (=*upakāryām*, see Raṅganātha's commentary), V. 5. 9, *ajja tihiviseso tti bhaa-*

vadīṇaṁ gaṅgājamunāṇaṁ saṁgame devīe saha kidāhiseo saṁpadaṁ uvaāriaṁ uvaviṭṭho; (3) *gandhavāhin*, 'wind' or 'breeze', coined after *gandhavaha* and *°vāha*, in K. 8. 19, *uchchhvasatkamalagandhaye dadau pārvatīvadanagandhavāhine*; (4) *durāgatam*, 'unwelcome', in the Prakrit form *durāgadaṁ*, coined after *svāgatam* [cf. *durāhā: svāhā* in AV.8. 8. 24, *svāhai 'bhyō durāhā 'mībhyaḥ*], in V. 2. $\frac{19}{20}$, *Rājā /—. . . .svāgataṁ devyai / Devī /—durāgadaṁ dāṇiṁ saṁvuttaṁ /*; (5) *durnimita*, 'ill-measured', 'irregular' (MW.), in K. 7. 61 = R. 7. 10, *pade pade durnimite galantī* ; (6) *pīṭhamardikā*, facetious feminine form of *pīṭhamarda*, 'a lover's bosom friend', in the Prakrit form *pīṭhamaddiaṁ* in M. 1. $\frac{13}{14}$, *ai, uaaṭṭhidā devī pīṭhamaddiaṁ paṇḍiakosiim purokaria tattabhodī dhāriṇī* ; (7) *bodhana* for *budha* in V. 5. 21, *amaramunir ivā 'triḥ sraṣṭur atrer ive 'ndur budha iva śiśirāṁśor bodhanasye 'va devaḥ* ; (8) *vītasūtra* for *upavīta* in V.5.19, *gorochanānikaṣapiṅgajaṭākalāpaḥ saṁlakṣyate śaśikalāmalavītasūtraḥ* ; and (9) *śaradhi*, 'quiver', [Cf. *bāṇadhi* in the Mahābhārata (MW.) and the more usual *iṣudhi*] in V.1.19, *vāyavyam astraṁ śaradhiṁ punas te mahoragaḥ śvabram iva praviṣṭam.*

§ 31. There are at least three words of rather obscure origin and signification, causing headache to interpreters : (i) *Jāmitra* in K.7.1, *athau 'ṣadhīnām adhipasya vṛddhau tithau cha jāmitraguṇānvitāyām,* which is undoubtedly identical with GK. διαμετρον and has not yet been traced to an earlier Sanskrit author, seems to have been misunderstood. MW. gives 'the 7th lunar mansion' as its meaning, which seems hardly accurate, while Mallinātha's difficulty is obvious in the sentence *'yady api jāmitraśuddhir lagnadharmas tathā 'pi taddvāra tither api vyapadeśe na doṣaḥ.' Jāmitra* properly signifies the seventh astrological house, counted usually from the sign at the eastern horizon (*lagna*)—but often also from that containing the moon—as the first. Here *jāmitraguṇa* means freedom from the inauspicious collocation called *jamitravedha*, which is the presence of malignant *grahas* (or any *grahas*, according to some) in the seventh house from the moon's [see Śuddhidīpikā of Śrīnivāsāchārya 5. 8 along with the commentaries and ŚK. s.v. *yāmitravedha*]. It does not, however, refer to the *lagna*, but to the duration of the moon in that collocation, and hence there is obviously no anomaly in calling the *tithi*, 'lunar day,' *jāmitraguṇānvita*.

(ii) *Baimbika* (not recorded in MW.) in M. 4.14, *dākṣiṇyaṁ nāma bimboṣṭhi baimbikānāṁ kulavratam*,—which has been unwarrantably altered to *nāyaka* [cf. the absurd '*nāyakās tadvaṁśyā rājānaḥ*' in the attached commentary by Kāṭayavema !] in the recent Nirnayasāgara Press edition, but which is guaranteed also by a quotation in Rāghavabhaṭṭa's commentary on Ś. 6. 5.—must have reference to the royal line. As the word is evidently derived from *bimba* [='the sun' ? Cf. the presence of the word *mitra*, 'sun', at the end of the names of these kings], this may be the reputed name of its founder. A Vārtika to P. 4. 1. 97, however, prescribes a different derivative, *baimbaki*, from *bimba*.

(iii) *Māḍiā* in M. 5. $\frac{0}{1}$, *vijjābhariāṇaṁ bahmaṇāṇam ṇichchadakkhiṇamāḍiā purohidassa hatthaṁ pāvaissaṁ*, which has been similarly altered into ....*ṇichchadakkhinaṁ māsiīṁ*...., is rather obscure. [Cf. *māṇikā*, 'a particular weight', and *māḍa*, 'measure', 'weight', 'quantity', MW.]. The commentator Kāṭayavema has '*nityadakṣiṇāmāḍikā niṣkāṇi*, while in the immediate context there is reference to a casket sealed with lac (*jadumuddālañchhidaṁ mañjūsaṁ geṇhia*) that was being carried by the speaker.

Inflexion

§ 32. A few cases of nominal inflexion call for comment. Of the pronominal forms three deserve notice : (1) *Te* in Ś. 2. $\frac{7}{8}$, *bho vaassa, te tāvasakaṇṇaā abbhatthaṇīyā dīsadī*, appears to violate P. 8. 1. 22 and 72, according to which the shorter forms of *yuṣmad* and *asmad* are not available as the first word of a sentence and a word in the vocative case is to be considered non-existent as a previous word for such a purpose. (2) *Me* in Ś. 6. $\frac{4}{5}$, *yadai 'va khalu svāṅgulīyakadarśanād anusmṛtaṁ devena satyam ūḍhapūrvā me tatrabhavatī rahasi śakuntalā mohāt pratyādiṣṭe 'ti*, used in the sense of *mayā*, has been justified by VĀMANA at 5. 2. 10, *te-me-śabdau nipāteṣu*, and is paralleled in RĀM. 4. 14. 14, *anṛtaṁ no 'ktapūrvaṁ me chiraṁ kṛchchhre 'pi tiṣṭhatā*. (3) *Vām* for *yuvām* in R. 15. 69, *geye kena vinītau vāṁ kasya che 'yaṁ kṛtiḥ kaveḥ*, is recorded as a genuine reading by Mallinātha, Śaraṇadeva in DV. p. 123, Durgādāsa on Mugdhabodha 221, and Suṣeṇāchārya in Kalāpachandra. The Durghaṭavṛtti, *l.c.*, gives three alternative explanations : (i) that it is a clipped form for *yuvāṁ* ; or (ii) that *dvitīyā* in P. 8. 1. 20 is representative (*upalakṣaṇa*) of the ending for Karmakāraka : or (iii) that it is just an instance of carelessness. Of these the first appears to be the most reasonable one: cf. *vām* for *āvām* in RV. 6. 55. 1, *ehi vāṁ vimucho napād āghṛṇe saṁ sachāvahai.* Another interesting use is that of *vām* for *yuvābhyām* in RĀM. 6. 29. 9, *āchāryā guravo vṛddhā vṛthā vāṁ paryupāsitāḥ| sāraṁ yad rājaśāstrāṇām anujīvyaṁ na gṛhyate||.*

§ 33. The form *subhru* (vocative singular of *subhrū*), found in K.5.43, *vimānanā subhru kutaḥ pitur gṛhe*, and V.3.22, *yadi tu tava samāgame tathai 'va prasarati subhru kṛtī bhaveyam*, is so popular [cf. RĀM. 4.33.32 ; BHĀG. 4.3.20 ; 25.31 ; 26.23 ; 9.20.15, etc.,; BHAṬṬI 6. 11] that some of the post-Pāṇinian grammarians sanction it by special rules [cf. SS. 6. 12 ; Mugdhabodha 154] or else justify it by an extended application of Pāṇ'ni's rules [cf. VĀMANA 5.2.48 ; Jayamaṅgala and Mallinātha on BHAṬṬI, *l.c.* ; and DV. p. 21.] The passage, *dūrād arālabhru vibhāti velā kalaṅkalekhāmaline 'va dhārā*, quoted by Durgādāsa on Mugdhabodha 154 as from the Raghuvaṁśa, but untraceable unless it be a variant of R. 13.15, would, if genuine, present a parallel formation.

§ 34. The case of *bhīru*, another vocative singular, in R. 13. 24, *tvaṁ rakṣasā bhīru yato 'panītā*, and elsewhere is paralleled by RĀM. 5. 20. 36, *vihara mayā saha bhīru kananāni*, and BHAṬṬI 4 39 [cf. also 5. 50, 66 ; 6. 68 ; 8. 77], *kutastyaṁ bhīru yat tebhyo druhyadbhyo 'pi kṣamāmahe.* It is justified by the Pāṇinians in the same way as *pīvaroru*, already discussed in § 28, while SS. 4.106 expressely sanctions a stem *bhīrū* in order to explain it.

B. VERBAL

Secondary Roots (Sanādyanta Dhātu)

§ 35. A few peculiarities incidental to the use of *ṇich* as forming causative and denominative roots deserve notice :

(1) The Vṛddhi of the radical vowel in *ākrāmayāmāsa*, found in K. 6. 52, *sa tair ākrāmayāmāsa śuddhāntaṁ śuddhakarmabhiḥ*, and *viśrāmaya*, found in R. 1. 54, *atha yantāram ādiśya dhuryān viśrāmaye 'ti saḥ*, has been objected to on the ground that it violates P. 6.4. 92, *mitāṁ hrasvaḥ*. The Kāśikā, followed by the Siddhāntakaumudī and the Durghaṭavṛtti, reconciles it by carrying down from the previous Sūtra *vā* with a definite scope (*vyavasthitavibhāṣā*). (2) On the other hand, want of the same in *niyamayasi*, found in Ś. 5. 8, *niyamayasi kumārgaprasthitān āttadaṇḍaḥ*, has been taken exception to as it apparently violates the Gaṇasūtra, *yamo 'pariveṣaṇe*, and reconciled through considering it a denominative formation from *niyama* or *niyamavat* [DV. p. 105 ; SS. 1. 27 ; SIDDH. 2353]. But Chandra as reported by Goyīchandra on SS. 1. 28 holds an opposite view, considering such uses as the right ones. So also MW. WHITNEY § 1042. **g.** admits optional Vṛddhi. (3) The denominative form *dūrayati* (as against the regular *davayati*, prescribed in P. 6. 4. 156), appearing in K. 8.31, *sīkaravyatikaraṁ marīchibhir dūrayaty avanate vivasvati*, is exceptional. It has, however, been justified by VĀMANA 5. 2. 79 with reference to the word *bahula* in the Gaṇasūtra, *prātipadikād dhātvarthe bahulam iṣṭhavach cha*. SS. 2.434 also gives optional sanction.

Stem-forming Suffixes (Vikaraṇa)

§ 36. Two cases deserve notice in this connection : (1) *Apahārita* in R. 3.50, *ato 'yam aśvaḥ kapilānukāriṇā pitus tvadīyasya mayā 'pahāritaḥ*, appears to have taken *ṇich* without change of meaning (*svārthe*), as rightly pointed out by Mallinātha. It thus appears to have taken the Vikaraṇa of the Churādi class. (2) *Khidyase* in Ś. 5.7, *svasukhanirabhilāṣaḥ khidyase lokahetoḥ*, appears as a member of the Divādi class, which inclusion is not recognised by some followers of Pāṇini, and therefore VĀMANA at 5. 2. 6 refers it to a Karmakartṛ as its subject. Sāyaṇāchārya in DHĀTU. 4. 62 expressly admits the inclusion and Kṣīrasvāmin in Kṣīrataraṅgiṇī 4.61 cites Durga as reading '*khida dainye*' after '*pada gatau*' in the Divādi class, while MW. recognises both the

Parasmaipada (rarely) and the Ātmanepada forms and refers to the Mahābhārata, the Rāmāyaṇa, the BHAṬṬI, etc.

The Voices (Upagraha)

§ 37. There are three cases of Ātmanepada, where Parasmaipada is expected according to the grammarians : (1) *Chuchumbe* in K.3.38, *priyāmukhaṁ, kimpurusaś chuchumbe*, which DV. p. 20 following the Anunyāsa justifies through assumption of *karmavyatīhāra*, while SS.-VṚTTI. 2. 175 does it by means of the dictum, '*ātmanepadam ichchhanti parasmaipadināṁ kvachit.*' (2) *Nidrāyate* in M. 4. $\frac{12}{13}$, *iti nidrāyate*, which, although not recognised by the commentators of the Dhātupāṭha, is admitted by MW. on the authority of the Śatapatha-Brāhmaṇa, the Mahābhārata, etc. (3) *Bubhuje* in R.15.1, *bubhuje pṛthivīpālaḥ pṛthivīm eva kevalām*, which is justified by SS., DV., and SIDDH. on the ground that here *upabhoga*, 'enjoyment,' (and not *avana*, 'protection', as envisaged in P. 1. 3. 66) is the sense.

§ 38. Parasmaipada appears in the following cases, where normally one would expect Ātmanedpada : (1) *Atarjayat* in R. 12.41, *aṅkuśākārayā 'ṅgulyā tāv atarjayad ambare* [cf. also Ś 1. $\frac{21}{22}$, *śakuntalā sakhīm aṅgulyā tarjayati*], which has been found fault with by Mallinātha and Durgādāsa on KK. p. 85 as not strictly in accordance with the Dhātupāṭha, is parallelled by BHAṬṬI 7.36, *vikṣāvais toyaviśrāvaṁ tarjayanto mahodadheḥ* [cf. also, *tarjayann iva ketubhiḥ*, cited in DHĀTU. and TATTVA.]. (2) *Dadhatuḥ* in R. 1. 26, *sampadvinimayeno 'bhau dadhatur bhuvanadvayam*, apparently violating P.1.3.14, has been considered a hard case requiring explanation in DV. p. 14, while SS.-VṚTTI 2. 30 passes it and others generally ignore it. (3) *Niviśati* in R. 12. 38, *ity uktvā maithilīṁ bhartur aṅke niviśatīṁ bhayāt*, has been impugned as violating P.1.3.17, *ner viśaḥ*, in DV. p.15, DHĀTU. 6. 140, KK. p. 208 and TATTVA. on 2683, where frantic efforts have been made to exculpate the poet by suggesting an emendation (to *niviṣati* or *aṅgāni viśati*),or by considering *viśati* as derived first and then combined with *ni*, or by the assumption that *ni* here is not an Upasarga, but a different Nipāta resembling it. (4) *Vininyuḥ* in R.3.29, *vininyur enaṁ guravo gurupriyam*, has been criticised (as violating P.1.3.36) by Śaraṇa, who suggests as an explanation that *āchāryakaraṇa* is not intended (*vivakṣita*) here, but others do not take notice of it, seemingly because they consider that *up-√nī* is the only proper case contemplated in the rule. (5) *Śiñjad* in MD. 2. 16, *tālaiḥ śiñjadvalayasubhagair nartitaḥ kāntayā me yām adhyāste divasavigame nīlakaṇṭhaḥ suhṛd vaḥ*, although considered a hard case by Vallabha and in DV. p.12, DHĀTU. 2.17, and the commentary to KK. p. 91, is paralleled by BHĀG. 3.23.15, *mañjuśiñjatṣaḍaṅghribhiḥ*, and 10.53.52, *śiñjatkalānūpuradhāmaśobhinā*. (6) The reading *sañcharan* in K. 8. 21, *tatra tatra vijahāra sañcharann aprameyagatinā kakudmatā*, found in Mallinātha's text and some MSS. for *sampatan* and apparently violating P. 1. 3. 54, has not been taken notice of by critics ; cf. the regular use in R. 13.19, *kvachit pathā sañcharate ghanānām*.

Modal and Temporal Forms (Lakāra)

§ 39. (1) *Āsa* <*√as*, found in K. 1. 35 (*lāvaṇya utpādya ivā 'sa yatnaḥ*) ; R. 11. 15 (*prādur āsa bahulakṣapāchhaviḥ*), 63 (*prādur āsa kila vāhinīmukhe*), 81 (*niṣprabhaś cha ripur āsa bhūbhṛtām*) ; 14. 23 (*tenā 'sa lokaḥ pitṛmān vinetrā*) ; etc., has been a sore point with commentators and critics, who have variously called it a solecism, an indeclinable resembling a verbal form, or a form of *√as*, 'to shine'. It is, however, really an archaism, found so often in the epics and current in the Vedas. (2) Similar is the case with *āha* [as also with *āttha* in K. 2. 31, *evaṁ yad āttha bhagavann āmṛṣṭaṁ naḥ paraiḥ padam*], considered a present form in P. 3. 4. 84, but used with a past reference in K. 5. 65, *athā 'ha varṇī vidito maheśvaraḥ* ; R. 3. 25, *yathā 'ha dhātryā prathamoditaṁ vachaḥ* (altered to *uvācha dhātryā* etc., but cf. DV. p. 61) ; and R. 9. 79, *pratyāha kosalapatiḥ prathamāparāddhaḥ* (also altered to *provācha* etc., but cf. SS.-VṚTTI 2. 8), which VĀMANA 5.2.44 considers an unpardonable solecism. BHAṬṬI 7. 63(65), *parighorubhujān āha hasantī svāgataṁ kapīn*, presents a similar use. (3) There are three cases of violation of P. 3. 1. 40, *kṛñ chā 'nuprayujyate liṭi*, as understood by the commentators : R.9.61, *taṁ pātayāṁ* *prathamam āsa papāta paśchāt* ; 13. 36, *prabhraṁśayāṁ yo nahuṣaṁ chakāra* ; and 16.86, *saṁyojayāṁ vidhivad āsa sametabandhuḥ*, for which commentators and critics have found no better explanation than a highly artificial one of treating *pātayām* etc. as accusatives of *pātayā* (=*pātaṁ yātī 'ti*) etc. and *āsa* as derived from √*as*, 'to get', signifying '*praptavān*' ! To this we can only say with Sāyaṇa in DHĀTU. 2. 7, '*satyam, śabdāḥ sidhyanti, arthās tu sahṛdayahṛdayaṅgamā na bhavanti.*' Others evidently find pleasure in bluntly calling these absolute solecisms. The remarks of WHITNEY § 1072. c., however, along with the examples cited [*mīmāṁsām eva cakre* (ŚBr.) and *vidāṁ vā idam ayaṁ cakāra* (JBr.)], put the case in its true perspective: 'The connection of the noun and auxiliary is not so close that other words are not occasionally allowed to come between them.' (4) A case of inversion of the order (cf. WHITNEY § 944. **b.**) of the two parts of the periphrastic future (Luṭ) seems to be found in MD. 1. 49, *antaḥ śuddhas tvam asi bhavitā varṇamātreṇa kṛṣṇaḥ.* The *asi* is retained only in the Trivandrum edition of the text with Nātha's commentary ; elsewhere it appears converted to *api.* But just consider the text of Mallinātha's commentary as it appears in the Nirṇayasāgara Press edition : *tvaṁ tāsām. . . .sevāṁ kṛtva. . . .śuddho. . . .bhavitā, 'ṇvultṛchau' iti tṛch / api sadya eva pūto bhaviṣyasī 'tyarthaḥ / 'vartamānasāmīpye vartamānavad vā' iti vartamānapratyayaḥ.* Nātha considers *asi* an Avyaya in the sense of *tvam.*

IV. Syntax

NOUNS AND PRONOUNS

Number

§ 40. Anomalies of number appear in at least two cases, which are easily explanable : (1) K. 5. 76, *vipatpratīkāraparеṇa maṅgalaṁ niṣevyate bhūtisamutsukena vā / jagachchharaṇyasya nirāśiṣaḥ sataḥ kim ebhir āśopahatātmavṛttibhiḥ //*, where Mallinātha remarks, '*pūrvaṁ maṅgalam ity ekavachanasya jātyabhiprāyatvād ebhir iti bahuvachanena nirdeśo na virudhyate.*' (2) K. 7. 19, *patyuḥ śiraśchandrakalām anena spṛśe 'ti sakhyā parihāsapūrvam / sā rañjayitvā charaṇau kṛtāśīr mālyena tāṁ nirvachanaṁ jaghāna //*, where the same commentator rightly remarks, *'rañjane dvayor niyamāch charaṇāv ity uktvā 'py auchityāt tāḍanavidhāv ekatara-parāmaśa ity āhuḥ.'*

Gender

§ 41. The use of *dos* (which is considered masculine by most of the grammarians and lexicographers) as neuter in R. 15. 23, *tam upādravad udyamya dakṣiṇaṁ dor niśācharaḥ*, has the weighty support of Patañjali in *kakuddoṣaṇī*, quoted by Mallinātha and TATTVA. on Uṇādisūtra 237, and Vedic usage (see MW.).

Person

§ 42. In the Prakrit verse Ś. 5. 1, *ahiṇavamahuloluvo bhavaṁ taha parichumbia chūamañjariṁ | kamalavasaimettaṇivvudo mahuara vihmario si ṇaṁ kahaṁ ||*, a verb in the second person is made to agree with *bhavat*. Although this is somewhat unusual in classical Sanskrit, there are Vedic parallels, cf. Macdonell, *Vedic Grammar for Students*, § 195. **A**.*c*., and the passage from the Śatapatha-Brāhmaṇa quoted there, *iti vāva kila no bhavān purā anuśiṣṭān avocaḥ*.

Case

§ 43. A c c u s a t i v e : (1) An accusative case, governed by the preposition *anu* forming part of a compound, appears in the use of *anvak* in K. 7. 71, *tam anvag indrapramukhāś cha devāḥ*, and R. 2. 16, *tāṁ devatāpitratithikriyārthām anvag yayau madhyamaloka-pālaḥ*, and in that of *anujātaḥ* in R. 6. 78, *asau kumāras tam ajo 'nujātas triviṣṭapasye 'va patiṁ jayantaḥ*. It is supported by Vedic and later usage, e.g., Aitareya-Brāhmaṇa, viii, 18, *tvām anvañcho vayaṁ smasi*, and Kātyāyana-Śrautasūtra 20. 7. 22 (BR.), *ekaviṁśatipradānān eke 'nvak chāturmāsyadevatāḥ*. Cf. Macdonell, *Vedic Grammar for Students*, § 197. B. α. ; WHITNEY § 272. (2) An accusative governed by *ārāt* as in Ś 5. 30, *sā nindantī svāni bhāgyāni bālā bāhūtkṣepaṁ kranditum cha pravṛttā | strīsaṁsthānaṁ chā 'psarastīrtham ārād utkṣipyai 'nāṁ jyotir ekaṁ jagāma ||*, has not been traced to any other writer. That the explanation of Rāghavabhaṭṭa and others that *jagāma* governs *apsarastīrtham* can hardly be right is clear from Ś. 7. $\frac{31}{32}$, *yadai 'vā 'psarastīrthāvataraṇāt pratykṣaviklavāṁ śakuntalām ādāya menakā dākṣāyaṇīm upagatā* etc. (3) In R. 2. 8, *adijyadhanvā vichachāra dāvam*, and K. 3. 31, *madoddhatāḥ pratyanilaṁ vicherur vanasthalīr marmarapatramokṣāḥ*, an intransitive verb is made to govern a noun denoting region (*deśa*), which according to the Siddhāntakaumudī 539 and the Tattvabodhinī on the same as well as SS. 5. 70 should have reference only to a country or its divisions such as Kuru, Pañchāla, Śrughna, etc., but according to the Mugdhabodha 283 to any extension of space including a river or a forest and Mallinātha agrees with it. (4) Double accusative is found with √*jñā* in Ś. 1. $\frac{21}{22}$, *iti sakhīṁ te jñātum ichchhāmi*, and with *ud*-√*diś* (which, being in the passive, has one of them as its subject) in Ś. 5. $\frac{29}{30}$, *tvaṁ sādhubhir uddiṣṭaḥ prathamam eva chakravartinaṁ putraṁ janayiṣyasī 'ti*. Although these two are not specially counted in the lists added to P. 1. 4. 51 in the Kāśikā and the Siddhāntakaumudī, a comparison of the lists in these two works as well as in SS. 5. 9 and Mugdhabodha 286 show that more and more roots have been included in course of time, and the last two have expressly contemplated others, according to usage. (5) The use of the agent as an object of the causative forms of the following roots have caused headache to critics : (i) √*grah* in K. 1. 52 [also in R. 15. 88 ; 17. 3], *ayāchitāraṁ na hi devadevam adriḥ sutāṁ grāhayitum śaśāka*, parralled by BHATTI 2. 42, *ajigrahat taṁ janako dhanus tat*, and Maitrāyaṇīyasaṁhitā (cited by WHITNEY §277. **a**), *oṣadhīr eva phalaṁ grāhayati*; (ii) √*muh* in MD. 2. 30, *tvām apy asraṁ navajalamayaṁ mochayiṣyaty avaśyam*,parrelleled by BHATTI 9. 67, *pṛtanāṣāḍḍviṣo dhūrṣu yuktān yānasya vājinaḥ / āyūṁṣi tvakṣu nirbhidyap rābhañjanir amochayat //* ; and (iii) √*tyaj* in R. 15. 88 [also at 4. 33 ; K. 7. 14. ; MD. 2. 33], *bharatas tatra gandharvān yudhi nirjitya kevalam / ātodyaṁ grāhayāmāsa samatyājayad āyūdhām //*, where Mallinātha remarks, '*grahityajor ṇyantayor dvikarmakatvaṁ nityam ity anusandheyam.*' Puṇḍarīka Vidyāsāgara in his Kalāpadīpikā on BHAṬṬI 2. 42 cites the view of Āpiśali optionally sanctioning such cases :

gatyarthādiṣu karmai 'va nīkhādyādiṣu kartṛtā / śeṣe karma cha kartā cha yathāsambhavam iṣyate //, referred to also by Bharatamallika on BHAṬṬI 15. 120, which he reads '*muṣṭinā kaumbhakarṇiṁ cha kruddhaḥ prāṇān atityajat*' and mentions *prāṇair* (the reading of Jayamaṅgala and Mallinātha) for *prāṇān* as a variant reading.

§ 44. Instrumental : (1) Mallinātha and Śaraṇadeva in DV. p. 42 support the instrumental *taiḥ* in K. 6. 52, *sa tair ākramayāmāsa* [°*krāma*°, DV. p. 105] *śuddhāntaṁ śuddhakarmabhiḥ*, on the ground that √*kram* here does not mean 'to go' as contemplated in P. 1. 4. 52, and the latter, on p. 27, even goes so far as to suggest a correction to *tān* along with the necessary changes. (2) SS. 5. 76 and DV. p. 44 support the ending in *uttareṇa* in MD. 2. 12, *tatrā 'gāraṁ dhanapatigṛhād uttareṇā 'smadīyam*, as *prakṛtyāditvāt tṛtīyā*, while others who look upon it as a formation with *enap* would correct °*gṛhād* straight away to °*gṛhān*. Mallinātha explains an analogous use of the same word in MD. 1.16, *kiñchit paśchād vraja laghugatir bhūya evo 'ttareṇa*, with reference to the same dictum.

§ 45. Ablative : Analogical use of the ablative is found in R. 3. 7, *purāṇapatrāpagamād anantaram* [Consider also R. 2. 71, *anantaraṁ bhartur arundhatīṁ cha*, and K. 6. 9, *viśvayoner anantaram*, along with '*tasyā 'nantaram*' cited from Patañjali by Mallinātha on K. 6. 9], and 17. 34, *dhūmād agneḥ śikhāḥ paśchād udayād aṁśavo raveḥ*. Of these the former is parralleled by '*ayam athaśabdo vṛttād anantarasya prakriyārthaḥ*', Śabarasvāmin on Mīmāṁsāsūtra 1. 1. 1, and the latter by '*tataḥ paśchād sraṁsyate dhvaṁsyate cha*', Patañjali quoted in TATTVA. on SIDDH. 609.

§ 46. Genitive : Mallinātha, SS. 5. 130, and DV. p. 42 resort to *ṣaṣṭhī śeṣe*, P. 2.3.50, in explaining the use of the genitive in K. 1. 44, *tato 'nukuryād viśadasya tasyās tāmrauṣṭhaparyastaruchaḥ smitasya*, and R. 1. 72, *ikṣvākūṇāṁ durāpe 'rthe tvadadhīnā hi siddhayaḥ*.

§ 47. Locative : Locative for the usually expected dative has been used in R. 13. 43, *sabhājane me bhujam ūrdhvabāhuḥ savyetaraṁ prādhvam itaḥ prayuṅkte* [cf. also Ś. 1. $\frac{15}{16}$ (Pischel's edition), *ya imāṁ valkaladhāraṇe niyuṅkte*], 3. 5, *spṛhāvatī vastuṣu keṣu māgadhī*;

and 14.45, *tapovaneṣu spṛhayālur eva*. The last one has been rightly referred to *vivakṣāvaśāt kārakāṇi bhavanti* in SS.5.36, and the others seem in no way different from it. Mallinātha's explanation of the first with reference to '*nimittāt karmayoge*', VĀRT. to P. 2.3.36, seems to be due to a misconception of the scope of the dictum, *vide* SS. 5.203 ; Mugdhabodha 312; SIDDH. 633 ; and DV. 2.3.36. Cf. also SPEYER § 81. β.

ADJECTIVES

§48. Certain adjectives have been used as nouns, for which parallels may mostly be had in ancient as well as later usage : e.g., (i) *utsuka* in RS. 1. 6, *prakurvate kasya mano na sotsukam*, and 2. 17, *samīraṇaḥ kaṁ na karoti sotsukam* ; (ii) *matsara* in R. 3. 60, *sa chāpam utsṛjya vivṛddhamatsaraḥ* ; 7. 3, *kākutstham uddiśya samatsaro 'pi* ; and 18. 19, *jarā vṛthā matsariṇī jahāra* ; (iii) *manthara* in RS. 6. 9, *tanūni pāṇḍūni samantharāṇi* ; and (iv) *maula* in R. 12. 12, *maulair ānāyayāmāsur bharataṁ stambhitāśrubhiḥ*, and 14. 10, *sa maularakṣoharibhiḥ sasainyaḥ*. On the other hand, certain nouns (as commonly recognised) have been used as adjectives : e. g., (i) *avaśeṣa* in K. 1. 16, *saptarṣihastāvachitāvaśeṣāṇi* ; (ii) *marmara* in K. 3. 31, *madoddhatāḥ pratyanilaṁ vicherur vanasthalīr marmarapatramokṣāḥ* ; R. 6. 57, *anena sārdhaṁ viharā 'mburāśes tīreṣu tālīvanamarmareṣu* ; and 19. 41, *marmarair agurudhūpagandhibhir vyaktahemaraśanais tam ekataḥ / jahrur āgrathanamokṣalolupaṁ haimanair nivasanaiḥ sumadhyamāḥ //*; (iii) *viśeṣa* in R. 2. 14, *āsīd viśeṣā phalapuṣpavṛddhiḥ* ; and (iv) *śeṣa* in K. 1. 35, *śeṣāṅganirmāṇavidhau vidhātur lāvaṇya utpādya ivā 'sa yatnaḥ*, and MD. 1. 30, *śeṣaiḥ puṇyair hṛtam iva divaḥ kāntimat khaṇḍam ekam*.

§ 49. A few cases of apparent anomaly in concord of adjectives are noticed : e.g., (i) *asāmpratam* in K. 2. 55, *viṣavṛkṣo 'pi saṁvardhya svayaṁ chhettum asāmpratam* ; (ii) *yuktam* in M. 5. $\frac{19}{20}$, *bhaavadīe ṇa juttaṁ ahme parichchaiduṁ* ; (iii) *varam* in M. 3. 15, *parasparaprāptinirāśayor varaṁ śarīranāśo 'pi samānurāgayoḥ* ; and (iv) *śakyam* in Ś. 3. 4, *śakyam aravindasurabhiḥ kaṇavāhī mālinītaraṅgāṇām / aṅgair anaṅgataptair aviralam āliṅgituṁ pavanaḥ //*, and K. 8. 62, 72 ; M. 3. 23 ; V. 2. $\frac{2}{3}$. Of these *asāmpratam* and *varam* have been considered indeclinable by all ancient grammarians, *yuktam* by Vardhamāna in Gaṇaratnamahodadhi and *śakyam* by Kāṭayavema on M. 3. 23. SPEYER §§ 220, 221 considers all of them to be derived from adjectives. Such anomalous uses, retained in these specific instances and in a few others [e.g., *duḥkham* in *duḥkham ātmā parichchhettum*, Hitopadeśa cited by SPEYER and *sukhaṁ* in *sukham ātmā bhaved dātuṁ sukhaṁ prāṇāḥ sukmha tapaḥ*, Svapnavāsavadatta 1. 10], appear to have arisen from a confusion of two idioms : (i) a transient one of construing the predicate and, consequently, the predicative adjective with the infinitive,still preserved in V. 2. $\frac{2}{3}$, *tahiṁ pañchavihassa abbhavahārassa uvaṇadasaṁbhārassa joaṇāṁ pekkhamāṇehiṁ sakkaṁ ukkaṇṭhāṁ viṇodeduṁ* ; M. 5. $\frac{10}{20}$, *bhaavadīe ṇa juttaṁ ahme parichchāiduṁ*, already cited ; K. 8. 72, *śakyam aṅgulibhir utthitair adhaḥ śākhināṁ patitapuṣpapeśalaiḥ / patrajarjaraśaśiprabhālavair ebhir utkachayituṁ tavā 'lakān //*; and Mahābhārata cited by SPEYER, *na yuktaṁ bhavatā 'nnam aśuchi dattvā pratiśāpaṁ dātum* [Cf. also Svapnavāsavadatta 6. $\frac{3}{4}$, *piaṁ me ñādikulassa kusalavuttantaṁ soduṁ*]; and (ii)the all but universally adopted one of construing it with the object of the infinitive, which is thus turned into its subject.

VERBS

§ 50. *Mā* has been used with the indicative (Laṭ) in V. 4. 63, *mai 'vai nam aśrūpahataṁ karomi*, which is paralleled by RĀM. (MW.), *mā gantum arhasi*, and BHĀG. 10. 4. 4, *snuṣe 'yaṁ tava kalyāṇa striyaṁ mā hantum arhasi*, while Prakrit presents a host of other forms accompanying it : e.g., the imperative (Loṭ) in M. 5. $\frac{10}{11}$, *bhodi, mā bhaāhi* ; the future (Lṛṭ) in Ś. 2. $\frac{10}{11}$, *mā kassa vi tavassiṇo iṅgudītellamissachikkaṇasīsassa hatthe paḍissadi* ; the infinitive (*tumanta*) in Ś. 4. $\frac{10}{20}$, *tā mā adimettaṁ mama kide ukkaṇṭhiduṁ* ; and the gerund (*ktvānta*) in Ś. 7. $\frac{20}{21}$, *mā kkhu edaṁ avalambia.*

§ 51. A few other cases of departure from the ordinary uses of the modal and temporal forms, which accord with the idiom of the language and therefore generally not taken exception to by critics, may be noted here : e.g., (i) the future (Lṛṭ) for the indicative (Laṭ) in K. 2. 31, *pratyekaṁ viniyuktātmā kathaṁ na jñāsyasi prabho*, and for the optative (Vidhiliṅ) in Ś. 5. 14, *tamas tapati gharamāṁśau katham āvirbhaviṣyati*, as well as 7. $\frac{20}{21}$, *ko tassa dhammadāraparichchāiṇo ṇāma saṁkītiduṁ chintissadi* ; and (ii) the imperative (Loṭ) for the future in M. 4. $\frac{4}{5}$, *pachchhā mama hatthe dehi ṇaṁ.*

§ 52. Mallinātha demurs to the use of the conditional (Lṛṅ) in K. 6. 68, *gām ādhāsyat kathaṁ nāgo mṛṇālamṛdubhiḥ phaṇaiḥ / ā rasātalamūlāt tvam avālambiṣyathā na chet //*, because, in his opinion, the non-realization of the action (*kriyātipatti*, P. 3. 3. 139) is not apparent. The case, however, seems exactly similar to that in K. 7. 66, *parasparena spṛhaṇīyaśobhaṁ na ched idaṁ dvandvam ayojayiṣyat / asmin dvaye rūpavidhānayatnaḥ patyuḥ prajānāṁ vitatho 'bhaviṣyat //*, and especially to that in Ś. 7. 4, *kiṁ vā 'bhaviṣyad aruṇas tamasāṁ bibhettā taṁ chet sahasrakiraṇo dhuri nā'kariṣyat*, which is cited by WHITNEY § 950. **a**. as a normal example. The fact is that here the non-realization of the negation (or futility) of the verbal action is in question, and Mallinātha's scruple smacks of superficiality, to say the least. Cf. also BHATTI 21. 13, *nā 'śotsyan maithilī loke nā 'chariṣyad idaṁ yadi.*

V. Semasiology

§ 53. Unusual meanings, mostly traceable first to Kālidāsa, appear in the use of the following words : (i) *anuyojya*, 'servant', in Ś. 7. $\frac{27}{28}$, *ubhābhyām api vāsavānuyojyo duṣyantaḥ praṇamati* ; (ii) *anu-√sthā*, 'to grant' [Mallinātha ; but *anvatiṣṭhat*—*anvasthāpayat*, Nārāyaṇa], in K. 1. 17, *yajñāṅgayonitvam avekṣya yasya sāraṁ dharitrīdharaṇakṣamaṁ cha / prajāpatiḥ kalpitayajñabhāgaṁ śailādhipatyaṁ svayam anvatiṣṭhat //* ; (iii) *udita*, 'accumulated (=*samudita*)', in K. 5. 41, *trilokasaundaryam ivo 'ditaṁ vapuḥ* ; (iv) *unmukhī*, 'talkative (=*mukharā*)', in K. 6. 2, *tayā vyāhṛtasandeśā sā babhau nibhṛtā priye / chūtayaṣṭir ivā 'bhyāśe madhau parabhṛtonmukhī //*; (v) *gandha*, 'pride', in *sagandha*, 'proud', found in MD. 1. 9, *vāmaś chā 'yaṁ nadati madhuraṁ chātakas te sagandhaḥ*, and in *āttagandha*, 'robbed of pride', humiliated', found in R.

13. 7, *pakṣachchhidā gotrabhidā 'ttagandhāḥ*, and Ś. 6. 25/26, *kenā 'ttagandho māṇavakaḥ* ; (vi) *chhāyā*, 'series (=*paṅkti*),' in Ś. 3. 24, *chhāyāś charanti bahudhā bhayam ādadhānāḥ sandhyāpayodakapiśāḥ piśitāśanānām* [Pañchatantra I. 16. 7 (406) also has '*grāhākīrṇam ivā 'bhirāmakamalachchhāyāsanātham saraḥ*'] ; (vii) *tāmisra*, 'night-ranger (=*tamisrāchārin*)'> 'demon', in R. 15. 2, *lavaṇena viluptejyās tāmisreṇa tam abhyayuḥ* ; (viii) *netra*, 'veil' or 'cloth' in R. 7. 39 *utthāpitaḥ saṁyati reṇur aśvaiḥ sāndrīkṛtaḥ syandanavaṁśachakraiḥ / vistāritaḥ kuñjarakarṇatālair netrakrameṇo 'parurodha sūryam* //, which is traced by MW. also to the Rāmāyaṇa; (ix) *nyāya*, 'accent' [Mallinātha ; but,=*vyavasthā* according to Nārāyaṇa], in K. 2. 12, *udghātaḥ praṇavo yāsāṁ tribhir nyāyair udīraṇam / karma yajñaḥ phalaṁ svargas tāsāṁ tvaṁ prabhavo girām* // ; (x) *prajāvatī*, 'brother's wife', in R. 14. 45, *prajāvatī dohadaśaṁsinī te*, and 15. 13, *tasyām evā 'sya yāminyām antarvatnī prajāvatī / sutāv asūta sampannau kośadaṇḍāv iva kṣitiḥ* //; (xi) *pratiyātanā*, 'image' or 'figure' (=*pratimā*), in R. 16. 17, *stambheṣu yoṣitpratiyātanānām utkrāntavarṇakramadhūsarāṇām* ; (xii) *prasiddha*, 'lofty', in R. 18. 41, *tasmād adhaḥ kiñchid ivā 'vatīrṇāv asaṁspṛśantau tapanīyapīṭham / sālaktakau bhūpatayaḥ prasiddhair vavandire maulibhir asya pādau* //; (xiii) √*lopi*, 'to cause to swerve from' (MW.), in R.12.9, *sa sītālakṣmaṇasakhaḥ satyād gurum alopayan* ; (xiv) *vaktavya*, 'dependent (on)', 'subject (to)', in Ś. 6. 8/9, *kadā vi sappurisā soavattavvā ṇa honti* [Cf. RĀM. 2. 117. 26, *kāmavaktavyahṛdayāḥ*, and AMARA III.3.159, *garhyādhīnau cha vaktavyau*]; (xv) *vanadhārā*, 'avenue of trees' (MW.), in V. 4. 27/28, *aye, dakṣiṇena vanadhārāṁ priyācharaṇanikṣepaśaṁsī nūpuraśabdaḥ* ; (xvi) *varṇa*, 'character', 'description', in Ś 6. 20/21, *edo dāva ummatto / ahaṁ vi edassa saṅgeṇa īdisavaṇṇo via saṁvutto* / ; (xvii) √*vāhi*, 'to traverse', in R.16.12, *sa vāhyate .rājapathaḥ śivābhiḥ* [Cf. Mallinātha's remarks], and MD. 1. 38, *dṛṣṭe sūrye punar api bhavān vāhayed adhvaśeṣam* ; (xviii) *vivāda*, 'utterance,' 'order', in R.18.43, *paryantasañchāritachāmarasya kapolalolobhayakākapakṣāt / tasyā 'nanād uchcharito vivādaś chaskhāla velāsv api nā 'rṇavānām* //; and (xix) *viśeṣa*, 'limb', in K. 1. 25, *pupoṣa lāvaṇyamayān viśeṣān*.

§ 54. The primary meanings appear to have s h i f t e d variously in the following cases : (i) *āloka*, 'sight' > 'hail to a king on sight (*jayaśabda*)', in R.2.9, *udīrayāmāsur ivo 'nmadānām ālokaśabdaṁ vayasāṁ virāvaiḥ*, and 17. 27, *sa rājakakudavyagra-pāṇibhiḥ pārśvavartibhiḥ / yayāv udīritālokaḥ sudharmānavamāṁ purīm //* ; (ii) *uparāga*, 'eclipse'> 'trouble as in eclipse'> 'trouble', in R.16.7, *bibharṣi chā 'kāram anirvṛtānāṁ mṛṇālinī haimam ivo 'parāgam*; (iii) *parāga*, 'pollen' >'pollen-like' >'dust', in R.4.30, *pratāpo 'gre tataḥ śabdaḥ parāgas tadanantaram / yayau paśchād rathādīni chatuḥskandhe 'va sā chamūḥ //*; (iv) *prasiddha*, 'accomplished' >'adorned', 'decorated', in K. 5.9, *yathā prasiddhair madhuraṁ śiroruhair jaṭābhir apy evam abhūt tadānanam* ; (v) *varha*, 'tail-feather (of a peacock)' >'feather-like'>'petal', in R. 6.17, *vilāsinīvibhramadantapatram āpāṇḍuraṁ ketakavarham anyaḥ / priyānitambochitasanniveśair vipāṭayāmāsa yuvā nakhāgraiḥ //*; and (vi) *subhaga*, 'graceful' >'suitable', in Ś. 4. 4, *niṣṭhyūtaś charaṇoparāgasubhago lākṣārasaḥ kenachit* [Not found in the N. S. Press edition, but appears in most of the other editions, and recorded by MW. as a *v.l.*].

§ 55. A n a l o g i c a l e x t e n s i o n of the acquired significations of certain words to their normal synonyms characterises the following cases : (i) *auṣmya* (=*santāpa*, 'heat' >'grief') in R. 17.33, *tasyai 'kasyo 'chchhritaṁ chhatraṁ mūrdhni tenā 'malatviṣā / pūrvarājaviyogauṣmyaṁ kṛtsnasya jagato hṛtam //*; (ii) *kriyā* (=*kṛti*, 'work' >'literary production') in V. 1. 2, *śṛṇuta janā avadhānāt kriyām imāṁ kālidāsasya* ; and (iii) *dhvānta* (=*tamas*, 'darkness'> 'ignorance' and 'the cause of ignorance, viz., the Guṇa called Tamas') in K.7.48, *adhvānam adhvāntavikāralakṣyas tatāra tārādhipakhaṇḍadhārī*.

§ 56. The semantic ranges of the following words appear to have been w i d e n e d : (i) *avatāra*, 'descent' >'descent, i.e. manifestation, of a deity' > 'manifestation (of anything)', in R.3.36, *agachchhad enaṁ guṇābhilāṣiṇī navāvatāraṁ kamalād ivo 'tpalam*, as also in 5. 24 ; V. 2. $\frac{6}{7}$ (Pr.) ; M. 3. $\frac{2}{3}$ (Pr.) ; (ii) *avadhi*, 'limit' >'time-limit' > 'time', in R. 16. 52. *manojñagandhaṁ sahakārabhaṅgaṁ purāṇaśīdhuṁ navapāṭalaṁ cha / sambadhnatā kāmijaneṣu doṣāḥ sarve nidāghāvadhinā pramṛṣṭāḥ* //; (iii) *kalpadruma*, 'one particular variety of the five divine trees' (*vide* AMARA)> 'the five divine trees as a class', in R. 6. 6, *teṣāṁ mahārhāsanasaṁsthitānām udāranepathyabhṛtāṁ sa madhye / rarāja dhāmnā raghusūnur eva kalpadrumāṇām iva pārijātaḥ* //; (iv) *samādhi*, 'absolute concentration of the mind' > 'any religious discipline', in K. 1. 22, *sā bhūdharāṇām adhipena tasyāṁ samādhimatyām udapādi bhavyā* ; (v) *sārathi*, 'charioteer' > 'companion', in R.3.37, *vibhāvasuḥ sārathine 'va vāyunā* ; and (vi) *hiṁsra*, 'a beast of prey'> 'any wild beast', in R. 14. 28, *sā daṣṭanīvāravalīni hiṁsraiḥ*.

§ 57. Narrowing of the semantic ranges, on the other hand, characterises some of the uses of the following words : (i) *kuśeśaya*, 'lotus' > 'red lotus', in R. 6. 18, *kuśeśayātāmratalena kaśchit kareṇa rekhādhvajalāñchhitena* [Cf., however, *padmarāga*, 'ruby', literally, 'having the colour or redness of the lotus', and *padmakāṣṭha* or *padmaka*, 'a kind of reddish-coloured wood'] ; (ii) *kautuka*,' festive occasion' > 'marriage festivity', in R. 11. 53, *kanyakātanayakautukakriyāṁ svaprabhāvasadṛśīṁ vitenatuḥ* ; (iii) *graha*, 'planet' > 'Rāhu', in R. 12. 28, *saṁdhyābhrakapiśas tasya virādho nāma rākṣasaḥ / atiṣṭhan mārgam āvṛtya rāmasye 'ndor iva grahaḥ* //, and M.4.16, *aparvaṇi grahakaluṣendumaṇḍalā vibhāvarī kathaya kathaṁ bhaviṣyati* ; (iv) *tridaśa*, 'god' > 'Indra', in R. 11. 42, *śraddadhe tridaśagopamātrake dāhaśaktim iva kṛṣṇavartmani*, as well as 11. 80, *kevalo 'pi subhago navāmbudaḥ kiṁ punas tridaśachāpalāñchitaḥ*, and elsewhere [Note that *sura* has been similarly used in K. 2. 20] ; and (v) *sambandha*, 'connection', 'relation'> 'friendship', and *sambandhin* or *sambaddha*, 'connected' > 'friendly,' in R. 2. 58, *sambandham ābhāṣaṇapūrvam āhur vṛttaḥ sa nau saṁgatayor vanānte / tad bhūtanāthānuga nā 'rhasi tvaṁ sambandhino me praṇayaṁ vihantum* //, and 14. 28, *sambaddhavaikhānasakanyakāni*.

§ 58. Etymological (*yaugika*) meanings appear to have been given preference over the conventional (*rūḍha*) ones in the following uses : (i) *atyanta* (=*ati*+*anta*) 'overstepping the limit', 'perpetual' or 'perpetually', in R.14.49, *ākhyātam asyai guru bhāvi duḥkham atyantaluptapriyadarśanena*; ibid. verse 65, *kiṁ vā tavā 'tyantaviyogamoghe kuryām upekṣāṁ hatajīvite 'smin* ; Ś. 1. 22, *atyantam eva madirekṣaṇavallabhābhir āho nivatsyati samaṁ hariṇāṅganābhiḥ*, etc. ; (ii) *namra* (=√*nam*+*ra*), 'bending', 'bowing', in R. 14. 58, *devi kṣamasve 'ti babhūva namraḥ* ; K.7.28, *akhaṇḍitaṁ prema labhasva patyur ity uchyate tābhir umā sma namrā* ; MD. 1. 55, *bhaktinamraḥ parīyāḥ*, etc. ; (iii) *pravīṇa* (=*pra*+*vīṇā*), 'expert in the lute', in K. 7. 48, *viśvāvasuprāgraharaiḥ pravīṇaiḥ saṁgīyamānatripurāvadānaḥ* ; and (iv) *sahāya* (=*saha*+√*ay*+*a*), 'fellow-traveller,' in MD. 1. 11, *sampatsyante nabhasi bhavato rājahaṁsāḥ sahāyāḥ.*

§ 59. Archaic senses in preference to the conventional ones seem to prevail in the following cases : *anu*-√*khid*, 'press' [cf. GRASS., s. v. *khid*], in M. 4.$\frac{1}{2}$, *tado tāe aṇukhijjamāṇāe bhavado aviṇaaṁ antareṇa parigadatthā kidā devī* [The text here is based on A. S. K. Rao's edition; *aṇukhijjamāṇā* of the older N.S. Press edition has been altered to *aṇubandhijjamāṇā* in the more recent ones]; (ii) *ā*-√*dhā*, 'to bear' and 'to conceive', in K. 6. 68, *gām ādhāsyat kathaṁ nāgo mṛṇālamṛdubhiḥ phaṇaiḥ*, and in R. 2. 75, *narapati kulabhūtyai garbham ādhatta rājñī*, respectively; (iii) *draviṇa*, 'strength', 'prowess', in R. 18. 14, *ahīnagur nāma sa gāṁ samagrām ahīnabāhudraviṇaḥ śaśāsa* ; and (iv) *śāśvata*, 'lasting many years', in V. 4. $\frac{70}{71}$, *purā bhaavadā mahāseṇeṇa sāsadaṁ kumāravvadaṁ geṇhia akaluso ṇāma gandhamādanakachchho ajjhāsido.*

§ 60. Archaism and purity (as contrasted with their later uses) seem to be retained also in the use of these two words : (i) *yāvat* (as an illustration of P. 3.3.4, *yāvatpurānipātayor laṭ*) in K. 3. 4, *kenā 'bhyasūyā padakāṅkṣiṇā te nitāntadīrghair janita tapobhiḥ / yāvad bhavaty āhitasāyakasya matkārmukasyā 'sya nideśavartī //*, and V. 1. 14, *sūta, upaśleṣaya ratham / yāvat punar iyaṁ subhrūr utsukābhiḥ samutsukā / sakhībhir yāti samparkaṁ latābhiḥ śrīr ivā 'rtavī //* ; and (ii) *vaśaṁvada*, 'expressing submissiveness', 'complaisant' (=*madhurabhāṣin*, Mallinātha), in R. 18.13, *vaśī sutas tasya vaśaṁvadatvāt sveṣāṁ ivā 'sīd dviṣatām apī 'ṣṭaḥ.*

§ 61. Certain apparently pleonastic combinations point obviously to differentiated meanings in the mind of the poet, which should be of considerable interest from a linguistic historical point of view. (i) *Aśvasādin* in R.7.47, *pūrvaṁ prahartā na jaghāna bhūyaḥ pratiprahārākṣamam aśvasādī*, and *turaṅgasādin* in ibid. verse 37, *pattiḥ padātiṁ rathinaṁ ratheśas turaṅgasādī turagādhirūḍham*, evidently do not envisage the *rūḍha* meaning, 'horseman', for *sādin*, but only its original meaning as derived from √*sad*, 'to sit'. [Note that VS. 30.13 has *aśvasāda*, but AV. 11. 10. 24, *ye rathino ye arathā asādā ye cha sādinaḥ*, appears to have already *sādin* for 'horseman']. (ii) *Kṛtrimaputraka* in K.1.29, *mandākinīsaikatavedikābhiḥ sā kandukaiḥ kṛtrimaputrakaiś cha*, apparently takes no note of the Gaṇasūtra, *putra kṛtrime*, on P. 5. 4. 29,. Or else, as rightly pointed out by Śaraṇadeva in DV. p. 91, *kṛtrima* might have been added just in order to avoid semantic confusion with the diminutive of *putra*, which also happens to be *putraka*. (iii) *Kauṭuka* in K. 7. 25, *ūrṇāmayaṁ kautukahastasūtram*, obviously elects 'marriage' or 'auspicious rite (*maṅgala*)' from amongst its several senses. [Note that in K. 5. 66, *karo 'yam āmuktavivāhakautukaḥ*, Kālidāsa has used the same word in the sense of *hastasūtra*, while in R. 11. 53, already quoted, in that of 'marriage']. (iv) *Tadavagraha* in K. 5.61, *tapaḥkṛśām abhyupapatsyate sakhīṁ vṛṣe 'va sītāṁ tadavagrahakṣatām*, appears to ignore the dictionary meaning of *avagraha*, viz., 'drought (*varṣavighāta*)', but is obviously paralleled by the illustration, *avagraho devasya*, given in the Kāśika on P. 3. 3. 51. (v) In *dhanurjyā*, appearing in Ś. 2. 4, *anavaratadhanurjyāsphālanakrūrapūrvam*, the word *jyā* seems to be reminiscent of a very old general meaning, 'string', still possessed by its later synonym *guṇa*, which, by the by, is also similarly combined. [Note that the Vedas already use it in the sense of 'bow-string,' but some of its I.-E. correspondents still possess the sense, 'string', 'nerve', or 'tendon'. Cf. Émile Boisacq, *Dictionaire Étymologique de la Langue Grecque*, s. v. *βιος*]. The form appears also in the Āśvalāyana-gṛhyasūtra and the Harivaṁśa (MW.).

§ 62. There are two cases which throw an interesting light on two of Pāṇini's Sūtras. (i) In R. 18. 7, *mṛgair ajaryaṁ jaraso 'padiṣṭam adehabandhāya punar babandha*, the word *ajarya*—formed in accordance with P.3.1. 105, *ajaryaṁ saṅgatam*—is treated as a substantive meaning 'friendship', just as the word *sāptapadīna* (K. 5. 39)—formed in accordance with P. 5. 2. 22, *sāptapadīnaṁ sakhyam*—has been done by all interpreters. The Kāśikākāra giving two illustrations, *ajaryam āryasaṅgatam* and *ajaryaṁ no 'stu saṅgatam*, obviously leans in favour of the word being an adjective. He is supported by SS 3. 213, *jiraś cha saṅgate kartari/ —ajaryaṁ no 'stu saṅgatam/*, and BHAṬṬI 6.54, *tena saṅgatam āryeṇa rāmā 'jaryaṁ kuru drutam*, where Mallinātha notes the difference in the point of view taken by Kālidāsa, but justifies BHAṬṬI all the same, while Bharatamallika, siding with Kālidāsa, holds *saṅgata* in BHAṬṬI'S text to be an adjective qualifying *ajarya* and meaning 'proper' and cites Halāyudha 4. 21,..*snehaḥ/ maitrī prītir ajaryaṁ sabhājanaṁ saṅgataṁ proktam*. (2) R. 6. 30, *athā 'ṅgarājād avatārya chakṣur yāhī 'ti janyām* [v.l., *yāte 'ti janyān*] *avadat kumārī*, presents a problem whether P. 4. 4. 82 is to be read '*saṁjñāyāṁ janyā*' or '*saṁjñāyāṁ janyāḥ*' and whether, accordingly, the second word is meant to be taken as feminine or masculine. Aruṇagirinātha admits only the reading in parenthesis, while Mallinātha also recognises and explains it as an imporgant variant. Both appear to read *janyāḥ* in Pāṇini, Mallinātha also citing the text of the Kāśikā, [*yad āha vṛttikāraḥ* /-]'*janīṁ vadhūṁ vahantī 'ti janyā jāmātur vayasyāḥ*', for which the Chowkhamba edition has '*janīṁ vahati janyā, jāmātur vayasyā*'. In Vedic usage *janya* is masculine and carries the sense 'friend or companion of the bridegroom', which is given also in the Vṛtti to SS. 3. 211 and 4. 807, *janyo jāmātuḥ snigdhaḥ*, and the various Koṣas. Cf. RV.4. 38. 6, *srajaṁ kṛṇvāno janyo na śubhvā*, and AV 11. 8. 1, *yan manyur jāyām āvahat saṁkalpasya gṛhād adhi/ ka āsaṁ janyāḥ ke varāḥ ka u jyeṣṭha-varo bhavat //*. The second reading of the text of the Raghuvaṁśa appears to be the better one, inasmuch as it is difficult to see Sunandā, expressly called a 'door-keeper' (*pratihārarakṣī*, verse 20), in the role of a chum of the Queen and *janya* in the sense of 'bearers of the bride' [*janīṁ vahantī 'ti janyā voḍhāraḥ*, Aruṇagirinātha] is recognised in the Koṣas. The sense '*mātur vayasyā*' attributed to *janyā(ḥ)* seems to be traceable to a misreading of the already cited text of the Kāśikā as *'janīṁ vahatī 'ti janyā yā mātur vayasyā'* [Cf. TATTVA. on SIDDH. 1634].

§ 63. Various figures of speech seem to be responsible for the aberrant senses in which a number of words have been used. (1) Simile, or rather Metaphor, can be traced as underlying the use of : (i) *ārdra*, 'fresh' <'moist', 'not dry' in R. 14. 4, *te putrayor nairṛtaśastramārgān ārdrān ivā 'ṅge sadayaṁ spṛśantyau*, and M. 3. 12, *praṇamitaśirasaṁ vā kāntam ārdrāparādham*; (ii) *kṛśa*, 'scanty' <'lean', in R. 5.65, *taṁ karṇabhūṣaṇanipīḍitapīvarāṁsaṁ śayyottarachchhadavimardakṛśāṅgarāgam*; (iii) *komala*, 'delightful', <'tender', 'delicate', in K. 3. 30, *rāgeṇa bālāruṇakomalena chūtapravāloṣṭham alañchakāra* ; (iv) *chatura*, 'charming' < 'clever', in R. 9. 47, *tyajata mānam alaṁ bata vigrahair na punar eti gataṁ chaturaṁ vayaḥ*, and K. 5. 49, *avaimi saubhāgyamadena vañchitaṁ tava priyaṁ yaś chaturāvalokinaḥ / karoti lakṣyaṁ chiram asya chakṣuṣo na vaktram ātmīyam arālapakṣmaṇaḥ* ; (v) *pragalbha*, 'mature' < 'resolute', in K. 1. 51, *guruḥ pragalbhe 'pi vayasy ato 'syās tasthau nivṛttānyavarābhilāṣaḥ* ; (vi) *rāga*, 'loveliness' (*rañjakatva*)' < 'colourfulness', in M. 1. 22, *dhairyāvalambinam api tvarayati māṁ murajavādyarāgo 'yam*, and Ś. 5. ½, *aho rāgaparivāhiṇī gītiḥ* ; and (vii) *visphūrjathu*, 'sudden manifestation' < 'thunderclap', in R. 13. 12, *velānilāya prasṛtā bhujaṅgā mahormivisphūrjathunirviśeṣāḥ*. (2) Metonymy seems to underlie the uses of : (i) *kuliśa*, 'edge (*koṭi*)' <'hundred-edged (*śatakoṭi*), i.e. thunderbolt' (Mallinātha), in MD 1. 61, *tatrā 'vaśyaṁ valayakuliśodghaṭṭanodgīrṇatoyaṁ neṣyanti tvāṁ surayuvatayo yantradhārāgṛhatvam*; and (ii) *durdina*, 'shower' <'cloudy day', in R. 4. 41, *dvisāṁ viṣahya kākutsthas tatra nārāchadurdinam / sanmaṅgalasnāta iva pratipede jayaśriyam //*, and 5.47, *tasyai 'kanāgasya kapolabhittyor jalāvagāhakṣaṇamātraśāntā / vanyetarānekapadarśanena punar didīpe madadurdinaśrīḥ //*.(3) The figure Synecdoche may be seen underlying the uses of: (i) *alaka*, 'toilet of the lochs' < 'lochs', in R. 9. 14, *samanukampya sapatnaparigrahān analakān alakānavamāṁ purīm* ; (ii) *karaṇa*, 'body' <'organ', in K. 4. 5, *upamānam abhūd vilāsināṁ karaṇaṁ yat tava kāntimattayā / tad idaṁ gatam īdṛśīṁ daśāṁ na vidīrye kaṭhināḥ khalu striyaḥ//*, and MD. 1. 55, *yasmin dṛṣṭe karaṇavigamād ūrdhvam uddhūtapāpāḥ saṁkalpante sthiragaṇapadaprāptaye śraddadhānāḥ* ; and (iii) *śarīra*, 'organ' < 'body', in R. 6. 39, *antaḥśarīreṣv api yaḥ prajānāṁ pratyādideśā 'vinayaṁ vinetā.*

§ 64. N o v e l t y o f s e n s e s, eminently remarkable, characterises the uses of certain indeclinables. For instance, (i) *antareṇa*, 'with regard to (=*uddiśya*)', in Ś. 2. $\frac{10}{11}$, *attabhavantaṁ antareṇa kīdiso se diṭṭhirāo*, and 5. $\frac{1}{2}$, *tasyā devīṁ vasumatīm antareṇa madupālambham avagato 'smi* [Also in M. 1.$\frac{3}{4}$; 4. $\frac{1}{2}$; 3. $\frac{11}{12}$. Cf., in this connection, a similar use of *antarā* in BHAṬṬI 8.94, *vaidehīm antarā kruddhaḥ kṣaṇam ūche viniśvasan*] ; (ii) *anyat*, 'otherwise (=*anyathā*) in V. 3. 16, *anyat katham iva pulakaiḥ kalitaṁ mama gātraṁ karasparśāt*; (iii) *astam*, 'at sunset', and *udayam*, 'at sunrise', in K.8. 52, *se 'yam astam udayaṁ cha sevyate*; (iv) *ūrīkṛtya*, 'including', in M. 5. $\frac{17}{18}$, *maudgalya, yajñasenaśyālam ūrīkṛtya mochyantāṁ sarve bandhanasthāḥ*; (v) *nanu*, 'not?' or 'is not?' (=*na*+*nu*) in M. 4. $\frac{1}{2}$, *Rājā/—nanu matsaṁparkam upalabhya/ Vidūṣakaḥ/—aha iṁ* ; ibid. 1. $\frac{6}{7}$, *etan nanu vo viditaṁ / yat tulyābhijaneṣu rājñāṁ vṛttiḥ /* ; and R. 8. 87, *kṣaṇam apy avatiṣṭhate śvasan yadi jantur nanu lābhavān asau*, etc.; (vi) *prati*, 'according to', in M. 3.15, *anāturotkaṇṭhitayoḥ prasidhyatā samāgamenā 'pi ratir na māṁ prati/ parasparaprāptinirāśayor varaṁ śarīranāśo 'pi samānurāgayoḥ//* ; (vii) *madhyekṛtya*, 'relating to (=*viṣayīkṛtya*)', in M. 5.2, *virachitapadaṁ vīraprītyā suropamasūribhiś charitam ubhayor madhyekṛtya sthitaṁ krathakaiśikān/ tava hṛtavato daṇḍānīkair vidarbhapateḥ śriyaṁ parighagurubhir dorbhir viṣṇoḥ prasahya cha rukmiṇīm //* ; and (viii) *vā*, 'like (=*iva*)', in MD 2.20, *jīrṇāṁ manye śiśiramathitāṁ padminīṁ vā 'nyarūpām*, and M. 5.12, *preṣyabhāvena nāme 'yaṁ devīśābadakṣamā satī/ snānīyavastrakriyayā patrorṇaṁ vo 'payujyate//* [also R. 19. 51]. Cf. RĀM. 2.105.31, *vayasaḥ patamānasya srotaso vā 'nivartinaḥ/ ātmā sukhe niyoktavyaḥ sukhabhājaḥ prajāḥ smṛtāḥ//*

§ 65. An equally r e m a r k a b l e d e p a r t u r e is noticeable also in the uses of the Upasargas in the following words: (i) *anuyojya* =*niyojya*, 'servant', in Ś 7. $\frac{27}{28}$, already cited §53 ; (ii) *ā-*$\sqrt{}$*hṛ*= *apa-*$\sqrt{}$*hṛ*, 'to rob', in R. 6. 75, *vāto 'pi nā 'sraṁsayad aṁśukāni ko lambayed āharaṇāya hastam* ; (iii) *udita*=*samudita*, 'accumulated', in K. 5.41, already cited §53 ; (iv) *upa-√diś=ud-√diś*, 'relating to,' in R. 8. 73, *atha tena daśāhataḥ pare guṇaśeṣām upadiśya bhāminīm/ viduṣā vidhayo mahardhayaḥ pura evo 'pavane samāpitāḥ//* ; (v) *ni-√yoji=saṁ-√yoji*, 'to join', in K. 4.42, *upalabdhasukhas tadā smaraṁ vapuṣā svena niyojayiṣyati* ; (vi) *ni-√vṛt=pratyā-√vṛt*, 'to return', in R. 8.5. *raghum eva nivṛttayauvanaṁ tam amanyanta naveśvaraṁ prajāḥ*, cf. also 3.67, ; 9.14 ; 11.57 ; and (vii) *vi-√vad=√vad* in the word *vivāda*, 'utterance', 'order', found in R. 18. 43, already cited §53.

AN ALPHABETICAL LIST OF THE WORDS AND FORMS DISCUSSED

[The references are to §§.]

ON THE INTERPRETATION OF SOME DOUBTFUL WORDS IN THE *ATHARVAVEDA* AND OTHER ESSAYS